CHINA-EU
A Common Future

edited by

Stanley Crossick
Founding Chairman,
European Policy Centre, Brussels

Etienne Reuter
Lee Kuan Yew School of Public Policy, Singapore

CHINA-EU
A Common Future

World Scientific

NEW JERSEY • LONDON • SINGAPORE • BEIJING • SHANGHAI • HONG KONG • TAIPEI • CHENNAI

Published by

World Scientific Publishing Co. Pte. Ltd.

5 Toh Tuck Link, Singapore 596224

USA office: 27 Warren Street, Suite 401-402, Hackensack, NJ 07601

UK office: 57 Shelton Street, Covent Garden, London WC2H 9HE

Library of Congress Cataloging-in-Publication Data
China-EU : a common future / edited by Stanley Crossick & Etienne Reuter.
    p. cm.
    Includes index.
    ISBN-13: 978-981-270-776-5
    ISBN-10: 981-270-776-X
  1. China--Relations--Europe. 2. Europe--Relations--China. I. Crossick, Stanley.
  II. Reuter, Etienne.
    DS740.5.E85C47 2007
    337.5104--dc22

                         2007040429

British Library Cataloguing-in-Publication Data
A catalogue record for this book is available from the British Library.

Typeset by Stallion Press
Email: enquiries@stallionpress.com

Printed in Singapore.

Editors' Introduction

Relations between China and the EU are at a crossroads. Negotiations for a new partnership and cooperation agreement formally started in January 2007. Both the EU and China are marking milestones in their history. The EU celebrates the 50th anniversary of its founding treaty, the Treaty of Rome, and goes through a "mid-life crisis", questioning its identity, its *modus operandi*, and its purpose. China is successfully pursuing a complete transformation of its economy, initiated in 1978 by the visionary Deng Xiaoping. At the same time, it is confronted by ominous challenges such as increasing inequality in its society, governance and degradation of the environment.

Against this background, this book offers to scholars and researchers, to observers from think-tanks and other civil society groups in Europe and in China, a platform to share their views and reflections on a number of issues that are relevant to the future of the EU-China partnership. Authors from Europe and China have come together to produce, often in unique pairs, essays discussing the big issues that dominate policies — economic prosperity, energy, environment, geopolitical security and stability. The views expressed in this book are those of the authors and cannot be attributed to the institutions and organizations to which they belong.

These diverse and multifaceted contributions benefit from the independence and freedom enjoyed by their authors, away from the green baize of negotiating tables. They constitute an augury to the fostering of exchanges between the cultural and academic circles in China and Europe, a prelude to more people-to-people contacts and better mutual understanding.

Stanley Crossick, Brussels
Etienne Reuter, Singapore

Foreword

It is a geopolitical cliché to observe that China will be one of the principal architects of events in the century that lies ahead.

This is not just because of economics, though we know that China will be in due course the largest economy in the world, as it has been for 18 of the last 20 centuries. It is true of political issues as well. While China is not a military superpower like the USA, it nevertheless has enormous and growing political influence. It is very difficult to think of a big issue on the international agenda that can be solved without China's active participation.

I have never myself believed that we should regard the ascent of China — or of India for that matter — as a threat to the transatlantic community. The growth and material improvement in the quality of life in these two great Asian countries is an opportunity for the whole world.

I very much hope that Europe will build on its historic links with China to create a partnership that can encompass economic as well as political issues. One area where we could start would be in recognizing the shared interest we have in enhancing free trade and preventing a resurgence of protectionism. We should also work hard together to help the development of poorer countries, for example in Africa, and increase our cooperation on the environment including in particular global warming and climate change. If we in Europe and in China can thicken up our relationship, it will not only be good for our citizens, but for the whole world.

Chris Patten

Contents

A New Agenda

On 27 November 2006, Presidents Hu Jintao and George W. Bush had a telephone conversation. Hu had just returned from visits to India and Pakistan following the APEC summit in Hanoi a week before, where the two Presidents had also met for bilateral talks. Bush was arriving at the NATO summit in Riga (Latvia). There was, however, no sign that the President of China was in any comparable direct contact with the leaders of Europe, of EU nations.

China and the EU held a summit meeting in Helsinki six weeks before. China's Prime Minister, Wen Jiabao, attended, and the EU was represented by the Prime Minister of Finland and the President of the European Commission. The joint statement emphasized the importance of high-level political dialogue and consultations, but it is obvious that the EU does not talk to China at the same level as the US. This is the case despite the fact that day-to-day relations between China and the US are much less serene than those between the EU and China.

Diplomatic relations between the People's Republic of China and the European Union as such started in 1975 with a visit to China by the then Vice President of the European Commission, Christopher Soames. The President of the Commission, Roy Jenkins, visited China at the end of February 1979 and met with senior politicians, among them Deng Xiaoping, who was to emerge as the paramount leader. Deng, who had visited the US in late 1978, told Roy Jenkins that to him, the European Community seemed to be coming together politically, economically and militarily, step by step. He wished to see a powerful, strong, united Europe which fitted into his concept of a world structured around specific poles of power. At that time, the Soviet Union represented the central threat both to Europe and to China, and he wondered whether the US was really fully committed to defending Europe. He thus implied that Europe needed to take care of its own security and should eventually cooperate with China, as both were threatened by the Russian bear. Deng said, "You hold the bear by its forepaws where he bites, and we hold him by the hind paws where he kicks, and . . .".

At the time, China was engaged in a brief war with Vietnam, which it saw acting as "Russia's Asian Cuba". Roy Jenkins told the Chinese that he thought China was neither wholly First World, nor Second, nor Third — referring to China's achievements as a nuclear power, in science and technology as well as its economic potential in the context of the implementation of the four modernizations, and the challenge to improve the well-being of its vast population.

A quarter of a century later, at the beginning of the 21st century, China and the EU have both greatly changed. With its booming economy, China is almost unrecognizable to the visitor who accompanied President Jenkins at the end of the 1970s. The EU, today a bloc of 27 countries focusing on economic interaction and integration, has not yet become the wholesome interlocutor that Deng had in mind. It is true that for both the US and the EU, relations with China top their agenda of concerns, in particular with reference to the consequences of globalization. The US, however, is an Asian power, particularly from a security standpoint. Europe is not. Europe's main engagement with China is about trade disputes, but there is no really meaningful political cooperation, so no telephone calls from Hu Jintao.

Following the summit in Helsinki, the EU and China have committed to redefine and strengthen their relations. For the EU, the fundamental objectives are to have China as an investment and trade partner, contributing to growth in Europe, and to have China as a responsible player in world affairs, sharing the responsibilities for stability and the preservation of the environment and natural resources. For China, relations with the EU are not on top of its foreign policy agenda. Its basic priorities are a need for stability in Asia, including the preservation of its territorial integrity in the "one China" concept, and the need of securing markets and access to technology as well as raw materials to sustain its development. Relations with the US are a crucial concern. The presence of the US 7th Fleet in the Pacific Ocean as well as of US troops in South Korea, Japan and the Philippines, attest the daily reality of the US's role in Asia's security.

A New Actor on the World Stage

Nowadays, China is indeed very active in international diplomacy. In a single week in November 2006, it hosted the ASEAN plus 3 leaders in Nanning as well as a summit conference in Beijing of 48 African countries, while at the same time bringing together the six countries involved in the attempt to deal with North Korea and its nuclear program. At the turn of 2006, a powerful delegation led by the Chinese foreign minister toured Africa, which had already received high-level Chinese visitors earlier that year.

Two weeks later the Chinese Prime Minister joined his counterparts from the ASEAN countries, Japan, Korea, India, Australia and New Zealand in a series of summits held in Cebu (13–15 January 2007). The ASEAN agreed on a plan to draft a charter for an ASEAN economic community — the leaders having the example of the EU's economic integration very much on their mind — with legally binding provisions and enforcement mechanisms. "We are happy to have China as our big brother in our region", said President Gloria Arroyo of the Philippines. China agreed with ASEAN to create a free trade zone.

The Chinese Premier visited Japan in April 2007. It was a most carefully planned public relations and charm operation, demonstrating Chinese goodwill towards its neighbor. The new administration in Japan under Prime Minister Abe is engaging in active diplomacy around the region. But plans to review the constitution as well as the creation of a fully-fledged Ministry of Defence and revisionist views of history expressed by this administration are unsettling news for the people in Asia. The true normalization of the China-Japan relationship might take another generation as proper reconciliation or closure over the Japanese atrocities during World War II has yet to be undertaken.

Europe Puts Trade First

At the time of Lord McCartney's mission to China in 1793, China was the largest economy in the world. Throughout the nineteenth and twentieth centuries, its share of global GDP fell as low as 0.5%. Industrial revolution and colonial exploitation increased the wealth of western Europe, and China fell behind. The last quarter of the twentieth century saw a reversal of this trend as China's program of the four modernizations unleashed an unprecedented economic revival.

In those 30 years since the establishment of diplomatic relations between the EU and China, both entities have undergone considerable changes. China today is the fourth biggest economy in the world and on its way through sheer force of numbers to become the world's biggest economy within 20 years. Nevertheless, its GDP is only about one-tenth that of the US or the EU. And its GDP per capita is today barely US$2,000 (although its GDP PPP is already US$7,200). It has experienced an annual growth rate of quasi 10% for the last 20 years — 10.7% in 2006 — but still faces tremendous problems in creating jobs for the 25 million new workers that join the labor market every year. Indeed, the tremendous transformation of its economy has deepened the gulf between the poor and the very rich. Long gone are the days of the egalitarian society 30 years ago.

The European Union then was the European Community of nine states. Developments such as the demise of the Iron Curtain and the collapse of the Soviet Union were difficult to imagine in 1975, as was the idea that the European integration project could comprise 27 member states as it does today. The challenge facing the EU now is to some extent of the same nature as China's problems. How to generate more wealth and create jobs for the 10% unemployed in the EU?

Deng Xiaoping's vision in 1979 of big players in a multipolar picture of the world, with a fully empowered EU being one of the poles, has not materialized. Although a great economic might, Europe is still to become a political and military power. The initial phase of the EU's relationship with China was characterized by cooperation arrangements designed to assist China's development, particularly in areas such as science, rural economy and training. There was some political dialogue, but the emphasis was essentially on economic opportunity as China's development would open vast markets for European goods and services. The Tiananmen massacre had a traumatic effect on this relationship. After a cathartic period of sanctions and frozen relations, China emerged as a different partner, a harder, self-asserting state rather than a soft friend. The issue of the arms embargo has not been resolved to date, both sides having tacitly agreed to put it in between brackets. In fact, it is doubtful that the lifting of the embargo at a future date would have more than a symbolic — important, nevertheless, politically — significance as by now China is buying arms more cost-effectively from Russia and developing its own (e.g. advanced fighter jet), not to mention its spectacular and successful space program.

Significant steps in the history of this relationship were the initial 1978 Trade Agreement, followed by a Trade and Economic Cooperation Agreement in 1985. The EU Commission opened a Delegation in Beijing in 1988. It also opened an office in Hong Kong in 1993 (with accreditation to Macao). The preservation of the business environment and the rule of law in the former British and Portuguese colonies was the objective of the EU's support of China's "one country, two systems" concept for the handover of these territories in 1997 and 1999. Ten years later, one can rate this policy as having been very successful.

The EU and China have held summit meetings since 1998. They reached agreement on China's accession to the WTO in 2000. China joined the WTO in 2001. China's accession to the WTO was a great achievement not only for China, but also for the EU. The EU actually offered assistance to China to prepare for the consequences and implementation of its membership. The pace of trade between China and EU, between China and the rest of the world accelerated. This trade is now three times more important than in 2001. China still has not gained market economy status and is a target for many anti-dumping actions. This reflects a situation where China is the workshop for the world, its cheap and abundant labor involved in low value-added processing and assembly, mostly by foreign funded enterprises. These are issues that will have to be addressed in the next round of negotiations between China and the EU, as China continues to enter high technology sectors, like the manufacturing of Airbus planes.

Looking Ahead

In 2008, the world will be drawn to China. In fact, the curiosity in the West for things Chinese has always been strong, and has strengthened much over the past few years. In particular, the number of tourists has increased, as has the number of Chinese visitors to Europe after the Approved Restriction Status Agreement signed in 2004. These exchanges play an essential part in fostering better understanding between the peoples of Europe and China.

China's fantastic growth over the last 30 years has had obvious benefits for the rest of the world, reducing for instance the cost of clothing, equipment, food and all those things that China supplies. But China's economy is working two-thirds for exports, while the EU and US by comparison only export about 25%, probably less, of their production of goods and services.

China's success due to the combination of very low wages with state-of-the-art technology has created a fantastic manufacturing capacity. In the West, there is now increasing concern that China is destroying "our jobs". At the same time, China has accumulated foreign exchange reserves of over US$1 trillion. 70% of these are held in US treasuries and other US dollar denominated assets. The US and Europe tend to accuse China of artificially keeping its currency undervalued to make its exports more competitive.

As the feeling of unfair competition from China becomes palpable with electorates in the EU (as in the US), there is a serious risk of a protectionist backlash. Restoring a balance or preventing excessive imbalances must be an objective for future negotiations between the EU and China.

Currently, cooperation between China and the EU spans many issues through seven formal agreements, 22 sectoral dialogues, covering anything from aviation and maritime transport to regional and macroeconomic policy. China participates in EU research programs and is also a partner in ITER and Galileo.

It certainly would seem desirable to strengthen EU-China cooperation in international organizations and forums, in particular to share information and coordination on terrorism, migration, drug and human trafficking, pandemics and so on. It will also be relevant to make China share the awareness that growth must be qualified by concerns for the environment, the management of natural resources as well as the impact of frenetic industrialization on global warming.

The reform of the UN is a common interest and the EU certainly welcomed China's participation in UN peacekeeping, clearly a step away from the insistence on non-interference in the affairs of third countries.

The reforms introduced by Deng Xiaoping liberated the economy, eventually making it the most capitalist economy in the world. China has become a brutal playground, where survival of the fittest is the rule. There is, however, no level playing field. Corruption and abuse of power by officials are a major problem both for Chinese and foreign operators. The EU can share its regulatory experience with China, but closer to hand are also the examples and models to be followed of Hong Kong and Singapore.

China's membership of the WTO should eventually make a contribution to reforming and strengthening China's legal system and rule of law. This is an essential requirement for the legal certainty and validity of contracts and conventions entered by foreign investors.

From an EU viewpoint there are a number of sticky issues, in particular the concern over China's failure to comply with some of its WTO obligations, such as market access in services. A classic example is the difficulty encountered by investors from Europe trying to create, ahead of the Olympic Games in 2008, a sports program television channel. Other problems are counterfeiting, unfair tariffs on automobile spare parts, and the difficulties created by the Chinese regulatory authorities for foreign news agencies and journalists.

Today's foreign affairs agenda is driven by domestic concerns. The priorities of government policies, both in Europe and in China, are to provide jobs for the citizens. In China in October 2006, the Communist Party's Central Committee adopted two priorities: one was looking after the poorest in society, the other space exploration. Thirty years ago China was very much an egalitarian society; today, the gap between the very wealthy and the very poor is widening in a spectacular fashion. Extreme poverty and abuse of power by local officials were the root causes for 17,000 riots in China in 2006. Thus, sustaining economic growth is indispensable to alleviating poverty. It also means that energy, raw materials and water management will determine much of China's foreign relations.

This typically shows up China's interest in Africa. The EU, in the context of the summit meeting with China on 9 September 2006, reaffirmed its attachment to the principles of good governance and human rights in Africa. China emphasized the five principles of peaceful coexistence, including the principle of non-interference in internal affairs, as well as the mutual respect of sovereignty and territorial integrity. China also takes an interest in the Middle East where it has reasonably good relations with all the parties and from where it obtains a substantial part of its oil.

Europe's Image in Asia

When visiting or staying in Asia, the opportunities of exchanging views with business communities, academics and government circles, confirm that the EU as such is not very present. Public opinion in Asia is aware that Europe is very busy with its enlargement, the attempts to reshape its operation and institutions, and the development of its single currency, and therefore understands to some extent that not enough energy and attention is given to relations with Asia. Meetings at various levels, in various forums, seldom attract all the leaders from the EU member states, while their Asian counterparts dutifully attend. The President of the Commission is less well-known than the Commissioner for External Trade, attesting the reality that the only issue that matters is trade.

It is also clear that this is the only area in which the EU can act as EU. The EU of 27 member states with all their national leaders, as well as its institutions and its complicated rotating 6-monthly presidency (Germany and Portugal in 2007, Slovenia and France in 2008), has become baffling for China and others in Asia. In the new EU, the assertion of national identities has had a diluting effect on the integration process that was so clearly a theme in the conversations between Deng Xiaoping and Roy Jenkins.

European economic operators in China do not see a big role for the EU institutions. They have set up an effective Chamber of Commerce, with the blessing of the EU, for lobbying against counterfeits, tariffs and so on. But the EU is of little help when investors and their joint venture partners have problems.

The Chinese and others in Asia are well aware that the EU makes the rules, but they also see that trade promotion is a national affair. High-powered trade missions from member states visit regularly, with the presence and assistance of government leaders. Brands (e.g., Ferrari, Mercedes-Benz, Louis Vuitton) are identified with their European countries of origin. Disputes over bras and shoes, prompted by individual member states' concerns, are perceived as denying the European consumer a good deal, and jeopardizing business ventures of Europeans in China.

A New Approach

As China and the EU embark on a new round of negotiations to overhaul their relationship, it might be worth considering a more pragmatic but double-pronged approach.

Trade and investment relations are the priority, but the EU must also continue to project its soft power. That soft power is relevant for rising China was illustrated by the success and interest generated by a November 2006 broadcast on Chinese TV documenting the rise, over the past 500 years, of nine major powers (Portugal, Spain, the Netherlands, France, Great Britain, Germany, Russia, Japan and the US). The program concluded that what makes a power great is "soft power" (education, skills, organization, etc.) and not force or war. Discussions and audience reaction showed that China now sees herself as a major power, but that her rising is peaceful. It would in this context appear logical that all the EU-China dialogues and technical cooperation in education in particular will continue and develop without requiring new codification. Extending and deepening development cooperation and joint programs in public health, education, scientific cooperation, the protection of the environment and climate change should engage scientists, think-tanks and non-governmental organizations from both sides. Issues such as an ageing population confront societies in Europe and Asia. Because of the success of the one child policy, China can control the number of job seekers, but might also, in one generation, become an ageing society like Europe or Japan. Cooperation between small and medium-sized enterprises (SMEs) from Europe and China should also be developed as SMEs can contribute to stabilizing the social fabric outside the big conurbations, creating jobs and encouraging innovation.

Political consultations take place in the rarefied atmosphere of high-level meetings and visits by political leaders from different member states. It is to be hoped that the EU will increasingly speak with one voice and develop an identifiable political face, making the office of Javier Solana, the present High Representative for Common Foreign and Security Policy, more effective. In this context, the EU should also promote China's inclusion into the G8.

If the Doha round fails, it would be appropriate for the EU to propose a Free Trade Agreement (FTA) with China. This might be more expedient in responding to the EU's demands for better market access, removing restrictions on foreign ownership and investment, for joint action on improving the protection of intellectual property rights, and equally, in responding to China's demand for technology transfer and more investments as well as fairer access to European markets.

The Voice of the People

In time for the Olympic Games, the EU and China should agree — possibly after the autumn 2007 meeting of China's Communist Party's National

Congress — on a joint declaration, something that in historical terms would correspond to a European version of the US-China Shanghai communiqué and demonstrate in a highly visible form the will to work together. In fact, the EU-China partnership has a double agenda: a hard one about trade, and a soft one about shaping a new relationship between the nations and people of Europe and China in other areas of mutual interest. Projecting the EU's soft power in China as well as in Asia should become a constant endeavor both for the EU's institutions and the member states. To be successful, any policy must be carried by public opinion; this is equally true in Europe and in China. In China, a civil society is emerging — the internet helps. The government is also promoting greater transparency and accountability for the operations of the Communist Party and the various national, provincial and local power systems. These developments should have a positive impact on the relations between Europe and China.

The relationship between the EU, its member states and China can only develop to mutual advantage if it attaches to a warp and weft of growing people-to-people contacts. It is important to build on existing networks with China: academic, cultural, sports, business — rooted in the national states that make up the EU. Based in Singapore, one is aware of the region's distaste for Europe's interest in and insistence on the issues of democracy, human rights, rights of minorities and fundamental freedoms. Asian interlocutors fail to see why Europe attaches importance to these when they often fear that freedoms undermine the stability needed for economic development. There are two points to make. People in Europe — and presumably elsewhere in the world — are concerned by what happens to their fellow human beings in other places. In a world of global, instant communications, in a world of global news channels, the suffering of people is broadcast directly into the homes of voters and taxpayers. In Europe's active civil society, causes such as the Tibetan cultural and religious identities have a substantial following.

Human rights are definitely on the political agenda when dealing with China, and this is why it is EU policy "to encourage the full respect of fundamental rights and freedoms, of freedom of speech, religion and association, the right to a fair trial and the protection of minorities" in China.

China's political establishment might not like this, but it will appreciate that at a time when anxieties about globalization and trade imbalances fuel clamors for protectionism against China, it would be unwise to increase the number of China bashers in Europe by ignoring the human rights issue. In addition, it is conceivable that new concerns on China's domestic agenda such as the need to make society more harmonious and to promote accountability and democracy within the Communist Party could make the EU-China human rights dialogue more relevant.

The Olympic Games in 2008 and the 2010 World Expo will offer tremendous opportunities for travel and exchange between Europe and China. The cultural attraction for things Chinese has been for centuries a factor in promoting better understanding between China and Europe. Today, as the number of students and tourists grows exponentially in both directions, it is important to strengthen the people-to-people dimension in the China-EU partnership. China has a strong national identity, whilst the Europeans are in a more complex situation, with participants from old and less old, but recently revigorated nation-states in a new venture of cooperation for peace and stability.

For this more complex new Europe, two developments that are foreseeable in China will contribute to shaping the new agenda for the future EU-China partnership. The first comes with China's growing affluence. China's economic success will lead to the emergence of a more affluent and demanding middle-class, resulting in a stronger internal market both for Chinese and foreign — including luxury — products. The second will be a consequence of the first in prompting structural adjustment caused by higher wages and higher manufacturing costs. Investment from the EU and China will seek to diversify, looking for cheaper sites elsewhere in Asia. The strengthening of China's currency will have an impact, as will protectionist measures by China's trading partners. European investors will be tempted to switch to countries in Asia that escape EU quotas and other restrictions. This prospect also corroborates the significance of China lining up with ASEAN for creating a free trade zone.

Indeed, there can be no doubt that trade is the key for the success of the future EU-China partnership, as it is for the future prosperity for the whole of Asia.

Etienne Reuter

Part I

STRATEGIC ISSUES

Key Elements of a Strategic Partnership

Introduction

The EU and China have both undergone dramatic changes in the past 20 years. With 480 million citizens, a single currency and the largest GDP in the world, the EU has become an important actor on the international stage. China, with over 1.3 billion citizens, has undergone dramatic reforms and enjoyed unprecedented economic growth that has also led to a greatly increased world role. Both the EU and China are now keen to develop and further deepen their relationship, but what do Brussels and Beijing mean when they talk of a "strategic partnership"? To what extent do they share the same conceptual ideas and principles? The EU proclaims it stands for a values-based foreign policy with the emphasis on "effective multilateralism". China asserts that its peaceful rise is aimed at developing a "harmonious world". But often, the two sides seem to talk past each other. It would seem to the authors that much more attention should be paid to increasing mutual understanding about each other's history, culture, values, aims and interests before one can really build a "strategic partnership". The authors also propose a number of recommendations that would assist both actors achieve their common goal.

Defining Strategic Partnership

If there is one word that is overused in contemporary politics, it is "strategy". Originally, the word had a strong military aspect and was used mainly in connection with warfare. This aspect remains true today (e.g., US strategy in Iraq, NATO strategy in Afghanistan), but the word has acquired a larger meaning and actors can now become involved in political or economic strategies (e.g., China's development strategy). The word "partner" can mean anything from a lifetime partner (spouse) to a short-term partner of convenience (e.g., the UK-Soviet alliance to defeat Hitler's Germany). When used together with "strategic", the term "partner" usually acquires a longer-term connotation. For the purpose of this chapter, therefore, we propose defining strategic partnership as a long-term commitment by two important actors to establish a close relationship across a significant number of policy areas. This does not mean that there will be no differences between the partners (after all, differences within a marriage are not unknown), but that the partners recognize the importance of their commitment to each other and are prepared to try and reach common ground wherever possible.

Chinese Views

For years, China has attempted to establish a "strategic partnership" with the EU. In an important 2003 policy paper, the Chinese government noted the impressive developments in the EU, stressed the number of mutual interests and similarities of view on many global issues and called for a deepening of relations. In contrast with its relations with the US, China considers that its relationship with the EU is free of strategic competition and rivalry. While the US has huge geopolitical interests in East Asia, especially on the Taiwan issue which China regards as its core national interest, the EU's interest in its relations is mainly in commerce and other non-geopolitical areas. In this sense, it seems to Beijing that EU-China relations are steady and pragmatic. From the Chinese perspective, the strategic partnership should be comprehensive, comprising cooperation in the field of traditional security (weapons of mass destruction, terrorism, etc.) as well as non-traditional security (trade, economics, energy, environment, satellite navigation, etc.). Many Chinese maintain that the partnership should also serve to promote a multipolar world and the democratization of international relations. China would seem to prefer European approaches to international relations to those of the US. China compares its own "peaceful rise" with the peaceful rise of the Union, maintaining that the EU and China will becomes "global balancing forces" pursuing similar international policy strategies. In the post-Cold War era, China is sometimes perceived in the US as a threat, and a containment strategy often becomes the main focus of the China policy debate. China is deeply concerned about the US's unilateral approach in international affairs, especially when it touches on Taiwan. China has tried to integrate itself into a multilateral world, the EU's multilateral approach being perceived in China as the more appropriate way to conduct world affairs.

Moreover, China acknowledges that some elements of EU-style integration could be applicable in the Chinese (and Asian) context. National unification has been identified as China's core national interest since its reform and open-door policy in the late 1970s. While China has successfully applied the principle of "one country, two systems", which was proposed by the late Deng Xiaoping, to Hong Kong and Macao, the Taiwan issue appears to be far more complicated. China cannot accept Taiwan's *de jure* independence and the resolution of the Taiwan issue continues to be an open question. At the official level, China does not publicly recognize that the EU integration model is applicable to Taiwan, but this model has been debated in academic circles and among think-tanks in China. With strong resistance of the "one country, two systems" in Taiwan, the EU model could become more attractive to China in the future. The advantage of the EU integration model is its gradual nature. Integration begins in one policy area, and then gradually expands to other policy areas, and begins with economic issues and then expands to strategic and political areas. Despite political tensions between Beijing and Taipei, China and Taiwan have actually developed a high level of economic interdependence. Think-tanks and academics are looking at the EU model to see how economic interdependence could lead to more integration between China and Taiwan.

China's views of the EU are not uncritical. In the early days, China had very high expectations of the EU model, and many people began to regard the EU as a highly integrated unit. But the failure to secure ratification of the constitutional treaty affected Chinese views of the EU's ability to continue moving forward. In recent years, China finds that its relations with the EU are structurally asymmetrical. While the EU can deal with China as a sovereign unit, China often finds that the EU is hardly a unit. For instance, in China's decentralized system, each province has a high degree of autonomy in policy enforcement. But when pressed by the EU, China's central government is responsible for all agreements it reaches with the EU. On the other hand, China has to deal with the EU's member states in some key issue areas such as market economy status and the arms embargo. Although the first issue is an area of EU competence, China considers that it has to make its views known with key member states. China has been keen to secure market economy status from the Union, arguing that the rising number of anti-dumping cases against Chinese companies stands in the way of implementing a strategic partnership. China also argues that maintaining the arms embargo against China, imposed after 1989, cannot correspond to the desire to establish a strategic partnership. But increasingly, China finds that EU member states cannot reach a consensus on these issues.

From China's point of view, another important factor that can affect China's efforts in building China-EU strategic partnership is the US. The US and the EU have a long tradition of alliance, a partnership without rival in the world. With their largely common values and similar political systems, one would assume that there would be broad agreement on how to deal with China. But China is in fact an area where the EU and the US disagree in terms of their overall approach, on Taiwan and indeed on the arms embargo. The new EU-US dialogue on China (called East Asia dialogue so as not to offend Beijing) has helped bridge the gap on some points, but revealed differences on others. It seems to Chinese analysts that the recent expansions of the EU have made it easier for the US to influence some EU member states when coming to strategic issues with China such as the arms embargo.

EU Views

The term "strategic partnership" has not been defined by the Union and there is little that the countries identified in the 2003 European Security Strategy (China, India, Russia, Canada, Japan) have in common apart from their size. Yet, few have questioned the decision to include China as a strategic partner. As Commissioner Benita Ferrero-Waldner said in February 2005: "There is no greater challenge for Europe than to understand the dramatic rise of China and to forge closer ties with it." Interestingly, some American officials and commentators have expressed concern that the EU might seek to play the "China card" against the US. Few in Beijing share this view, although many seem to prefer the EU as opposed to US approach to foreign policy. As for the EU, no one argues that it should seek to replace its transatlantic alliance with a strategic partnership with China.

While the EU has endorsed the concept of "strategic partnership" in its relations with China, the concept is not as frequently used as on the Chinese side. There is a consensus in the EU that the strategic partnership seeks to build on the current economic and trade relationship with a country whose global political and economic influence and power have grown substantially and will inevitably grow further in the future. The EU considers its policy dialogues with China an effective means to further deepen EU-China relations. Certainly, the EU has to face many consequences resulting from China's rise, and there is broad agreement that the various policy dialogues with China continue to be the best tool to solve their common problems. Also, while China is searching for the strategies developed by the EU in solving problems which European states started to tackle years ago, the EU and China are facing many common problems in various areas. During the years of reform and open-door policy, China has accumulated a rich experience in dealing with internal development and external relations, especially with the developing world such as Africa and Latin America. In some areas, the EU can also learn from Chinese experience. Some EU member states (e.g., the United Kingdom) are beginning to consult China in its dealing with Africa, although with the aim of trying to persuade China to change policy.

Nevertheless, EU-China policy dialogues have so far been focusing mainly on domestic issues, such as further opening up China's economy, protecting intellectual property rights, tackling the social disparities, etc. Due to the lack of shared values and very different political systems, the EU-China strategic partnership can hardly go beyond commercial and economic areas. How to "construct" a strategic partnership with China is thus a serious challenge for the EU.

Key Elements of a Strategic Partnership

First and foremost, the parties must be clear about their objectives in developing a strategic partnership. The authors consider that the main goals should be:

- To promote mutual understanding
- To strengthen the rules-based systems of global governance
- To promote regional and global security

- To promote respect for the rule of law, including human rights
- To increase economic and social sustainability.

Any such strategic partnership must be based on equality, mutual trust, respect and understanding. It must also be comprehensive, holistic and long-term, and there must be an intensive, on-going and stable commitment to it. Ideally, the broad, underlying values of the two parties should be similar, or at least compatible.

Towards Mutual Understanding

As a strategic partnership has to be built on the basis of mutual trust, respect and understanding, the most important challenge is how to build a solid foundation for the relationship. Despite increasing tourism, many Chinese know little about Europe, and Europeans have little appreciation of China's history, politics and culture. While the Sino-European partnership has to be forged government-to-government, it needs to be supported by all elements of civil society. In particular, think-tanks, academics, the media, business and NGOs should be directly involved. Journalistic exchanges are also an important way to promote mutual understanding. Proposals have already been made to promote European studies in China and Chinese studies in Europe. Twinning between Chinese and European cities should be encouraged. A dedicated EU-China website could be created to provide information and a mechanism for exchanges of views, as well as to facilitate networking contacts. A China-EU Committee of Understanding should also be set up, composed of representatives of government, legislators, think-tanks and academia, business and NGOs, who should direct the implementation of a long-term (10–20 years) plan, beginning with schools and universities, including the promotion of exchange programs covering numerous areas such as culture, language, technology, social sciences, natural sciences, etc., at all levels.

Mutual understanding also involves a greater degree of social participation when major decisions are made in EU-China relations. Decision-making processes in the EU and China are drastically different. Prior to taking decisions on dealing with China, there are debates within the EU (as also in PRC). There is also a greater degree of transparency within the EU. In China, decision-making remains authoritarian and lacks social participation and transparency. Social groups sometimes are not so clear about the government's policy towards the EU. For instance, business groups can hardly have any policy input when the government makes its trade policies with the EU, and such policies are also not widely promoted among relevant business groups. Wider participation of civil society in China's EU policy-making can certainly increase understanding of the EU, and thus build a sound foundation for EU-China relations.

The EU Member States and Chinese Regionalism

The political process and competences for different policy areas within the EU is highly confusing. China has, in the past, chosen to address the Union as an institution when this approach is likely to result (at least from a Chinese perspective) in a joint EU-China position on a particular issue. It should continue to deal with Europe in a multilateral framework as well as fostering bilateral relations with the member states. This should be a mutually reinforcing process. Confusingly for the Chinese, individual EU member states — particularly the big ones — promote their own political relationships with China, using this as leverage for trade deals. It is of paramount importance that the member states agree common policies towards China and support, rather than undermine, the goal of an EU-China strategic partnership.

China also has similar problems. Although China is a unitary state, its political system is highly decentralized. While the central government makes decisions in international affairs, the provinces have substantial powers in implementing policies that the central government has reached with foreign governments. In recent years, many Chinese provinces, especially those in the coastal areas, have sought to develop their own relations with EU member states. The lack of policy coordination among Chinese provinces often leads to intensive competition among them in the EU market. Many forms of trade conflicts with the EU are often the results of this lack of coordination capacity on the part of China's central government. The EU should take Chinese regionalism into consideration when its China policy is made. In dealing with China, it is not enough for the EU to deal with its central government alone. More regional offices should be established in order to monitor policy enforcement and policies reached between the EU and China's central government. By taking Chinese regionalism into account, the EU will be able to understand what the real problems are in some key issues such as trade conflicts between the

EU and China. For example, sub-provincial authorities are often key to implementation (e.g., IPRs and anti-corruption measures).

International Cooperation

The EU and China share an overriding objective of a peaceful and stable world order. Both Brussels and Beijing have stressed the importance of working through international institutions. But both actors have not punched their full weight on the global stage. China has given priority in the past two decades to economic growth and has only recently begun to play a more active global role. While China's "going global" strategy is sometimes tied in with purchases of raw materials, especially energy, the country has broader interests in developing relations with resource countries in Africa and Latin America. To become a responsible state, China has taken its role as a permanent member of the UN Security Council (UNSC) more seriously in recent years. It has become more engaged in issues such as Iran and North Korea, while applying the brakes in other areas such as Darfur and Zimbabwe. Although Beijing has taken a back seat in discussions of reform at the UN, it has been reluctant to change the composition of the UNSC, especially the granting of a UNSC seat to Japan, and to accept Kofi Annan's drive to introduce new concepts such as the responsibility to protect. Concerns over national sovereignty remain very important for Beijing.

The EU has its own problems in promoting effective multilateralism. It too cannot agree on a change in the composition of the UNSC, and while it has been supportive of many UN reforms, it has failed to speak with one voice in bodies such as the International Monetary Fund or World Bank. The authors suggest that both the EU and China have a major interest in promoting a fairer and strengthened rules-based international system and that this should be a key feature of their strategic partnership. To improve their cooperation in international affairs, the EU and China will have to develop a higher degree of mutual trust through their strategic partnership. In addition to existing multinational forums, more platforms are available for EU-China interaction due to China implementing its "going global" strategy in recent years. For instance, many EU member states had good and bad experiences in Africa in the past, and China can certainly learn from these EU states. While the EU is concerned about aspects of China's Africa policy, China considers that it is engaged in constructive cooperation in this region.

Political Values

There are some who argue that it is impossible to develop a strategic partnership when the two sides have different concepts of fundamental values such as democracy, the rule of law and human rights. It is clear that the EU and China have divergent views on democracy. However, it is important to remember that many countries in Europe are only very recent democracies. It is also worth noting that China does not oppose the EU concept of democracy; what Chinese elites insist is that EU models of democracy do not fit China's current situation. There is no strong democratic tradition in China, but its citizens enjoy more freedom today than ever before. The Chinese Communist Party (CCP) appears to be inching towards more democracy, but in its own manner and at its own pace. It has a difficult balance to strike between full freedom and stability (akin to the West's problem in achieving a balance between freedom and terrorism). In general, China is following the East Asian model of democratization, namely, economic and social freedom first, and political freedom later. It is broadly understood by many senior officials in Beijing that economic liberalization is likely to lead to political reform and increasing democratization. However, the Party clearly seeks to control its pace and manner, arguing that economic rights have priority over human rights, and economic and social freedom have priority over political and civil freedom/rights.

In the EU, political parties more often than not are means for political participation. But in China, the CCP is not only an organization for political mobilization; more importantly, it bears responsibility to promote socioeconomic transformation. As the only reliable national political institution, the CCP is unlikely to be replaced by any other organizations. Multiparty democracy remains an ideal only among Chinese liberals.

Despite its authoritarian nature, China fully appreciates the importance of ensuring the application of the rule of law both to comply with its WTO obligations and to ensure continued inward investment. China is also strongly motivated by its own "going global" strategy to follow a rules-based international system since it needs such rules to protect its overseas interests and solve international conflicts.

There will certainly be different views on any subjects related to political values in China and Europe, but the important point is to maintain an open and frank discussion to try and narrow the areas of difference. Through political dialogues between the two, China will be able to find the advantages of democracy in solving socioeconomic problems, while the EU can establish a more effective strategy to encourage the Chinese political system to be more transparent and accountable.

Social and Economic Issues

Partly as a result of its staggering economic growth, there are growing economic and social problems, in China. The EU also has economic and social problems, but of a different scale. Given the international impact of some of these problems (climate change, health hazards, immigration, etc.), there is a real need for both sides to engage in a wide-ranging discussion on subjects from energy security and the environment to social and regional policy. While the Chinese dimensions are of a very different order, there may be areas here where the EU experience could be of some value. EU experience of dealing with regional disparities and promoting sustainable development are just two such areas. It is important to emphasize that China is particularly interested in the EU model of socioeconomic development. After the failure of the Soviet model of socialism, China is now turning to the EU model of social and economic development. Ideologically, China finds no difficulty in accommodating European socialism. In recent years, many think-tanks in China, especially the Central Party School, are studying European socialism, and the leadership is keen to learn from the EU to remedy mounting social problems resulting from ruthless capitalistic development in the past decades. The EU certainly has rich experiences in developing welfare capitalism.

Conclusion and Recommendations

A strategic partnership means nothing if it is just a scrap of paper. It needs the whole-hearted commitment of both sides and must focus on promoting mutual understanding. It must also be a partnership between all the constituents of society and ensure an on-going strategic dialogue. It is particularly important to involve civil society if the strategic partnership is to take root among the peoples of Europe and China. There are many issues facing the two sides which require the actors in civil society to agree on a much stronger narrative. A strategic partnership based on diplomacy alone will fail.

An EU-China strategic partnership presents an opportunity for both sides to understand and manage the forces that are shaping a globalizing world, so as to deliver the outcomes which both the EU and China want; namely, peace, prosperity and progress. Our success in doing this will do much to determine whether we spend the rest of this century responding to events beyond our control or putting in place the conditions necessary to make interdependence work. It is within this global context and with a sense of urgency that the EU and China must forge their strategic partnership.

- A small high-level China-EU Committee of Understanding should be established, comprising representatives of government, parliament, think-tanks, business and NGOs. The committee's objective would be to monitor developments in the strategic partnership and draw attention to potential problem areas and, where appropriate, make recommendations.
- The annual summits are important, but often largely symbolic. Although these are occasions to sign agreements and to publicize the relationship, there is limited time for in-depth discussion. Summits could be better prepared by sherpas building on the ministerial and sectoral dialogues. Summits could also be usefully flanked by business and think-tank roundtables.
- The strategic dialogue should be all-embracing and could be facilitated by a new *troika* of three Chinese ministers meeting twice a year with three EU representatives. Such a dialogue should facilitate the resolution of issues such as the lifting of the arms ban and the textiles dispute. Senior officials and others should exchange views on how to strengthen the institutions of global governance. This group could also give guidance to other dialogues on social and economic issues.
- There should be a regular dialogue involving civil society from both sides on sensitive political issues. Issues like the rule of law and human rights are often too sensitive to bring to the leadership level, especially on the China side. But these issues can be discussed and debated at civil society level. After consensus is reached, they can be brought to the leadership level. Therefore, government-to-government dialogues must be accompanied by people-to-people dialogues.

- A judicial dialogue should be established to help achieve a speedy and effective redress system for commercial disputes, including arbitration and mediation. A China-Europe Law School should be established, to be run jointly by a Chinese and a European non-governmental organization, benefiting from the experience of the successful China-Europe International Business School in Shanghai set up by the Commission and the Chinese Foreign Trade Ministry in 1994.
- A dialogue should be promoted between the National People's Congress (NPC, China's parliament) and the European Parliament. The Chinese have not yet fully understood the European Parliament's growing powers and interest in China. Beijing has criticized its resolutions on China without attempting seriously to inform or influence the Parliament. Such a dialogue will increase mutual understanding of the functioning of the parliament system on both sides.
- A high-level EU-China Business Dialogue should be set up (along the lines of the Transatlantic Business Dialogue), bringing CEOs together and giving them the opportunity to meet with political leaders from time to time, including participating in one session of the annual summit.

Implementation of some of these recommendations would help give substance to the development of a sound EU-China relationship. Trust comes from working together, and the above agenda should help create the basis for a genuine strategic partnership.

Fraser Cameron
Zheng Yongnian

2

Environment

State of China's Environment

In recent years, China's environment has been making headlines the world over and usually it is bad news. From the 2005 Songhua River toxic spill to the mounting water crisis and the prediction that China will become the world's highest CO2 emitter at the start of the next decade, it is hard to find positive reports about the huge environmental challenges facing this nation. What is talked about little is how China is tackling these challenges. As it explores its increasingly influential role in the global economy, China is setting ambitious, domestic environmental and energy targets for itself. In the economic context, China is too often "presented as a threat to European prosperity even as they take advantage of cheap Chinese goods and compete vigorously to supply goods and services to China". The interrelationship between China and Europe is much more complex than that. In this chapter, we will explore China's environmental issues and how they relate to Europe and the world.

China is one of the most diverse countries in the world, encompassing such varied ecological landscapes as the Qinghai-Tibetan plateau, the Yangtze River network and the Inner Mongolia desert. It has about 6,266 species of vertebrate and more than 30,000 species of higher plants, of which nearly 20% of the vertebrate species and about 50%–60% of high plants are endemic. China has established 2,349 nature reserves with a total area of 150 million hectares, which amounts to 15% of the nation's total land area.

However, in the past, in China's long history of agrarian civilization, forests and wetlands were treated as "wastelands". Much of the forest cover along the Yellow and Yangtze rivers, and the southeast parts of the country, was converted into agricultural lands and settlements, removed for developmental purposes or reduced to secondary forests, shrubs and wastelands. Large-scale industrial harvesting of forests and conversion of the wetlands began in the early 1950s. The ecological functions of the wetlands were not recognized until the mid-1990s after the Rio Conference. By that time, China had lost large areas of lakes, mangrove forests and wetlands in the central and lower parts of the Yangtze and Yellow rivers, and the coastal areas of Songliao, Songnen and Shanjiang plains.

Many contradictions and problems in China's economic and social development are closely associated with the issue of population, which has become the primary factor restricting the nation's economic development. There is no historical precedent to China's modern population growth since 1950 when its 550 million population doubled in less than 40 years. According to the January 2007 news release of the State Council of China, the total population of the nation has reached about 1.31 billion with an annual growth rate of 8 to 10 million. China has an immense population with relatively inadequate resources per capita. With 1.31 billion people in the world's fastest-growing economy that does not have sufficient resources within its borders, China's environmental problems are obviously not going to remain just its own. Its rising consumption and human wealth per capita will increasingly rely on natural resources from outside the nation.

China is facing not only shortages in natural resources, but also severe environmental pollution, particularly air and water pollution. China started its industrialization fairly late, in the last 60 years. By the 1960s, it had become one of the most polluted nations on earth. Its rivers and groundwater were fouled by industrial chemicals and the air in its cities was blackened with soot. Since 1979, China's open-door policy and economic reform has accelerated its rapid industrialization and foreign investments, which in turn have increased the development of township and village enterprises (TVEs).

The rapid development of TVEs over the past two decades is the backbone of China's huge industrial growth. At the same time, it has caused an enormous impact on China's water quality. Industrial waste from TVEs is rarely treated before it is dumped into local waterways. The main problem with China's industrial development is that not enough is invested in pollution control measures. To add to the problem, existing industrial pollution control equipment is not fully operated or only occasionally operated during inspections by monitoring agencies. Several environmental campaigns have failed. In 1994, the government embarked on a campaign to clean up what was considered the nation's most polluted river, the Huai River. In 2004, after investing more than US$7 billion in the project, it was deemed a failure.

China has participated in most of the United Nations environmental conferences and conventions since 1972, and environmental awareness has been steadily on the rise. In the past decade, China included environmental protection in its constitution and built an extensive body of laws and statutes to protect the environment and natural resources. But implementation of these laws, regulations and international conventions remains a big challenge. Chinese government officials in 2005 reported that half of the world's 20 cities with the worst air quality are in China. The Public Report of China's Environment Status by the State Council of PRC on 27 July 2006 reported that the air quality of 40% of 522 cities in China did not meet the national standards. The reason for this air pollution is that China's major energy source is coal, one of the country's most abundant resources and the world's dirtiest sources of energy.

In Europe, efforts to protect environmental quality rose from the consequences of industrialization in the 18th and 19th centuries. These efforts were strengthened, particularly in the past 30–40 years, in response to demand by its citizens for a sustainable path of development. China is undergoing the most accelerated process of industrialization that the world has ever seen. This unprecedented growth over the past 30 years has resulted in environmental degradation, undermining economic growth. The World Bank calculated that China lost 8% of GDP through environmental pollution in 2004. However, in the past decade, a number of important events have acted as a major check to this negative trend. The 1998 Yangtze flood resulted in the 2000 logging ban on watersheds in western China and a new approach within the government on watershed management. More recently, the 2005 Songhua chemical spill brought about increased enforcement of regulations. As more local disputes arise from communities affected by environmental pollution, Chinese citizens are realizing the importance of environmental quality. This will certainly result in a stricter Environmental Protection Agency and tougher controls by the end of this decade.

2006 may well be viewed historically as China's turning point for environmental protection. Some bold steps have been taken and billions of dollars in government funding are starting to be invested in protecting natural resources and pollution control. The Chinese government has started the implementation of its scientific development concept and issued the following national strategies under its 11th five-year national plan:

• Promote regional and coordinated development based on zoning that restricts human activities in key protected areas as well as in priority areas which have significant ecological services and biodiversity. Policy will be applied to increase the level of payment for ecological services of these key/priority areas.
• Develop a resource-saving and environment-friendly society by developing a recycling economy focused on saving energy, water, land and raw materials and strengthening integrated resources utilization, and further protecting and restoring natural ecosystems.
• Strengthen pollution control of air, water and soils.
• Strengthen the management of natural resources, including water and land resources.
• Improve management of mines and extractive operations.
• Ensure wise use of marine and climate resources.

EU-China Exchange on the Environment

China and the European Union have had exchanges on environmental issues of common interest in the past. The European Union (and member states) have strongly pushed the concept of sustainable development. Both the EU and Chinese government have made commitments to sustainable development. The European Commission (EC) Mainstreaming Environment Paper and the European Union's Biodiversity plan offer strategies for mitigating environmental degradation. In China, the 11th five-year plan came out with a clear directive from the central government on the need to balance the environment with economic growth.

From the Chinese perspective, the environment is seen as an important area of collaboration. China is keen to learn from EC member countries on how to address environmental protection in the context of economic development. At the same time, technological exchange remains a high priority, as the Chinese government sees this as one of the most important tools of "leapfrogging". The Chinese government has placed great emphasis on energy and water efficiency. As a result, commercial opportunities for European technology are multiplying. EU standards also play an important role in increasing standards in China by, for example, raising fuel efficiency and standards in cars.

The 2005 Draft EU-China Environmental Profile identified essential areas where the EU can participate and assist Chinese authorities in sustainable development. These are: environmental education, governance, research and data provision relevant to environmental management decision-making, environmental capacity building and institutional development, and assistance in technology transfer for renewable energy and "clean development" processes.

In fact, the European Commission and many of the EU member states' international development and environmental agencies (for example, DFID, DEFRA, IMELS, KFW, GTZ, AFD, Danida and SIDA) have over the past decade collaborated with Chinese government departments on environmental and sustainable development efforts including biodiversity protection, desertification, water and energy. The Sino-Italian Cooperation Program has provided more than €100 million to China for environmental projects in the past decade. These address issues from water management to green construction for the Olympic Games. The European Commission's Director-General for Environment is a member of the CCICED promoting exchange of ideas between Europe and China. In addition, many international civil society organizations have contributed resources for piloting sustainable concepts in China. For example, WWF was invited to work in China by the Chinese government in 1979. It supported the CCICED taskforce on integrated river basin management (IRBM) in collaboration with the European Commission, which in turn helped to promote the concept of IRBM throughout China and established the Yangtze IRBM Forum.

Priorities for EU-China Relations on the Environment

The authors have identified three priority areas that will be critical to sustainability within China and in EU member countries.

Water crisis in China

One of China's most urgent problems is water. This includes water shortage, periodic flooding, drought and heavy pollution. China has only 7% of the earth's fresh water and about one-quarter of the global average per capita water supply. China not only has very limited fresh water resources, but also uneven spatial and temporal distributions. Its monsoonal climate concentrates precipitation in the summer months, which is unevenly distributed, with lower precipitation in the north and northwest and higher in the south and southeast. Droughts and water shortages in the northern part of the country have long been integral to the Chinese experience. A recent example is the severe drought in the summer of 2006 in Chongqing city in the upper reaches of the Yangtze River, where drought had rarely happened before. China has dealt with major floods along the major river basins of the Yellow River and the Yangtze River in the past thousand years. Periodic flooding is one of the most destructive factors in China and has become more frequent over the past two decades. Two well-known flood disasters are the Yangtze flood in the south and Song-Nen flood in northeast China in 1998.

Changhua Wu *et al.*'s (1999) research review on water pollution and human health in China identified a triple threat: supply is scarce in the populous north, flooding endangers lives and land in the south, and growing municipal and industrial pollution jeopardizes regions throughout the country. The major causes of water pollution are industrial waste, excessive use of fertilizers and pesticides in rural areas and untreated human waste. Groundwater now accounts for 19.5% of water consumed in China, with 80% from lakes and rivers, and 0.5% from recycled water (CLSA, 2006). More than 300 million people in China lack access to clean drinking water. The number of water-related disputes rose by 60% between 2001 and 2004. Groundwater under 90% of China's cities is polluted. It is overused in the dry north of China by industry and agriculture.

Heavy water pollution is increasing water shortage. The Public Report of China's Environment Status by the State Council of PRC, 27 July 2006, reported the monitoring results of surface water quality. It indicated that about 59% of the total 411 monitoring sections in the seven largest rivers and 72% of the 28 most important lakes in China are category IV and V and worse (these categories are not suitable for drinking). Five lakes inside China's big cities, including Kunming Lake in Beijing and Xuanwu Lake in Nanjing, are category V. The two largest freshwater lakes linked with Yangtze River, *viz.*, Poyang Lake and Dongting Lake, are category IV and V respectively.

There are a number of important challenges that need to be addressed to tackle the water issue. Although many new industrial infrastructure projects and factories are installing new technology that reduces pollution and increases efficiency, there is still an urgent need for existing industrial factories to replace old, inefficient and polluting equipment. Financial incentives and stronger regulatory mechanisms are needed to ensure that this transition takes place. Enforcement of good national environmental standards has been difficult because provincial governments have been solely focused on economic development for the past 30 years. Ensuring that provincial governments have the mechanisms, capacity and will to implement national environmental targets is a priority for China.

The CCICED policy recommendations report suggested that the State Environmental Protection Agency (SEPA) be strengthened to tackle the environmental challenges facing China. It noted, "in case of market failure, government should take responsibility, enhance scientific decision-making, strengthen enforcement efforts and intensify the supervision mechanism". It suggested the initiation of a "centrally-funded program to upgrade local and provincial capacity and willingness to improve environmental data gathering". Implementation of recommendations like this would certainly help to address the weaknesses at the provincial level on environmental governance.

The China water crisis has implications for both China and Europe. Water shortages have reduced industrial output by an average of US$25 billion per year, and agricultural output by US$19 billion per year, according to the Chinese government (CLSA). Losses to industrial and agricultural outputs and lack of clean drinking water have enormous implications for the future direction of China's macroeconomic growth and efforts toward a harmonious society. At the same time, the impact on Europe cannot be underestimated given the current interdependence of trade and investment.

Climate change: An issue linking Europe and China

The issue of energy and climate change remains central to the current relationship between Europe and China. China and Europe between them account for around 34.6% of global emissions, 17.4% and 17.2% respectively. Excluding the urgent need for US action, it is clear that an appropriate response to the clear and present danger of climate change to humanity will in a large part depend on the actions of both Europe and China.

The incentive for moving towards a low carbon economy for both Europe and China is an inescapable consequence of climate change. The first national Climate Change Assessment 2006 in China was a four-year government study carried out by over 80 leading Chinese experts. The assessment indicated that China is very vulnerable to the impacts of climate change. Projections have China's mean temperature rising by 1.3°C–2.1°C by 2020 and 2.3°C–3.3°C by 2050. Average annual precipitation is expected to increase by 2%–3% by 2020 and 5%–7% by 2050. Historically, the report found that between 1956–2000, precipitation has changed in different Chinese regions. For example, the annual average rainfall in the middle and lower reaches of the Yangtze River and in southeastern China increased by around 60 to 130 mm. It also found that in the watersheds of the Yellow River, the Hai River, the Liao River and the Huai River, the average annual rainfall declined by 50 to 120 mm over the past 50 years. Further research is urgently required to determine the cost to Chinese society of these and future impacts of climate change. The Himalayas have also seen major environmental impacts from climate change. This is the source area for the Yangtze and Mekong rivers that encompass the high altitude wetlands of Yunnan, Qinghai and the Tibet Autonomous Region (TAR). A WWF 2005 study found that in the past 40 years, "glaciers have shrunk by more than 6606 km^2 in the Tibetan Plateau". If temperatures in China increase by 1.3°C–2.1°C as projected by 2020, then further glacial melting and drying of high altitude wetlands will have serious consequences for annual water flows in, for example, the Yangtze River, which supports a population of 450 million people and accounts for approximately 40% of China's annual GDP.

China is notching up its environmental targets domestically. In 2005, China announced an ambitious energy efficiency target aimed at increased energy efficiency. The goal is to reduce energy consumption per unit GDP by 20% in the five-year plan from 2006 to 2010. To achieve the 2010 target will require major macroeconomic structural adjustment and technological leapfrogging along with provincial governmental reform. At the 2007 National People's Congress Conference (NPCC) meeting, Premier Wen Jia Bao acknowledged that progress towards the target has been slow, but urged greater effort by all departments, industry and citizens to achieve the 2010 goals. In addition, the State Council approved the drafting of a comprehensive Chinese Energy Law in 2005. This would cover all aspects of energy within China as well as overseas obligations under international treaties with the aim of improving the overall delivery of Chinese laws on energy. The process for drafting the Energy Law included consultations with international experts and agencies, uncommon in PRC law development. It reflects changes within the Chinese government on collaboration efforts with the international community on energy.

Despite the government's efforts, awareness of energy efficiency is still very low within Chinese industry and society. The government's National Development and Reform Commission (NDRC) ten-point plan for energy efficiency has as objective 10, to raise awareness and educate society. This is where civil society can and is playing a role, with a consortium of non-government, academic, private sector and international organizations supporting a "20 ways to 20%" campaign (www.20t020.org), which provides Chinese consumers with a guide on how to increase efficency, save money and decrease greenhouse gas emissions.

Critical to any dialogue on Chinese energy and emissions reductions is technology for ensuring higher efficiency standards for coal use and the introduction of new technologies. The EU and member states have been working with Chinese departments like the National Development and Reform Commission (NDRC) and Ministry of Science and Technology (MOST), providing support to explore Carbon Capture and Storage (CCS) in China. For example, the China-UK Near Zero Emissions Coal (NZEC) Initiative, announced at the EU-China Summit in September 2005, will over the next decade look to develop and demonstrate near zero emissions coal technology through carbon capture and storage. Whilst this iniative holds promise for the next decade, the first choice of the Chinese government now is to increase efficiency in coal plants through use of existing state-of-the-art technology.

Energy is a key priority of the current EU-China dialogue, which is structured around an annual summit between leaders and senior officials. The EU-China Energy Environment Program (EEP) seeks to promote sustainable energy use. The five-year, €42.9 million program was established to "correspond to the political intent of the Chinese government and the European Commission, to further strengthen the EU-China cooperation in the area of energy".

Supply chains and consumption — Timber and food

A common misconsception in Europe is that China is solely to blame for its environmental problems. The reality is a lot more complex. Although it is widely recognized that China has become a manufacturing hub for Europe, the less acknowledged aspect is that Europe has exported its energy demand and pollution to China for goods to consume at home but preferably to be manufactured abroad. European governments, corporations and NGOs are keen to provide expertise, services, resources and technologies to improve the environmental quality in China. However, there is little awareness, voice or action on Europe to reduce its unsustainable consumption. This interdependence is of critical importance when looking for solutions to water needs, climate change and forest cover loss.

The situation in the timber industry illustrates the interrelationship between Europe and China. At present, China (and India) consume less than 10% of the world's industrial wood, while in Sweden and the United States, per capita consumption of wood products is currently at least tenfold that of the developing countries. A Forest Trends report in 2006 stated, "The quantity of timber which is processed and exported is equivalent, in terms of volume, to over 70% of the timber imported by China. Markets such as the US and EU increased imports of Chinese manufactured wood products by 700%–900% between 1997 and 2005".

Much of the timber processed in China, destined for European and US markets, comes from the forests of Southeast Asia (Borneo and New Guinea) and Africa. Timber exports from Africa to China grew enormously in the past decade; for example, the value of timber exports from the Congo to China has risen from US$1.9 million in 1997 to US$120 million in 2005. Similarly, soyabean consumption of both China and Europe are causing detrimental impacts elsewhere. Europe and China account for 80% (45% and 35% respectively) of soya exports from the Amazon, where soyabean farming (and cattle ranching) is driving deforestation. EU and China must increasingly work together on market solutions to counter unsustainable forestry and deforestion of the last intact tropical forests.

Active collaboration has begun between Europe and China on practical solutions to address issues on the supply chain from production to consumption. European demand for Chinese manufactured products from Forest

Stewardship Council (FSC) like certified timber has resulted in collaboration between the Chinese State Forest Administration, Chinese timber companies and the Forest Stewardship Council. The China Forest and Trade Network (CFTN) now has over 12 Chinese companies signed up to use timber from sustainably managed forests. China has the largest area of FSC certified forests in Asia, and more than 220 companies received FSC Chain of Custody (CoC) certification by the end of 2006. Exchange of information through mechanisms like the Roundtable on Sustainable Palm Oil, supported by European retail companies like Migros, has seen the Chinese Oil and Food Company (COFCO) agree to adopt Roundtable for Sustainable Palm Oil (RTSPO) standards and explore certification processes.

"The opportunity exists for the developed consumer economies of the EU, US and Japan to make use of existing bilateral trade discussions with China, and broaden the scope of these to include a resource consumption aspect". China is, in many ways, the factory of the world. To ensure sustainable resource utilization and equitable economic development globally, discussions for sustainable globalization must involve all these concerned countries.

Conclusion: Global Leadership for Sustainability

China's environment has become a matter of increasing global concern over the past decade. Within China, recognition of the need for scientific development has risen with dramatic increases in pollution and degradation of the natural resource base. Outside China, concern has focused on the impact that China is having and will have on global resources and its contribution to climate change. The seeds of a pragmatic, sustainable approach to development already exists in China. The government is being forced to take a hard look at the sustainability of key resources. It is clear that the Chinese government is willing to invest in the protection of the environment even if it means sacrificing some short-term growth. Moreover, the government has shown an increasing openness to dialogue and innovation in the search for solutions.

With its huge population, shortage of domestic natural resources, fast growing economy, plus increasing foreign investments and international trade, China cannot follow the economic development model and the current unsustainable lifestyles of EU and North America. The earth will not be able to withstand the impact of China reaching the same level of ecological footprint per capita as the EU today. At the same time, western societies cannot continue their current exploitative consumption patterns, but must become more ecologically responsible. The current and future lifestyles of Chinese and European citizens will have a crucial impact on the overall sustainability of the planet. Within China, the growing middle-class will increase demand for natural resources. The interrelationship between European consumption and Chinese manufacturing will require market solutions, like supply chain certification and other negotiated agreements that can change the lifestyle patterns of European citizens and determine a new path for the future middle-class Chinese consumers.

The fate of the global environment in the 21st century depends largely on the development path China chooses and how much Europe can transform its own. The authors conclude that the EU and China are equal partners who can play a global leadership role in sustainable development. In order for this to take place, China will need to continue its current policy of engaging in more international negotiations and exchange. The EU can provide assistance to China, but will ultimately be required to change its own development paradigm as well as its people's lifestyles towards sustainability. Together, China and Europe can forge a new partnership that supports the transition towards a sustainable global economy for their mutual benefit.

Dermot O'Gorman
Zhu Chunquan

3

Energy

EU PERSPECTIVE

While the two extremities of the Eurasian land mass may be expected to become increasingly embroiled in competition for resources from such regions as the Middle East, Russia and the Caspian Sea, Europe and China are also on the verge of beneficial cooperation towards what could become a new model of energy governance.

Governments, economies and industries everywhere are now being challenged and judged on the basis of how they are planning and delivering energy, as well as providing security, jobs, health and social services, educational and other crucial elements of stability, cohesiveness and prosperity. Yet, in much of the world, decisions affecting such critical energy choices are sometimes taken in piecemeal fashion, without appropriate evaluation or consultation regarding the consequences, or are the subject of intense and sometimes distorted pressures or perceptions.

At one end of the geopolitical spectrum, major economies appeared in the recent past to be launching a frenetic and potentially disastrous competition in their quests for their share of energy resources from traditional producers and suppliers as well as continuing to explore for possible new reserves of oil or gas. At the other end of the spectrum, an estimated 1.5 to 2 billion people live in perpetual darkness and poverty, unconnected to any electrical power source or grid, and illuminated only by the scant quantities of firewood, other biomass or kerosene they can obtain with their subsistence budgets. Taking one specific Asian situation, there are expert estimates that as many as 100 million persons in Indonesia are not connected to an electricity network.

Somewhere in the midst are government decision-makers, international industries, energy producers and consumers seeking to maintain a steady, sufficient and economical supply of energy to meet economic, political and social demands to prevent the risk of plunging into an economic recession or depression. While many of these options reflect the workings and realities of political economics, there is also an urgent need for a certain de-politicization and de-dramatization of the process in order to achieve more informed judgments. Despite the endless flow of words and debates, there is a need for more enlightened information and discussion.

In some countries, this process appears to be underway or at least beginning, while in others it is manipulated or merely window-dressing for a predetermined decision. Some have anticipated the major issues of the 21st century, while others seem to be complacently awaiting having to resort to some form of shock therapy when confronted by a crisis which could destabilize or even bankrupt some economies overly dependent on energy. Countries that fail to face up to these challenges of energy saving, security and sustainability, like those who fail in their responsibility in health, education, debt and other sectors, will leave a poisoned legacy for future generations.

The challenges and choices of energy governance concern not only the selection of an appropriate mix of energies for each society or economy. They also carry with them the possible choosing of societal, industrial and lifestyle options, which could in all likelihood imply geopolitical consequences for contemporary and perhaps future generations. Together, Europe and China can make a huge difference in the choices and models of energy governance for the planet as it faces what may be its most serious existential challenge in the coming decades. The two are involved in a process of cooperation that could and should include a grand bargain to jointly undertake what some in Europe refer to as "a new industrial revolution" in cleaner and more efficient energy. Basically, Europe may be the initial source of alternative energy technology and efficiency, with China providing both the production and application that will, as it has in so many other industrial sectors, result in the critical mass and economies of scale to change the global energy path and practices.

While no one in either region can pretend that the energy paradigm can be changed from one day, or even one year or one decade, to the next, both have recognized that the existing mix of energy sources and consumption patterns cannot be sustained on a "business-as-usual" basis. Virtual information over-load in both China and Europe has involved official actions, studies and pro-nouncement, academic and think-tank seminars and reports and industry and business plans, as well as a media avalanche, to call attention to and raise aware-ness of the twin risks of energy costs and supply scarcity and the threat to the environment of fossil fuels.

By now, there is so much data and information swirling around the com-plex questions facing the world and its political and economic leaders that they no longer need repeating. There, of course, exist disagreements, polemics and dialogue about the nature and urgency of the risks and therefore the actions required. But even now, the geopolitical risk of the competition for tradi-tional energy resources and the potential havoc have been evident for several decades. The recent 2006 study and report about this dilemma by Britain's former World Bank economist, Nicholas Stern, amounts to this generation's equivalent of the 1970s Club of Rome epochal, "Limits to Growth".

The European Commission has drafted plans for a new "industrial revolu-tion" in energy that looks forward to a breaking up of the concentrated power in the energy sector and a more environmentally friendly system of production and distribution. China, for its part, in its 11th Five-Year Plan, has set itself a national target of reducing the energy intensity of its economy by 20% in the period 2006–2011. But clever plans and slogans are insufficient to overcome the multitude of obstacles, preconceptions and interests in the way of making any abrupt changes. Early indications in both Europe and China are that such targets will not be met or will amount to tokenism or window-dressing that will require more political will and economic change if future environmental and energy disasters are to be mitigated.

While the two have also initiated a promising web of collaboration on these issues involving alternative energies, cleaner and more efficient technologies and other consultation on energy supplies, this synergy will have to be intensi-fied to meet their joint and the global challenge. Such exchanges have begun at both the business and industrial levels as well as on the official planning level. For example, major suppliers of renewable energy equipment have already realized the potential offered by operating globally across markets. The Dan-ish firm Vestas, a giant in production of wind power equipment, has entered the Chinese market in recent years, as have many other European industrial leaders. The firm sold 75 wind turbines in China in 2005, saw the number double to 150 in 2006, and has orders for 1,200 for 2007. To accommodate for this surge in the demand for windmills in China, the firm has established a production plant in Tianjin. Conversely, the leading China manufacturer of solar photovoltaic panels, Suntech, also considered a world leader with sales of several hundreds of million dollars annually, ships most of its production to the European market, most specifically in Germany.

Germany, Spain, Austria and a few other European countries stand out as the forerunners of this industrial energy revolution. Since making the political decision to diversify its energy sources, embark on renewable energy and plan the closing of its nuclear power plants, Germany has become perhaps the world leader in renewable power. The sector has surged as a source of employment producing nearly 200,000 new jobs and exported its technology and know-how. The country's engineering and capital equipment sector has also benefited handsomely from its sales and exports of energy-efficient technology. Such calculations also have their weight in the EU's plans to create a more energy-efficient economy throughout its zone, while at the same time becoming a world leader in both environmental protection and its related technologies.

To a certain degree, such plans and choices toward a more sustainable economy and future are in keeping with previous decisions. While some circles in Europe and elsewhere have criticized the modest economic 1.5%–2% growth rates in Europe in the past decade, in comparison to the more eye-catching surges in China, the US and elsewhere, a few others have seen in such a performance the result of a choice of more mature models of development that devotes a higher priority to environmental, social, health and other concerns than to unbridled economic growth. Most serious economic surveys also emphasize that energy efficiency is indeed more efficient and cost-effective for companies, and that for entire societies, the costs of prevention are infinitely lower than the costs of trying to cope with the consequences of environmental degradation.

That energy security and environmental protection have risen to become major national and international strategic priorities hardly needs repetition.

At the start of the new century, both Europe and Asia are standing — still undecided, confused and in some disarray — at a crossroads about which direction to take. Could they decide to essentially maintain the course of the previous century which was dominated by fossil fuels and nuclear energy, despite serious misgivings and costs? Will they instead open the door to a new era of new and renewable energies along with greater efficiency, despite uncertainty about the potential of such actions? Or will they follow different paths, reconsider, double-back, start again, in some continuing uncertainty?

Such choices inevitably carry with them historic implications that should be analyzed in full knowledge of the consequences of the alternative options. Both Europe and China appear in the vanguard of public policy-making in this regard, while other leading actors, such as the US, have been mired in a mixture of complacency and ideology and appear only on the verge of entering this dialogue. Other major economies and world actors, ranging from Japan, India and most industrial consuming countries dependent on energy imports, are also stakeholders. Asia and Europe could become driving forces for achieving such an historic transition and special steps should be taken within the Asia-Europe Meeting (ASEM) process and in other frameworks. The ASEM process should mainstream within all its cooperation and collaboration projects and discussions, sound, efficient, sustainable and ecological principles and planning and technologies that include a priority for renewable energy.

"There are broad similarities in the energy situation in Asia and Europe, such as a high import dependency and dependence on the Middle East," noted one recent study devoted to Asia-Europe energy cooperation. The team of authors also suggest that "Any policy option chosen by one region will also have an impact on the other." Later, the report notes that "In the broader context of economic integration, the EU countries opted very early on for some form of regional cooperation in the energy field… By contrast, energy security issues are still primarily addressed at the national level in Asia." In Germany and China, there appear to be such examination at the highest levels. Others in Europe, the US and elsewhere have launched national policy dialogues which consider a wide array of options or orient the debate toward a predetermined policy or industrial objective.

Germany and other countries like Denmark, Austria and the Netherlands, became experimental showcases for alternative energies, which have also encountered hesitation or reversals of policy following electoral swings. Largely in the aftermath of the rise of the Green party in the 1990s and its entry into a governing coalition, Germany placed increased emphasis on development of alternative energy capability. It also decided, following a government proposal backed by a parliamentary majority, to phase out its existing nuclear power plants. Since then, the country has become the world's leading market for alternative energy sources, including both wind power and solar energy, but also emphasizing greater energy efficiency and reduction. This is despite the fact that other countries have much better conditions for solar, wind and other new energies. 2005 data indicated that electricity from wind energy sources had surpassed the output from the country's nuclear facilities.

In 2005, a total of 10% of Germany's electricity came from renewable energy, and employment in the sector reached 170,000, many in small and medium-sized firms, installing solar panels on roofs or maintaining windmills. Much of this shift has resulted from legislation guaranteeing a fixed price for electricity produced from renewable energy, calculated to compensate and offset the environmental costs of other traditional energy sources. The resulting phenomenon has witnessed, for example, top Japanese, Chinese, American and other producers of solar panels exporting most of their output to the German and other European markets rather than furnishing their own. The top Chinese manufacturer of solar panels, Sun-Tech, considered among the world's top five producers and listed on the New York Stock Exchange, indicates that some 80% of its production is destined for the European market, most of that for the German market.

Chinese economic planners in 2006 launched an historic mid-stream correction to reorient its astounding growth toward remedying potentially explosive gaps which have opened up social and environmental dysfunctions that could pose systemic threats. The Chinese leadership is in the midst of a complex process that could determine whether it can cope with a number of the social and environmental problems which its rampant economic development has unleashed and which, according to many officials and outside analysts, could threaten its continued rise. Chinese leaders and planners have decided to shift the orientation of the country's astounding economic growth of the past decades to a more balanced, just, social and ecological pattern at the recent October 2005 meeting of the Party plenum, but without revealing how this policy conversion would be implemented or worked out in practice.

But the urgency of coping with these potentially lethal economic traps was underlined by the environmental pollution disaster in Jailin and Harbin in Heilongjiang that threatened a major city's water supply and spread to neighboring Russia. It is also present and latent in the repeated reference to the more than 74,000 recorded and announced public demonstrations of grievances throughout the country in 2004.

Approval of the new five-year plan for 2006–2012, which was preceded by an oral presentation by Prime Minister Wen Jiabao, came during a week that also saw an announcement that the Chinese economy had continued to grow at a rate of 9.4% rather than slowing down as generally sought, although the growth was said to be more driven by domestic demand than in the past. This is also in keeping with and giving substance to the leadership's expressed desire of achieving a "harmonious society" through a "scientific method". Also in the same timeframe, the Deputy Director of the State Environmental Planning Agency (SEPA) again warned that environmental degradation at the rate of the past was unsustainable and a profound risk. He indicated the country might adopt a "black list" of cities where air pollution had reached unacceptable levels and would ban new investment in those cities.

Numerous leadership figures and expert analysts have warned of the possible disruptive consequences of income and regional economic disparities, environmental and resource strains, and political and social unrest, among other problems. They acknowledge that remedial action will have to be prepared. Wen Jiabao, in presenting the five-year plan, and other officials later, including during visits to Europe, emphasized that only two numerical targets were included in the program — a goal of quadrupling per capita GDP growth in the coming period, and reducing the energy intensity of the economy by 20% per unit of production. Officials stressed that much of the remainder were declaratory objectives and that market mechanisms were important to fulfilment of the program, as was the case in the previous five-year version. It was also underlined that the program was not compulsory, but that the intension of channelling more investment into the rural economy and applying stricter environmental standards are clear priorities.

Energy experts have noted that there is indeed a long way to go in energy efficiency since the country consumes 50% more per unit of output than the world average, five times more than the US and 10 times more than Japan. China's landmark renewable energy law took effect on 1 January 2007, prompting the government to issue a number of pertinent new rules and technical criteria. In particular, financial subsidies and tax incentives for the development of renewable energy sources — including wind power, solar energy, biomass and others — are in the enactment process, said Zhang Guobao, Vice Director of the National Development and Reform Commission, at a press conference on 12 January 2007. The Chinese system is to be based on the "feed-in laws" that have been successful in advancing renewables in Germany and other European nations.

After gaining a reputation in recent years for its astounding urban growth and the more or less spontaneous creation of new cities, China has also recently launched a bold new experiment to create one of the world's first planned ecological cities on an island site near Shanghai. Not far from the new business and financial center of more than one million which sprang up in a decade or so at Pudong, city authorities are visualizing the first phase of another major urban metropolis at Dongtan for 2010 when Shanghai hosts the World Exposition. The internationally-prominent London-based engineering consulting firm Arup was named during the summer by the Shanghai Industrial Investment Corporation (SIIC) to prepare a master plan for an entire city with lower energy consumption and which is as close to being carbon-neutral as possible within economic constraints. The planners say it should be the world's first sustainable city to attract a range of commercial and leisure investments.

Dongtan will be on 630 hectares, which is said to be three-quarters the size of Manhattan, and strategically located near Shanghai on the third largest island in China at the mouth of the Yangtze River, which is now mostly agricultural land adjacent to a huge wetland of global importance. A road infrastructure is currently under construction to connect Dongtan to the Shanghai mainland. The site is also close to one of Shanghai's airports. The first phase is foreseen to include a wide range of developments with urban parks, ecological parks and "world-class leisure facilities". Priority projects are said to include capturing and purifying water in the landscape to support city life, community waste management recycling to generate clean energy from organic waste, reducing landfills that damage the environment, and combined heat and power systems linked to the use of renewable energy for clean and reliable energy.

There are therefore many signs indicating a growing consciousness in both Asia and Europe of the issues and an accompanying desire to move forward towards a new energy paradigm. There are also suggestions that the corporate industrial and financial communities are joining such a trend, which in principle seems to enjoy broad public support. But the existential question remains whether such signs and trends will move Asia, Europe and the rest of the international community towards what some refer to as the "tipping point" into a new energy era, or whether these suggestions of progress still face insurmountable resistance and obstacles from still dominant energy interests. It remains to seen whether the technological and economic momentum of alternative energies will reach the critical mass required to reach its full potential in the time required.

David Fouquet

CHINA PERSPECTIVE

The EU-China relationship has been characterized as a comprehensive strategic partnership for some years. But, despite both parties' goodwill, this comprehensive partnership has been only partly realized by increasing trade volumes between the EU and China.

Although China and the EU pay a lot of attention to multipolarity and try to create multilateral international mechanisms, they have not really found a way to achieve their strategic goals. Now the Chinese government is carrying out its 11th five-year plan, the commitment to reduce the energy intensity by 20% at the end of this plan offers a window of opportunity to the European Union to show its goodwill to strengthen the comprehensive strategic partnership.

Rationale for EU-China Cooperation on Energy Issues

The EU has some comparative advantages with regard to energy efficiency and for historical reasons. Since two oil crises in the 1970s, the United States and the European countries have adopted different approaches to ensure their respective energy security. The Nixon administration decided to fend off the effects of oil prices soaring by liberalizing world oil supply and an alliance with Saudi Arabia to provide more oil to the world market. This strategic choice was decided because the US dollar is the settlement currency for energy and most commodities. So Americans can influence the price of oil and commodities in the international market by using their monetary instrument.

At the end of the 1970s, the dollar interest rate was very low and oil prices very high, and borrowing dollars to invest in oil-related industries became a lucrative affair. A lot of countries took part in oil exploitation and oil prices began to fall in the 1980s. Moreover, as the former Soviet Union occupied Afghanistan, the US formed an alliance with Saudi Arabia in order to protect Saudi oil production and prevent Soviet influence from coming down to the Persian Gulf. For this deal, Saudi Arabia agreed to provide extra oil to the world market. As 2–3 million barrels per day of extra oil came onto the market, the price fell from $30/barrel to $12/barrel.

The strategy for oil supply diversification and liberalization of the world oil market adopted by the US had very important global effects, including the sovereign debt crisis in the 1980s, because many developing countries that invested heavily in oil exploitation with borrowed dollars did not foresee either the rise of the dollar interest rate under the Reagan administration or the fall of the oil price on the international market. They were trapped into a dollar debt crisis.

European countries have adopted a different approach after two oil crises in the 1970s; as middle-sized powers, they could not afford to adopt a global strategy to influence world oil prices, unlike the US. Thus, European countries tried to ensure their energy security by diversifying energy resources, including the development of nuclear energy and renewable energy, such as solar and wind. At the same time, most European countries adopted an energy policy aimed at improving energy-saving technology and raising energy efficiency.

During the subsequent two decades, the difference between US and EU strategies for ensuring their energy security led to different outcomes. In European countries, energy use is more efficient (energy intensity is something like 60%–70% of that in the US), which is why EU countries decided to adopt the Kyoto Protocol while the Bush administration refused to implement this important international agreement.

The difference between US and EU experiences provided China with some food for thought. Indeed, although China is a big energy-producing country with more than 90% of its energy need satisfied domestically, China has been suffering from international energy price fluctuation. In the 1980s and 1990s, China experienced a period of fast economic growth and energy consumption increased considerably. Logically, China should have paid more attention to energy-related issues, such as the exploitation of new energy resources or the development of energy-saving technology. But, as mentioned above, international oil supply was so affluent and the price so low that it became more profitable to buy oil from the international market. Many Chinese firms, especially power plants, converted their coal-burning systems into oil-burning systems, which was perfectly rational.

Moreover, the Chernobyl nuclear tragedy of 1986 traumatized many Chinese people. So, with cheap international oil, the development of a civil nuclear industry was not a Chinese government priority. Since the beginning of the new century, with the burst of the technological bubble in the US, the Federal Reserve decided to turn on the monetary tap in order to save the market. The extra liquidity released by the Fed flooded the commodity market, pushing the oil prices higher and higher.

With China's economy entering a new period of fast growth, its expansionary manufacturing sector consumes a lot of energy and thus, high oil prices in the international market have become a headache for China. Faced with an electricity shortage, many Chinese firms chose to equip their factories with diesel generators, which pushed China's oil import increase to an historically high level. Oil prices forced many Chinese electricity plants to reconvert to coal. Although cheap and abundant in China, coal poses a serious problem of environment pollution. How to make coal clean is a big concern in the Chinese government's 11th plan. Clean coal technology has been developed in some European countries and it is a mature technology, so there is much room for cooperation between the EU and China in this respect.

Obstacles to Overcome

When the US was massively investing in information and computer technologies in the 1990s, some European companies were doubting the effectiveness of this kind of investment. They invested in environment protection-related technologies, thinking the future world market would be in this field. After more than a decade of development, these European firms have, technologically speaking, comparative advantages in the world. Now that China faces growing problems of energy efficiency, these problems unfortunately are related to environment protection. As EU firms have comparative advantages in both fields, they can help China overcome this kind of problem.

EU companies that developed very sophisticated technologies on energy use or on environment protection need to expand their market in order to get their investment return as quickly as possible, and China can provide them with a much larger-scale market. So by investing in technologies related to raising energy efficiency and environment protection in China, European firms can speed up the processes of capital return on their investment, which will help them keep their technological advantage.

European firms may be tempted to sell their products at a higher rate because they want to get their investment back as quickly as possible, and as they do not trust the Chinese market, they may surcharge potential Chinese clients because they may want to include the cost of counterfeiting in the price of genuine products. This may be the logic of a vicious cycle. To avoid this kind of trap, European firms should take into account the fact that China is a bigger market than what they are used to working with. So they can afford to lower the price of their products in such a way that they can recover their investment on a larger scale and at a smoother pace. On the Chinese side, the government should pay more attention to energy and environmental protection-related intellectual property in order to give European investors better assurance on their investment return: protecting intellectual property is not only a benefit to foreign investors, it is also an incentive which will encourage Chinese firms to innovate and create their own technologies.

The last but not least reason why EU firms should help China develop new technologies related to raising energy efficiency is that, if they do not, Chinese research institutions and firms will develop their own anyway. Chinese technologies would then compete with European technologies in the international market, reducing the profit margins of European firms. If European firms develop energy efficiency technologies in cooperation with Chinese counterparts, they may raise their productivity by reducing costs and find a useful collaborator, instead of a competitor, to explore the bigger world market.

How to Implement a Strategy of Energy Cooperation

China and the EU have a lot to gain by cooperation in the areas of energy and environment protection. But how should they proceed to create favorable conditions for such a cooperation? Firstly, government officials from the EU and China should coordinate efforts on the exploitation of new energy resources. Many EU countries have been involved in the exploitation of new energy resources, such as solar and wind. Sharing these new technologies will allow European firms to lower the costs of their exploitation and Chinese firms to make progress more quickly.

Secondly, Europeans and Chinese should share experiences on traditional energy use. The average energy use intensity in China is much higher than in most EU countries, due to outdated production equipment and mismanagement of energy use. If European firms help Chinese firms improve their energy use, both will benefit. European firms will receive royalties and Chinese firms will benefit from reduced energy use. Thirdly, they can also try to find a way to coordinate their efforts to influence prices on the international energy market by forming a sort of cartel of energy-consuming countries, although it is a very hard enterprise and most efforts in this regard have failed.

Fourthly, they should be engaging in dialogue in order to find a way to facilitate European transfer of energy use-related technologies to China in exchange for easier access to the Chinese market. Fifthly, European and Chinese firms should find a way to coordinate the norms of their products in order to make their products interchangeable.

In the political landscape of the 21st century, the EU and China are not playing a zero-sum game in terms of energy consumption. Although both the EU and China are energy producers and energy consumers, their relationship is not necessarily competitive in terms of energy demand. If China and the EU can coordinate their efforts and help each other to ensure their respective energy needs, this will create a win-win game for both. Indeed, if the EU can help China reduce its energy needs, that will alleviate the pressure on the international energy market, and thus, the EU will benefit from a decline in energy prices. By helping China improve its energy efficiency, European countries can develop their new products on a much bigger market scale, recovering their investments sooner and maintaining an advanced position in the world market.

Ding Yifan

4

Security Issues

EU PERSPECTIVE

Until recently, European security planners had little to say about and not much interest in China. The People's Republic was the place of ancient and rich culture where Europeans liked to travel and make money, taking advantage of the country's economic dynamism. China's place and its role in the global security was more or less left to the Americans, with the Europeans following Washington's lead. This has changed to the point that most of the recent European policy papers and bilateral EU-China summits place security at the heart of the relationship. In the meantime, it has also become clear that the European and American security perspectives on China are not identical and that they are indeed increasingly divergent. Two developments are responsible for this change: the continuing development of the EU into a global security actor, and the expansion of China's interests into areas (Africa, Middle East) which overlap with the European security interests.

This paper presents a European perspective on the relationship's security aspects. It looks first at the most essential aspects of bilateral Sino-European relations, and subsequently, at their transatlantic implications.

EU-China: Closer Partners, Growing Responsibilities

The EU and China agreed to form a strategic partnership in 2003. At this point in time, the EU came to the conclusion that China's rise was an enduring process, which would change the nature of the international system. Rather than object to the inevitable, the EU decided in favor of embracing the process, engaging China and influencing its strategic culture through dialogue and cooperation. Of course, the EU continued to have a number of concerns about China's international posture and especially about cross-strait relations and China's relations with Japan — traditionally a close partner of the EU. On the other hand, with US unilateralism in the background, China's international behavior did not appear uncooperative or irresponsible. Whilst retaining its differences, China was open to discussions and often agreed (or abstained from voting) with the western powers at the United Nations. Like most Europeans, China opposed the war in Iraq, although unlike France, it did not threaten to use its veto power at the Security Council. In 2004 in a landmark decision, China agreed to send its peacekeepers to Haiti, hence overcoming its traditional opposition to intervening in other countries. Since then, China has become one of the major contributors to UN missions, currently having around 1,500 troops (the 12th biggest contribution) in various blue-helmet missions including Liberia, DR Congo and Sudan.

It was not yet apparent that the pluralistic international system both the Europeans and the Chinese spoke about meant different things to each. In 2003, the expansion of the Chinese presence in Africa and the Middle East was only beginning, as was the process of China's military modernization, neither of which caused much concern in Europe at the time. As a result, security issues were either absent or certainly not at the forefront of European considerations when embarking on the strategic partnership with Beijing in 2003. The same was true for the initial European decision to lift its embargo on arms exports to China. The subsequent reversal of the EU decision on this issue was largely motivated by the fact that strategic implications of the move (most notably linked to transatlantic relations, but also concerning the security situation in the region) began to filter into the calculations of European policymakers.

Three years after into the landmark 2003 agreement, the EU carried out a major revision of its China policy. This time, security became one of the top factors motivating the EU's China policy, and this is likely to continue in the future. Security-related aspects of the EU's three most important documents (Commission Communication of 24 November 2006, Finnish Presidency's EU Council Conclusions of 11–12 December 2006, and the Joint Statement of the Ninth EU-China Summit of 9 September 2006) fall into four categories: global governance, energy security, East Asia and China's defense policy. They are discussed below.

Global governance

The overall tone of the EU's recent China policy papers unmistakably suggests that Brussels expects and calls for Beijing's greater contribution towards the maintenance of international stability. A few years ago, the EU's comments on China's global role were limited to commending Beijing's re-entry into the international system and its overall cooperative posture at the UN. This time, however, the expectations of the EU have grown with Brussels saying that as one of the major world powers, whose global importance will only continue to rise, it is essential that China takes a greater share of responsibility. The EU also argues that China has clearly benefited from its integration into the international system and that global stability remains essential for China's economic development and its security interests. What concrete steps and policy posture is the EU calling for here? They fall into the following categories:

- Strengthening the role of the UN, other international organizations and regimes. Embracing a genuine commitment to international law and multi-lateralism. The Chinese tend to replace multilateralism with multipolarity, arguing in favor of a more pluralistic international system — both of which are greeted with unease by the Europeans. Multipolarity has negative con-notations for most Europeans, who associate it with the balance of power politics of the 19th and early 20th centuries. In the European mind, "multi-lateralism" (which the Europeans promote) means the rule of international law, whilst "multipolarity" means the rule of a few big, powerful states and perennial instability. A prospect of a more pluralistic international system is also received with ambivalence in Europe, especially by those who do not question their reliance on the American security protection.
- Enhancing cooperation on non-proliferation. The EU cooperates with China in non-proliferation on the basis of the Joint Declaration issued at the 2004 EU-China summit. The EU expressed its appreciation of the role China played in reaching the six-party agreement in February 2007, which may pave the way for the de-nuclearization of the Korean peninsula. The EU also compliments China's role in trying to resolve the Iranian nuclear issue, although Beijing rejects the EU's call for a more assertive action *vis-à-vis* Tehran. It is with the Iranian and North Korean cases in the background that the EU urges China to promote global compliance of the non-proliferation regime. Brussels also calls for the strengthening of the WMD (weapons of

mass destruction)-related materials and technologies. This provision alludes to China's cooperation with Iran as well as some African states.

Energy security

The EU has watched the expansion of China's energy demand with growing unease. China has become the world's second energy consumer and is on its way to take over from the US as the biggest consumer of the world's energy resources. This is, of course, a natural consequence of China's economic development, which in itself is welcomed by the EU. However, the following aspects of China's energy policy cause concern in the EU:

• China invests in some energy-rich "states of concern", for example in Iran, Sudan, Burma/Myanmar, Turkmenistan and Uzbekistan, whilst ignoring the nature of political leadership there. Refraining from interfering in other states' internal affairs is a long-standing cornerstone of China's foreign policy, but in this case it directly undermines whatever leverage the EU could have in promoting reforms in these countries.

• Almost all Chinese energy companies remain state-owned or state-controlled, and their investment plans are heavily influenced by the government's calculations rather than expectations of profitability. In the view of the EU, these practices often run against the principles of open market and free competition as well as contributing to the rise of energy prices.

• There is no doubt that China's economic development and its dynamically growing energy consumption are posing an environmental challenge and are one of the main factors contributing to global warming. According to some experts, whilst the US remains the world's primary polluter, in some areas (acid rain, particulars and toxic metals) China has already "caught up" with the US. Recent EU documents emphasize the need to enhance cooperation with Beijing over the reduction of emissions and promotion of clean energy.

East Asia

The EU commends China for its role in promoting regional integration and for the improvement in relations with India as well as for being a taming influence on North Korea. The EU expressed some concern about China's relations with Japan, noting recent tensions and arguing in favor of stronger diplomatic engagement. However, Brussels recognizes that history divides these two neighbors and that Japan has not been as forthcoming with settling these past differences as it should have been.

Most importantly, however, Brussels is concerned about the state of cross-strait relations, fearing a possible escalation of tensions, especially during the forthcoming election year in Taiwan. The EU always stresses its commitment to the "One China" policy, but strongly opposes forceful ways of achieving unification. A threat of the use of force by the mainland was, in the view of the EU, characterized by the PRC's passage of the anti-secessionist law, which was one of the main factors motivating the reversal of the EU decision to lift the arms embargo on China. But the EU has also warned Taipei against pursuing any measures that could unilaterally change the existing status quo, such as a declaration of independence.

China's defense policy

The modernization and the growth of the PLA (China's People's Liberation Army) does not raise the same concern in the EU as it does in the US. The EU recognizes that China's rise has a military and defense dimension. However, whilst the growth of China's military spending does not alarm the Europeans, Brussels is increasingly concerned about the lack of transparency in this process. In particular, the EU is sceptical about the actual level of the PLA's budget (assessed by the Pentagon as two or three times higher than official figures) and its military objectives. Consequently, the EU has taken steps to develop its capacity to assess the PLA and China's defense policy.

Transatlantic Implications

The China factor has begun to figure in transatlantic relations following the EU's debate on ending its arms embargo. At the moment, the EU's decision on the embargo has been delayed and it does not seem likely that the matter will be resolved any time soon, although in its recent conclusions the EU Council has reasserted that it would work towards ending the restrictions. Still, the United States remains staunchly opposed to any policy change on the embargo and the EU is concerned about not making a move that could undermine the post-Iraq transatlantic rapprochement. However, the importance of transatlantic considerations in this decision seems exaggerated, if not misjudged. After all, America's other close allies, Israel and Australia, are selling arms to China, which produced some frictions in Washington's relations with these states but no strategic policy shifts.

Whilst the arms embargo has been the focus of the transatlantic debate on China, there is no doubt that the significance of this issue has been blown out of proportion. The majority of issues concerning East Asia reflect very close positions of the EU and the US. For example, like the US, the EU has an interest in the peaceful resolution of the Taiwanese issue and in preventing instability in East Asia. Like the US, the EU is concerned about the link between China's energy investment and its leniency towards Iran, Sudan and other unsavory governments.

However, whilst similar, the interests of the EU and the US *vis-à-vis* China are not always identical. Most importantly, unlike the US, the EU is not militarily present in East Asia and is not an element of balance of power in the region. As argued above, China's military modernization bothers the US to a much greater extent than the EU, which tends to see it as a natural consequence of the PRC's growing international status. The US debate remains focused on the rapid growth in China's defense spending, but the Europeans point out that even if China spends twice as much as it declares ($35 billion), this is still a small fraction of the Pentagon's nearly $500 billion budget.

Europeans do not always share America's security assessment in the region; in particular, they are not willing to participate in the China "hedging" strategy. As the EU further develops its foreign policy role and as its political presence in East Asia grows, it is perhaps inevitable that, although minor at the moment, some transatlantic differences of perspectives in East Asia will become more apparent and perhaps more policy consequential. It is, however, far more important that both Europe and the US share the view that a stable, prosperous and internationally responsible China is in their common interest.

Assessment

Until recently, EU-Chinese relations have been almost exclusively driven by commercial considerations with little attention given to security and strategic issues. This situation has evolved since 2003, but the European security perspective on China is still fluid and sometimes short on detail. The three following elements of Europe's strategic thinking on China can be already identified:

- Europe does not see China as a threat, but as a potential close partner. This represents a significant difference from a certain body of opinion in the US, especially strong in the Congress, which looks at China as an emerging threat. In the US, this is still a minority view, but in Europe it is practically non-existent.
- There is some uncertainty in Europe as to what kind of international actor China is becoming. On one hand, the Europeans applaud China's role *vis-à-vis* North Korea; on the other hand, they are concerned about Beijing's policy towards Sudan and the Darfur conflict. It is still unclear to the Europeans if China will strengthen or undermine the role of international law and its institutions.
- The Europeans are now paying more attention to China's regional role and they are beginning to recognize that Beijing makes a much more assertive actor *vis-à-vis* its neighbors than in other parts of the world.

There is a strong possibility that the Sino-European relationship will only grow stronger, perhaps becoming one of the key elements of global stability in the future. However, much will depend on the internal evolution of both China and the European Union.

Marcin Zaborowski

CHINA PERSPECTIVE

Main Players on International Stage with Increasing Responsibility

Both China and the EU have made good use of a world situation favorable to peace and development in the post-Cold War period and have substantially reinforced their influence in international affairs and capability of diplomatic action.

For roughly 30 years, China has been carrying on a policy of reform and openness. The enlarging and deepening of such a policy during quite a long period could not have happened without internal and external implications.

The lasting economic and commercial open-door policy has resulted in an unprecedented openness of China's mind, giving her a new way of thinking. In China, the new leading concept is to keep abreast of the times, meaning that internal and foreign policies evolve according to the changed situation at home as well as abroad, and are not bound and frozen by rigid unchanged dogma. China understands more than ever that the country's fundamental interests increasingly merge with those of the international community. Recently, explaining the essence of the "China's peaceful development", Chinese Prime Minister Wen Jiabao stated that China tries to "gain profit from the international environment of peace for the development of the country and make this development contribute to the world peace".

In this sense, China is determined to act more positively on the international stage in a bid to play a constructive role in the promotion of both regional and global stability and prosperity. In doing so, China has taken and is taking many more responsibilities and is showing a new diplomatic posture, one of initiative and creativeness, in cases ranging from UN peacekeeping operations to the Iranian nuclear problem, and especially the hosting of the thorny six-party talks on the denuclearization of the Korean peninsula.

In the post-Cold War period, Europe, no longer facing the fatal threat of major military and political confrontation between the two superpowers, had the opportunity to substantially advance its integration process. In 1993, the European Communities became the European Union, reaching a higher integration level and covering enlarged fields of functions. In the meantime, the European Union succeeded in absorbing three former neutral countries and later 10 countries from the former Soviet camp together with Cyprus and Malta, becoming a pan-continental bloc and the central powerhouse for Europe as well as its surrounding area. This historically successful development gave the EU sufficient material, moral and political resources to assume far larger and more important responsibilities in world affairs.

The Laeken Declaration of the European Council of 15 December 2001 raised such a question: "Does Europe not, now that it is finally unified, have a leading role to play in a new world order, that of a power able both to play a stabilizing role worldwide and to point the way ahead for many countries and peoples?" The other motivation, equally important for the EU to seek an effective global role, is its recognition of the new challenges generated from a "fast changing, globalized and very fragmented world" threatening the stability and prosperity of Europe and the whole world. Europe is fully aware of the urgent need to cope with the challenges in a European as well as a global manner. Two years later, in its "European security strategy", the Union reinforced its intention to seek a global role, declaring "Europe should be ready to share in the responsibility for global security and in building a better world"; "An active and capable European Union would make an impact on a global scale".

Both China and EU possess mature and clear-cut strategies on regional and global security and have rich experiences in putting into practice their strategies. Based on its vision on the profound changes which have taken place in the international environment since the end of the Cold War and the resultant update of its diplomatic thinking, China has worked out a new conception of security which stands for mutual trust and benefit, consultation and cooperation on equal footing, as the ultimate conditions for solid security between countries. In improving and promoting good relations with its Asian neighbors, China is convinced that the vitality and efficiency of this new security approach has been effectively demonstrated.

In 2003, during the course of the Iraq war, the EU drafted its first common strategy on security, trying to find a collective response among the divergent opinions of member countries to the new and complicated elements in the international situation. This strategy analyzed the security environment, indicated global challenges and key threats facing Europe, and set three strategic objectives. In practice, the Union is in the process of developing a common foreign and security policy and subsequently common security and defense policy, forming a European force of rapid reaction, enlarging its diplomatic and even military intervention capabilities not only in Europe but also in other parts of the world, gradually but effectively "taking responsibility for global security", as stated by a conclusion of the EU Council of Defense ministers.

Grounds for Cooperation between China and EU on International Security Matters

With their growing global visions and actions on security, China and the EU are set to meet frequently on international grounds. They do not have any conflicts of fundamental interests — neither feels threatened by the other. Furthermore, their strategies on security are more similar than different. They each assess positively the role the other is playing in international security matters. In the latest Council conclusion on policy towards China, the EU expressed its "appreciation for China's constructive role in regional security and dialogue organization, as well as increasing commitments to UN peacekeeping operations". So, with the mutual trust fostered during several decades of relations, the two sides cooperate when there is a possibility, consult each other and exchange views when their positions are somehow distant from each other, or when there is a lack of information and understanding.

Under the pressure of the complex changes in the international security environment and their increasing responsibilities, China and EU felt it necessary to open a new platform for exchanges of view on security matters, apart from the numerous mechanisms of political consultation, and started a strategic dialogue at the end of 2005. Both sides agree that this dialogue gives them the opportunity to elaborate their strategic thinking and explain further their policy related to diverse problems of common concern, in a bid for better mutual understanding and more cooperation.

Convergent points in their security strategy

The security strategies of China and EU have, in essence, substantial convergence and resemblance. Especially since 9/11, as the international community faces unprecedented challenges, they share further common points of view in seeking an appropriate approach towards a very dangerous and very complicated situation.

Similarity in the examination of the security situation

China and the EU, to a large extent, see the world's security situation and define their strategic security objectives in a similar way. They both strive to guarantee stability and promote global development. Both of them pay attention to conventional as well as to non-conventional security threats.

Common option for multilateralism

Neither China nor the EU follows systematically an anti-American diplomatic orientation. Instead, most EU member countries are allied with the US in a transatlantic security guarantee bloc. China, for its part, makes efforts to stabilize and improve its ties with the US. Yet, both believe that no single country is capable of resolving international problems and taking major decisions on international security on its own. Both oppose a unilateral approach and favor international consultation and cooperation in handling security issues. They are in favor of maintaining the UN's authority and respect for international laws and regulations.

Focus on political solution of international conflicts

The essence of Chinese and European diplomatic thinking is to seek peaceful solutions to all international security problems and to avoid using military means as much as possible. Their resolute opposition to American military operation against Iraq highlighted this. Certain EU member states supported the US invasion of Iraq and even sent troops to join the "coalition of the willing", but their participation was motivated more by concern for maintaining their relationship with the US than preferring a military approach to resolving interstate disputes. Moreover, China and the EU prefer to focus on consultation and reconciliation to prevent international disputes ending in armed confrontation. They now cooperate in the mechanism of the five permanent members of the UNSC plus Germany in coping with the Iranian nuclear problem . And under very difficult circumstances, both still spare no effort to save even the least possibility of a way out through negotiation. In sum, it is the belief of China and the EU that generally speaking, the so-called "soft" forces are more productive and correct, even if the notion of soft forces remains to be more precisely defined.

Development as essential element for security

To different degrees but along the same lines, China and the EU believe that the growing gap between developed and developing countries fuels a hatred that promotes terrorism. They similarly state that to fight international terrorism, there must be a good understanding of the sources of this evil. In line with this thinking, they believe that the struggle against terrorism has to avoid leading to antagonism between civilizations and religions and that no religion should be assumed to be identified with terrorist activities.

Divergent points on the security problem

Subtle difference in interpreting and putting into practice multilateralism

By and large, China and the EU are in favor of a multilateral approach in answering to international security challenges. But the EU, particularly a certain number of EU member countries, insist that the diplomatic choice of multilateralism is not an anti-American orientation. Based on this consideration, most European countries dislike the term "multipolarization". While opting for the multilateral approach, the EU has taken the precaution to indicate that multilateralism should be "effective" in a bid to rule out a polarized understanding and application of this concept. China continues to believe that multipolarization is an objective trend in the evolution of the international situation, that such a positive tendency should be encouraged since it signifies sound equality and democratization of international relations and helps a more balanced resolution of global problems. In the meantime, China agrees with the European concept of "effective multilateralism".

Behind this different understanding about multilateralism, there is an interaction between Europe, China and the US. Most European countries rely on the alliance with the US for the final guarantee of their state security. Even making efforts to build up their own means of security, they still attach vital importance to their links on security with their "big brother" on the other side of the Atlantic. Because of the dependence of Europe on American military protection in international security matters, the US has considerable influence on European decision-making on security matters. In recent years, the EU intention to lift the military embargo against China was blocked by the US. So, the American factor surfaces in an eye-catching manner in relations between Europe and China, obstructing to some extent the development of their military and political trust and cooperation. China has no objection to the maintenance of transatlantic security links, nor does it attempt to use its good relations with Europe as an anti-American instrument. But China wants the EU to be less influenced by the US in taking measures to reinforce mutual confidence and cooperation with China. China does not worry very much about the recently opened European and American strategic dialogue on the East Asia security situation focusing on China's rise. China understands the growing attention of the EU to the East Asia security problem, but hopes, frankly speaking, that the Union keeps, in viewing and dealing with Asian matters, a spirit of independence and objectivity and guards against any manifestation of a sense of blocs that originated in the Cold War.

Different attitude regarding internal affairs of other countries

The EU affirms and reaffirms that safeguarding and expanding its values is essential in European diplomacy, pointing out that good governance is, in the final analysis, the most reliable guarantee for internal and cross-national security. State failure being designated as a source of not only internal but international instability, the EU judges that it is its obligation and need to make an "early, rapid and when necessary, robust intervention" in countries regarded failed, as a preventive measure against security threats. China for its part adheres to the principle of non-intervention in internal matters of other countries and respect for their sovereignty. China states that such a principle is the most important and valuable one guiding international relations, and the absence of this principle would risk the world falling into disorder and the law of the jungle. Nevertheless, China admits that the internal problems of one country can, under some circumstances, have regional and even global implications, and the international community should not be indifferent in facing the potential of one country's troubles being exported. China is participating more and more actively in international cooperation under the auspices of the UN in seeking solution to humanitarian disasters in diverse parts of the world. Amongst the permanent members of the UN Security Council, the input of China to the UN peacekeeping operations is one of the most important. So far as the governance of a country is concerned, China believes that developed countries, no matter how powerful they are and how self-confident they are in their own model, should respect diversity of patterns of development and the right of states to choose their own one, and to be careful when they are prepared to take sanction measures against a country in respect of its internal problems.

The Taiwan issue

By and large, the EU, by insisting on a "One China" policy with regard to the Taiwan problem, takes care of China's most important security concern, thanks to the good political relations between them. China still hopes that the EU will have greater awareness of the fact that China's wish to solve the Taiwan question peacefully is stronger than any other country's and that China will do its utmost with maximum sincerity to solve the Taiwan question peacefully. At the same time, China thinks it necessary for the Union to understand better that the Taiwan question relates to China's sovereignty and territorial integrity and that the fundamental interests of the Chinese nation are at stake. In Chinese minds, Europe does not appreciate sufficiently the utmost importance of the Taiwan question for China and where the danger threatening the peace and stability in the Taiwan strait comes from. This divergence sometimes produces negative influences on China-EU relations. China cannot accept certain contents in the EU declaration on the "Anti-Secession Law", nor the statement concerning Taiwan in the latest Commission communication on policy towards China which expresses "strong opposition to the use of force". The excuse of the Anti-Secession Law used by the EU for delaying the decision to lift the arms embargo is, in China's view, groundless. The fact that a few member states do not draw a clear demarcation line between official and non-official contacts with Taiwan authorities and persons can generate discord, damaging the friendly relations between the two sides.

Proposals for More Effective Security Cooperation between China and EU

There is reaffirmed will from both sides to enhance their cooperation in global matters, especially in the security field. The Council's conclusion relating to the latest European Commission's Communication on relations with China stated, "The partnership is increasingly focused on addressing global challenges, and China plays a key role in the effective international response to these issues". China, fully aware of the positive role played by the Union in international affairs and the large possibility of cooperation between the two sides, has warmly agreed to reinforce consultation and cooperation on safeguarding international security. The two sides should make good use of the above-mentioned sound base for more effective security cooperation.

Optimize the utility of canals of dialogue

- Bilateral ways: Apart from the annual summits and strategic dialogues between China and individual EU member countries, the China-EU strategic dialogue is of particular importance and full of possibilities to be developed so as to reinforce mutual trust and enlarge the room for cooperation on practical security problems.
- Multilateral ways: ASEM is quite a useful channel for political dialogue between the EU, China and other Asian countries. ASEM has already published a certain number of statements on security issues, such as fighting terrorism and multilateralism, and gained positive reactions. China and the EU should tap this forum further to seek more common understanding of security problems and more agreements on responses to security challenges.

Themes for possible cooperation

- Promotion of arms control: more vigorous efforts in disarmament negotiations, for safeguarding the international non-proliferation system.
- Closer coordination and cooperation, more exchanges of views and information on the Iranian and Korean nuclear crisis management.
- Further consultation on major hot issues such as the Middle East problem.
- Finding a way for effective consultation and cooperation in resolving non-conventional security issues such as climate change, contagious diseases, illegal immigration, organized crimes and food security.

Xing Hua

5

The Reform of the UN

China and the European Union are emerging as major players in global security governance. As strong supporters of multilateralism, both actors recognize the central role of the United Nations in safeguarding global stability and peace. This chapter aims at exploring the respective positions of China and the EU in the debate regarding the UN Security Council reform, the enlargement of its membership, the issue of the "responsibility to protect" as well as conflict prevention, peacekeeping and peace building. The main goal is to identify the commonalities and differences together with possible areas for cooperation between China and EU in transforming the Security Council, the central body of global security governance, to better cope with the daunting challenges of the 21st century.

UN Security Council (UNSC) as Key Security Governance Actor

The United Nations was created by powerful states under the leadership of the United States as an instrument to deal with peace and security. The echoes of the League of Nation's collapse and the devastation of the most calamitous war in human history prompted the leaders of the states officially at war with the Axis powers, to create a world body with "teeth" to obviate the outbreak of another world war and to guide statecraft toward a peaceful future. In essence, the inception of the UN largely reflected Roosevelt's belief that the Great Powers should determine the outcome of the war and exercise global leadership in the subsequent preservation of peace. This conviction was enshrined in the provisions of the UN Charter, which formalized the primacy of the Security Council and its five permanent members for the maintenance of international peace and security. To this end, the Security Council was devised to function as an enforcement mechanism with substantial authority, albeit subject to Great Power veto. Such an arrangement was designed to engage the Great Powers in this collective security mechanism, while at the same time making the Security Council more effective in reaching decisions when circumstances require. This strong structure was put in place so as to contrast the deficiency of the failed League of Nations, where all members of the council and of the assembly could veto substantial decisions.

The UNSC was entrusted with substantial authority to deal with future threats or breaches of international peace. The Council was endowed with powers to both legitimize and legislate. It can legitimize by determining which actions do and do not constitute a threat to international peace and security, and authorize certain actions accordingly. It also legislates by issuing resolutions on substantial matters that are potentially binding for members and non-members alike. While the Security Council did manage to mitigate interstate conflict in some regions and to some extent, it failed to fulfill its designated mission as the central organ for the maintenance of international peace and security. The Cold War between East and West, with their respective leading states holding permanent memberships in the Council, rendered the organ unable to perform its security role to a large extent.

The end of the Cold War unfolded a new chapter for the UN Security Council. After decades of marginalization throughout the Cold War stand-off, a new opportunity opened for its revitalization as a key security governance actor. Its engagement became visible in various parts of the world. The unity among the Council's members in their stern response to Iraq's invasion of Kuwait in 1991 indicated that this global organ finally found it could perform the role assigned to it by the founding states 45 years ago. Although the Council has functioned relatively better when compared to the Cold War period, it remains characterized by allegations of ineffectiveness and lack of representativity.

Making the Security Council More Representative: The Membership Issue

The Security Council established in 1945 consisted of 11 members, with five veto-bearing permanent members (P-5) — the United States, Russia/former Soviet Union, China, Britain and France — and six rotating non-veto-bearing members, out of 50 member states of the newly founded United Nations. Changing the Security Council's membership or veto power requires amendment of the UN Charter (Article 108) and necessitates the approval of two-thirds of the UN General Assembly. A further requirement is the ratification by two-thirds of all member states — in accordance with their own respective constitutional procedures — including the mandatory backing of the P-5. Hence, only one such *de jure* amendment has been made to the UN Charter since its formal signing on 26 June 1945. In 1965, with a view to the expansion of UN membership, the Security Council was enlarged from 11 to 15 members and the required majority from seven to nine votes.

As the UN has grown more universal, many countries complain that the representativity of UNSC membership has decreased accordingly, and as a result, its rules and decision-making no longer reasonably reflect the will of the international community. Since the end of the Cold War, calls for further expansion of the Council to reflect the new political landscape have been mounting from various parts of the world, but no membership plan has so far acquired the necessary support.

The UNSC is clearly an arena where pragmatism instead of reformism carries the day. The chances for an eventual enlargement of its membership are little better than zero due to a myriad of political and legal hurdles. The very notion of reform entails different things to the different member states involved, depending on their respective national interests. Obviously, the five permanent members have vested interests in the current structure of the Council. In addition, each potential candidate for a permanent seat has so far faced opposition from its major opponent (Japan-China, Germany-Italy, India-Pakistan, Brazil-Argentina, etc.).

In the mid-1990s the reform debate picked up momentum. Special working groups were tasked to find a way to reform this outdated relic of 1945. Two options were set out in the 2004 report of the High-Level Panel on Threats, Challenges and Change, which was endorsed by the then UN Secretary-General Kofi Annan in his 2005 report, *In Larger Freedom: Towards Development, Security and Human Rights for All.* The first option, Model A, provides for six new permanent seats, with no veto being attached, and three new two-year term non-permanent seats, divided among the major regional areas. Model B provides for no new permanent seats but creates a new category of eight four-year renewable-term seats and one new two-year non-permanent (and non-renewable) seat, divided among the major regional areas.

Mr. Annan's strong support for a quick overhaul of the UNSC gave hope to a small number of countries which have long been aspiring for a seat. Japan, Germany, India and Brazil formed a so-called "Group of Four" (G4), seeking the Model A solution. Meanwhile, other nations such as Italy, Pakistan, Argentina and Canada formed a "United for Consensus" (UFC) movement, strongly opposing adding new permanent members. In the end, due to the strong opposition or reluctance of the Chinese and American governments, the 59th General Assembly postponed its deliberation.

According to the official discourse of the Chinese government, enlarging the membership is an important aspect of the reform of the Security Council. The Chinese priority is to increase the representation of developing countries and allow small and medium-sized countries to be given more opportunity to enter the Council on a rotating basis. While China seems open to the idea of adding new permanent members, she does not explicitly endorse any plan. By emphasizing that the reform should be conducive to enhancing the authority and efficiency of the Council and strengthening its capacity to deal with global threats and challenges, China implicitly rejects the idea of granting veto power to any possible new members. China also stresses the principle of achieving consensus through consultation, and opposes setting a time limit for the Council reform or forcing a vote on a consensus-lacking proposal.

Clearly, the Chinese position reflects its key priority in 2005 to rebuff Japan's bid to obtain permanent membership, as China's relations with Japan further deteriorated in 2005 due to the then Japanese Prime Minister Koizumi's repeated visits to Yasukuni Shrine, which also honors 14 first-class war criminals. In contrast to the European reconciliation after WWII, the Sino-Japanese relations are still plagued by animosity on both sides, despite growing economic interdependence. Even if Sino-Japanese relations have improved from late 2006, the Chinese position will not change substantially for the moment.

On the European side, there is no common policy. The UNSC Council reform is a most striking source of disagreement among EU members. There are differing approaches due to the sharply diverging interests of its most powerful members. The majority favors enlargement of both permanent and non-permanent members. Most EU states support Model A. However, the German aspiration to obtain a permanent seat met with fierce opposition from Italy. From the early 1990s, Italy has been openly campaigning against a German seat out of concern for being reduced to a second-rank player within the EU.

Italy is opposed to any proposal that adds new permanent members and instead supports a substantial increase in the category of non-permanent members or permanent rotating regional seats. The Italian position is based on two reasons: firstly, an increase in rotating members can better check the power of the permanent members; secondly, permanent membership creates arbitrary distinctions among member states and freezes them in place indefinitely, and new permanent members would be unaccountable. Consequently, Italy proclaimed a regional-based representation and the need for the creation of a single EU seat. Such an idea was favored by EU's foreign policy chief, Javier Solana. On several occasions, he said that a European seat was a "good idea", and that a "possible cause" for the rift among the EU member states is the fact that the EU is not represented by one seat on the Council. In the light of the Iraq saga, Solana reiterated the need for the EU to speak with one voice internationally. It is, however, virtually unthinkable that the United Kingdom and France would relinquish their seat for a single EU one as long as there is no single European foreign policy. The French and British governments are aware that any talk of a single EU seat on the UNSC might put their privileged position under pressure. That is why, as Jeffrey Laurenti argues, Britain and France have a strong incentive to bring Germany into the Council inner circle: if left outside, the Germans will surely press for a consolidated EU seat at the expense of separate British and French permanent seats, but if the Germans gain their own permanent seat, the British and French can feel secure in retaining theirs in perpetuity. Overall, the role of the EU on UN Security Council reform is disappointing and undermines the credibility of its commitments to effective multilateralism by supporting well-functioning international institutions. The mutually neutralizing positions of its members result in EU passivity in the reform debate.

Regulating the Use of Force

Regulating the use of force is the primary function of a collective security system. The core of the idea of collective security deals with how to bring about and preserve peace. Article 2.2 of the UN Charter expressly prohibits member states from using or threatening force against each other. It specifies the only two occasions when force can be used legally by states individually or collectively. One such occasion is "self-defense if an armed attack occurs against a Member of the United Nations" under Article 51, and the other is military measures authorized by the Security Council under Chapter VII in response to "any threat to the peace, breach of the peace or act of aggression".

These universal rules of using force have been under challenge over the past years on two fronts. The first concerns the broad reinterpretation of the self-defense clause to allow for preemptive and preventive military actions against imminent or potential threats; the second touches on the embracement of the principle of "responsibility to protect", which would allow states to undertake humanitarian intervention in other countries.

The ongoing debate regarding Article 51 is whether a country which is not attacked but faces an imminent or potential security threat can, "without going to the Security Council, claim the right to act, in anticipatory self-defense, not just preemptively (against an imminent or approximating threat) but preventively (against a non-imminent or non-proximate one)"? The High-Level Panel report does not favor the rewriting or reinterpretation of Article 51 to allow states to take preventive military action. Yet, the panel report admitted that states may have the right to take military action against an imminent threat according to "long established international law".

The Chinese view is consistent and clear. In its position paper on UN reform, the Chinese government insisted that "use of force should not be resorted to without the authorization of the Security Council with the exception of self-defense under armed attack. Whether an urgent threat exists should be determined and handled with prudence by the Security Council in accordance with Chapter 7 of the Charter and in light of the specific situation". The Chinese stand is based on several arguments. First, any relaxing of Article 51 will open a Pandora's box that will lead to the abuse of self-defense right by major powers. As America's invasion of Iraq indicated, accusing some countries of posing a security threat could be used as a pretext for a state to use military force to achieve regime change, and further destabilize the country and the region. Second, there is a gradual acknowledgment in China that there might be some occasions where states, acting within the collective security system, have to deal with the potential threats posed by some countries, through preventive diplomacy backed by possible military actions in the future. The spread of weapons of mass destruction makes such a task more urgent than before. However, China strongly insists that any decision should be taken by the Security Council, the only legal and legitimate organ in today's collective security system. Third, while supporting the centrality of the Council in making decisions regarding the use of force, China calls for extreme prudence in the use of force, requiring the relevant actors to seek all possible peaceful means to solve the conflict. Only after all peaceful means are exhausted would China think of the possibility of using force authorized by the UNSC.

Since the EU is committed to multilateral and rule-based international order, the mandate of the Council is central for the use of force. The EU recognizes its primacy for the maintenance of peace and security and wants it to act effectively. This is what the EU called "effective multilateralism" in its security strategy of 2003. However, it also emphasizes that action must be taken when rules are broken.

The Responsibility to Protect

The second debate centers on the concept of "responsibility to protect". This is closely related to the evolving concept of security after the demise of the Cold War. It is a response to the changing nature of conflicts and their victims, which puts human security onto the top agenda of security. Sovereignty is conceived as a responsibility to protect rather than a license to slaughter the defenseless population inside the state. Since the end of the Cold War, western countries started to promote the idea of humanitarian intervention, that is, military action taken to prevent or terminate serious violations of human rights that is directed at and is carried without the consent of a sovereign government. British Prime Minister, Tony Blair, initiated the doctrine of humanitarian intervention and, in his view, the principle of non-interference must be qualified in important respects. Acts of genocide, oppression producing massive flows of refugees, and regimes based on minority rule, are not purely internal matters; they can be properly described as threats to international peace and security. Under such circumstances, other states should have legitimate, even legal, reasons to intervene militarily.

The trauma of the genocide which took place in Rwanda in 1994 added moral support for humanitarian intervention in the West, such as the US-led NATO military campaign against Serbia in the Kosovo war in 1999. While the US invasion of Iraq in 2003 was in the beginning based on alleged Iraqi possession of weapons of mass destruction, such weapons were not found and the humanitarian argument, removing the dictatorship in Iraq, became the main rationale for the invasion. Nevertheless, the military operation did not receive UNSC authorization, and its legitimacy was also compromised by the involvement of the national interests of the major powers. Mr. Blair specifically referred to the national interest in his fifth principle of humanitarian intervention. The legitimacy is further eroded by the catastrophic aftermath of the invasion. As CNN reported recently, the British medical journal *The Lancet* claimed that since March 2003, 655,000 Iraqis or an additional 2.5% of Iraq's population have died as a result of the conflict.

Acknowledging the backlash resulting from past humanitarian interventions, both when it happened (Kosovo) and when it failed to happen (Rwanda), a reformulation of the concept of "humanitarian intervention" into "responsibility to protect" was put forward in 2001 in a report of the International Commission on Intervention and State Sovereignty (ICISS), which was set up by the Canadian Minister of Foreign Affairs in 2000 after a call by UN Secretary-General Kofi Annan. Later, the High-Level Panel on Threats, Challenges and Change, a panel of eminent persons set up by Kofi Annan, largely adopted the recommendations of the ICISS in its report of 2004. While it acknowledges that the responsibility to protect the population of a country rests primarily with the state concerned, should that state not be able or willing to take that responsibility, it then becomes the responsibility of the international community to take action. The international community, through the United Nations, also has the responsibility to use appropriate diplomatic, humanitarian and other peaceful means, to help to "protect populations from genocide, war crimes, ethnic cleansing and crimes against humanity". Should peaceful means be inadequate and where national authorities are manifestly failing to protect their populations, the international community is entitled to take collective action, in a timely and decisive manner, through the Security Council, in accordance with the Charter, including Chapter VII, on a case-by-case basis and in cooperation with relevant regional organizations as appropriate.

The EU welcomed the reaffirmation at the UN Summit of 2005 of the unprecedented recognition of the responsibility to protect. Accordingly, the Union has fully endorsed the doctrine of "responsibility to protect". From the EU's point of view, it is encouraging that China in the end supported the embracement of the general concept of "responsibility to protect", and agrees that the international community does have legitimate concern to ease and defuse a massive humanitarian crisis within a country, considering its traditional strict adherence to state sovereignty and the principle of non-interference in internal affairs. Having said that, as the Chinese position paper on UN reform states, China places strong emphasis on prudence in judging a government's ability and will to protect its citizens, as internal unrest in a country is often caused by complex factors. China also insists that, in responding to those humanitarian crises, the UNSC should exploit peaceful means "as far as possible". Whenever this involves enforcement actions, there should be more prudence in the consideration of each case. China's strong emphasis on prudence reflects China's persistent concern that the West would use the human rights issue to interfere in its own domestic affairs.

A concrete case like Darfur makes clear where both the EU and China stand. During the Darfur crisis, up to 400,000 people have died and more than 2.5 million have been displaced. The European Parliament has been most vocal in its stance and has urged the UN to act according to the "responsibility to protect", and the EU has been more willing to impose targeted sanctions against the regime of Khartoum as it has done against other repressive regimes like Burma and Belarus. On the China side, economically, as the biggest investor in the Sudanese oil industry, China has a substantial economic interest in Sudan. Politically, along with Russia and other Arab countries, China thinks the Darfur crisis is a much more complicated issue, and urged parties concerned to seek diplomatic solutions before imposing any sanctions on the Sudanese government. Therefore, the Chinese government prefers to use private diplomacy to persuade the Sudanese government to accept the deployment of UN peacekeeping forces in the Darfur region. In mid-April 2007, the Sudanese government finally agreed to the deployment of 3,000 UN troops to strengthen the earlier-deployed African Union peacekeeping troops in the Darfur region. However, to bring this agreement into effect and bring more UN troops in the region, requires the EU, China as well as all other relevant actors to work much harder than what they have done so far.

Enhancing Security Council's Peacekeeping and Peace Building Capacity

The Charter of the United Nations does not mention the term "peacekeeping". However, during the Cold War era, the Security Council authorized a number of peacekeeping operations based on the provisions in Chapters VI and VII.

The first generation of peacekeeping operations during this period had its own characteristics: (1) it was usually aimed at maintaining peace between states; (2) the consent of the parties involved in an interstate conflict had to be obtained; (3) peacekeeping forces were deployed after the parties reached a ceasefire agreement; (4) they were generally composed of small military contingents, lightly armed, and mostly from neutral or non-aligned countries; and (5) force was only allowed to be used for purposes of self-defense.

Since the end of the Cold War, the second generation peacekeeping operations (PKO) has embarked on a road that is qualitatively and quantitatively different from the first generation: (1) it increasingly serves to maintain peace in intra-state conflicts, involving multifunctional missions such as peacekeeping and peace building; (2) it often does not obtain the consent of all the relevant parties to a conflict; (3) forces are composed of both civilian and military personnel, and the contingents are larger and armed with heavier weapons, increasingly coming from larger states; and (4) peacekeeping forces are authorized to use force to fulfill their mandates.

Since China regained its seat on the UN Security Council in 1971, for almost a decade, UN-sponsored peacekeeping operations were seen as interference in countries' internal affairs and as the undesirable result of US-Soviet hegemonic power competition. Therefore, China hardly participated in any vote on UN peacekeeping operations, nor did she bear any financial responsibility for such operations. In 1981, China voted for the first time for the extension of UN peacekeeping in Cyprus. In 1982, China paid dues to the operation in Lebanon. In 1988, China officially became a member of the UN Special Committee on Peacekeeping Operations.

In the 1990s, China started to participate in UN-led peacekeeping operations: she dispatched a total of 522 military observers, liaison officers and military advisors, and 800 engineering contingents. Since this modest beginning, Chinese participation in UN peacekeeping operations has surged over the past six years. At the end of 2006, China was participating in 11 of 18 on-going UN PKOs and deploying a total of 1,666 military personnel, and thus became the 12th biggest contributor in troops among all UN member states. Financially, China now shares about 2% of the total annual PKO budget, ranking 9th, and is the biggest contributor among the developing countries. While so far only military observers, engineering, transportation and medical contingents have been sent, China is also preparing itself to send heavily armed troops capable of undertaking more demanding PKO tasks. During discussions on increasing Chinese troops in Lebanon to a level of 1,000, China suggested sending an armored contingent, although in the end she decided to send an engineering and medical team again following a UN request.

While China now actively participates in UN-led PKOs, many of them being second generation operations, China still insists in participating only in UN-led PKOs, and would like to see the Security Council control and oversee these operations. China also insists that UN PKOs comply with the UN Charter and all the basic principles, including neutrality, consent of parties concerned and non-use of force except for self-defense. China does not see PKOs as the only means of the UN to maintain peace and security, the fundamental approach being to eliminate the source of the conflict.

The EU and the UN share very similar objectives and values in promoting peace and stability in the world. They both defend a comprehensive approach to security and emphasize structural conflict prevention by tackling the root causes of threats and conflicts. The EU cooperates with the UN on all levels of peace and security. The Union makes a major contribution to virtually the whole range of UN activities. EU members together are the largest financial contributor to the UN system. The EU pays 38% of the UN's regular budget, more than two-fifths of UN peacekeeping operations and about one-half of all UN member states' contributions to UN funds and programs. The cooperation has been increasingly institutionalized in different areas, such as crisis management, through regular joint consultations and exchange of information. The Union plays a unique role in the non-military dimensions of complex peacekeeping. EU cooperation in peacekeeping has been increasing steadily since 2000, active in different parts of the world — in the Balkans, Middle East and particularly Africa. However, it is the EU rather than the UN that sets the agenda for UN-EU relations. While the EU member states recognize the primacy of the UN Security Council's legitimizing power, the UN mandate does not appear to be a *sine qua non* condition; witness, for instance, the operation ALTHEA in Bosnia-Herzegovina and Proxima in Macedonia. Moreover, the EU member states contribute more to UN-mandated peacekeeping than to UN-led operations. There is reluctance on the EU side, similar to that of the US, as to the reliability of the UN structure in managing such operations. The consequence is two-speed peace operations.

Seeking EU-China Cooperation in Global Security Governance

An EU-China global strategic partnership requires the two sides to seek collaboration beyond bilateral issues. As two parties aspiring to play a bigger role in global affairs, they need to think through the areas where they should develop cooperation.

As demonstrated above, the EU and China share some strong interests in strengthening the United Nations Security Council as the key institution for global security regime. Although the two sides hold some different views on the reform and strengthening of the UNSC, they should concentrate on the present efforts at coordination and collaboration and explore potential areas for further development and improvement.

On the expansion of UNSC membership, both sides recognize the need for a more representative security council in the coming years. However, on the future configuration of the Security Council, as well as the procedure of reform, differences do exist between EU member states and between the majority of EU states and China. As the issue involves all member countries of the United Nations, a concerted action is much needed within EU, between EU and China, and among key players in the United Nations. This calls for an improved dialogue between the EU and China, to ensure that the reform would not only enhance the representativity of the Council, but also make it into a more effective institution in governing global security.

On conflict resolution, both parties put political solutions of interstate and intra-state conflicts to be their priority, as demonstrated by China's harmonious world vision and Europe's civilian power tradition. Both parties stress the need to respect the central authority of the UNSC in the authorization of the use of force in enforcing global security. The two sides do find themselves in disputes over the scope and necessity of using coercive measures, including the use of force, in global security governance. As the most successful multilateral organization ever, the EU multilateral approach stresses the effectiveness of a rule-based international order. China, being a strong supporter of national sovereign rights, mostly sees the UN as the multilateral institution to safeguard sovereign status, and to promote intergovernmental cooperation based on broader consensus. Therefore, China was reluctant in the past regarding the use of coercive measures to solve security and humanitarian problems. Nevertheless, in 2006, China's support for the UNSC resolutions on imposing sanctions against North Korea and Iran indicated that China is becoming more aware of the need and value of coercive measures in global security governance. Therefore, in the coming years, in order to work together where both parties share similar views or to narrow their differences where they have divergent views, the EU and China should establish mechanisms in joint fact-finding, problem definition, policy-making and policy implementation on the field.

The evolution of China's PKO policy indicates that a new area has opened for global cooperation between the EU and China. As the European Union seeks to play a bigger role in global security governance, China and Europe can develop cooperation in various aspects. Firstly, China and the EU should develop mechanisms to better coordinate their positions in PKO decisions within and outside the Security Council framework. Within the Council, it is important that the two major EU member states, France and Britain, closely consult with each other on matters related to the management of on-going operations and the deliberation of possible future operations. Outside the Security Council, China and the Union should strengthen bilateral consultation on PKO-related issues.

Secondly, China and the EU should better cooperate in the task zones where PKO troops from both sides have been deployed. Currently, in the 11 PKO zones where China has troops in service, there are also troops from EU member states. Enhanced cooperation between Chinese and European contingents will contribute to the fulfillment of the PKO mission.

Thirdly, as a newcomer in the UN-led PKOs, China still has a long way to go in developing its PKO capacity. As European states have been engaging in peacekeeping operations for several decades, there is much to be learned from their experiences.

Fourthly, as there are also EU-led PKOs with the development of a European Security & Defense Policy, China also hopes that these operations will comply with the UN Charter and be better coordinated with the UN to ensure full utilization of each other's advantages. China, being a permanent member of the Security Council, has a legitimate interest in an enhanced dialogue with the EU on this matter.

Gustaaf Geeraerts
Chen Zhimin
Gjovalin Macaj

Part II

GEOPOLITICS

6

The US Factor

For Europe and China alike, the most important bilateral relationship is with the United States. Although often described as a "strategic triangle", neither the Chinese impact on the transatlantic relationship nor Europe's role in the Sino-US relationship is remotely comparable to the significance of the United States for the Sino-European relationship. Describing the United States as the elephant in the room does not even begin to do it justice: the size and shape of the room are themselves shaped by the US factor.

To start with the Sino-European relationship and then look at the US influence is to look in the wrong place. It is the structure and dynamics of the other two relationships — the underlying tensions in the Sino-US relationship and the underlying strength of transatlantic ties — that provide the critical frame.

The Primacy of the Transatlantic Relationship

It is not much of an exaggeration to suggest that major developments in EU-China relations over the past few years have been a subsidiary consequence of the fraying and strengthening again of the transatlantic relationship. The 2003–2004 "honeymoon" period in EU-China relations, during which the two sides launched the "strategic partnership" concept and agreed, in principle, to lift the arms embargo, was substantially driven by a major transatlantic falling-out over Iraq. It was led, moreover, by two European political leaders — Jacques Chirac and Gerhard Schroeder — who were simultaneously burning their bridges with the Bush administration. The end of the honeymoon, in 2005, coincided with Schroeder's fading the scene, and the efforts of both Europe and the United States, largely successful at an elite (if not a popular) level, to put transatlantic relations back on track.

More important than these particular twists though is the basic structure of the two primary relationships. Despite their differences, Europe and the United States have a long tradition of strategic cooperation, a fully-fledged military alliance, deeply integrated economies (not least in the defense sector), and shared commitments to a number of basic values. China and the United States have an increasingly integrated — if sometimes testy — economic relationship, but despite growing diplomatic coordination over issues such as the North Korean nuclear crisis, the broader political and security relationship is still characterized on both sides by hedging, mistrust over intentions and a perceived gap in values. Most obviously, the US security commitment to Taiwan and Chinese threats of force against the island ensure that the two sides are engaged in on-going preparations for the eventuality of war with each other. The net result is a mix of cooperative and competitive elements that amounts neither to full partnership nor to overt rivalry.

Deep transatlantic cooperation could not coexist with these structural tensions in the US-China relationship without there being certain implied constraints on the scope of Sino-European relations. The United States expects that even if the Europeans are not going to provide active support to US security policy in East Asia, there will at least be no serious moves to undermine it by selling arms or key technologies to China that could place US targets at greater risk during a war. A similar expectation is seen in the case of Israel, another key US ally without security responsibilities in East Asia, whose potential arms sales to China have been treated by the United States as inconsistent with the maintenance of strong US ties. Both Israel and Europe have faced the prospect of restricted transfers of US military technology, blocks on Pentagon purchases and other steps with serious repercussions for future military cooperation.

The imbroglio over the lifting of the EU arms embargo clarified one issue — in the near future, the Europeans are not going to inflict serious damage on transatlantic relations for the sake of a deepened "strategic" EU-China relationship. But although there are many shared views between Europe and the United States about China, this apparent transatlantic comity conceals many underlying questions that are unresolved:

- To what degree does Europe agree with US strategy in East Asia?
- To the extent that it does, is Europe prepared to move to align itself more closely with the United States in its strategy towards the region?
- To the extent that it does not, are there circumstances over the longer-term where Europe would adopt a competing strategy to the United States in East Asia?

European Alignment with the United States in East Asia — Four Scenarios

Focusing on East Asia can sometimes appear restrictive to Europeans. China is now a global actor and its policy towards Sudan is in many ways closer to home than its policy towards Vietnam. But aside from the fact that China is, first and foremost, an East Asian actor and its global role will be significantly defined by the nature of its rise in this region, European attitudes are gradually starting to change.

The debates over the arms embargo have already stimulated broader EU-US dialogue about policy in the region and this is only likely to intensify as the embargo question resurfaces, as it is likely to in the run-up to the agreement of the EU-China partnership and cooperation agreement (PCA). This coincides, moreover, with two other major drivers. First, the transatlantic military alliance, NATO, has been shifting its focus to deal with new global threats and take in new global partners. This has already brought European troops into combat in Afghanistan, China's neighbor, and seen the deepening of ties with East Asian security partners, Australia and Japan. Decisions are looming for the European side as this more global NATO moves into its next phase and the argument for a more closely integrated role for these new partners becomes harder to resist — however implausible it is to imagine the extension of Article 5 commitments. Second, China's economic rise has been transforming East Asia into an ever more important region for European economic and commercial interests. As well as being by far Europe's largest regional trading relationship, it is now the major source of new growth for European companies and of inward investment flows to Europe. Europeans are increasingly conscious of how little influence they have over strategic questions, such as Sino-Japanese or cross-strait relations, in a region whose stability is vital to the European economy.

The net effect of these developments will inevitably be to site Europe's China policy in a broader political and security context, with greater attention now being paid to its impact on key allies and to the regional picture.

But these are still early days and at the moment, European policy fluctuates between two relatively weak positions, either of which could nevertheless persist:

(i) *Absence of European strategic policy.* It is possible that the European role will not develop at all. With no European strategic presence in East Asia, the United States had not previously treated the EU as a consideration in its thinking about the region and was only moved to do so when it appeared possible that Europe could start playing an actively negative role. Transatlantic discussion about East Asia may gradually wind down as Washington decides that the value of the conversation came only from ensuring that the Europeans understood why certain lines should not be crossed. China, after observing both the European climb-down over the lifting of the arms embargo under pressure from Washington and then the failure of the constitutional referendums, has concluded that it was probably too early to view the EU as an important and independent strategic actor. Divisions over China within the EU, whether on the degree to prioritize human rights or the differential impact of the Chinese economy across various countries and sectors in Europe, make it a difficult subject around which to agree on robust common policies. The net outcome could be a constrained EU role all round: easily leant on by Washington if Europe again appeared to be taking steps viewed as unhelpful, but easily leant on by Beijing too if transatlantic cooperation on East Asia appeared to be gathering pace.

(ii) *Tacit European alignment with the United States.* Another potential outcome is a European decision not to cause difficulties for US policy in East Asia, but not to lend it any active support either. Without necessarily subscribing to the virtues of the US hedging policy, the Europeans could continue supporting the engagement dimensions of US strategy while opting out of the balancing dimensions, knowing that there will be few real objections from Washington as long as Europe does not take any steps viewed as directly harmful. Even if the Europeans agree with US policy, they may see open support for it either as counterproductive ("ganging up") or simply harmful to European interests, creating risks for good relations with China that could damage economic and commercial ties. At one level, this would not differ significantly from the first scenario — choosing to play a modest role rather than doing so by default — but it would mean a far more stable and predictable policy framework than has existed over recent years, including a clear set of parameters for arms sales and technology transfer.

There are two further plausible scenarios, however, both of which would largely be driven by the imperative of influence:

(iii) *Active European cooperation with the United States.* The Europeans could decide to align their policies more closely with the United States. Seeing rising Chinese power as a potentially destabilizing force in the region unless democratic allies are given due attention and support, Europe could step in to play a more active role. Such a move could be prompted not just by a spirit of transatlantic cooperation or belief in the correctness of US strategy, but by anxieties over waning US influence in the region. The steps this could involve range from European involvement in contingency planning for worst-case scenarios over Taiwan, to support for deeper partnerships with NATO for countries such as Japan, as well as active efforts to strengthen political and economic relationships with other countries in the region to provide ballast to additional centers of power aside from China. Underpinning it would be a European decision that the risks involved in damaging commercial relations with China would be outweighed by the necessity of ensuring stability in the world's most important economic region and the advantages of having a weightier European voice on the strategic situation in the region. The obvious fact that the United States is able to maintain a vibrant economic relationship and an increasingly cooperative diplomatic one at the same time as hedging against Chinese security threats may also overcome European caution, and it could reasonably be expected to coexist with a cooperative Sino-European position on solving shared global problems.

(iv) *European competition with the United States.* Another potential outcome would be a situation where the Europeans decide that US policy in the region is ill-judged. Driven by many of the same motivations in the third scenario, Europeans may decide that stability in the region is important, that Europe should play an active role, but that US strategy is not the best way of achieving it. This decision would stem from a European analysis that balance of power politics goes against lessons from Europe's own history and that, for instance, the regional integration agenda should be the focal point for support, with the priority being to embed China in a network of consensual consultations, mutual obligations and pooled sovereignty. The degree to which this cuts against US strategy rather than complementing it will depend on the relative premium Europeans place on institutions and values. If the goal is to support the development of a regional architecture underpinned by democratic values and norms, this may be seen by the United States as a justifiable difference in emphasis but nevertheless consistent with US strategy. If the Europeans support institutionalization as a good in its own right even where the consequence is to squeeze the US role (creating, for instance, pressure for the United States to withdraw its military presence), exclude Taiwan and other such steps, this is liable to be seen as antithetical to US interests. Other steps that have been mooted, such as European cross-straits "mediation", would likely be viewed with a similar degree of suspicion. There is, of course, a hypothetical fifth scenario, in which Europe aligns more fully with China, but it is hard to see why such a provocative step would be taken unless there was a serious and sustained transatlantic rift.

These scenarios have intentionally been drawn up in static terms, based on an extrapolation of existing trends in the relationships. In practice, the US and Chinese agency roles will be substantial and will do much to decide which scenario pertains.

China, the Transatlantic Alliance and the World Order

At the broadest level, it will hinge on the direction in which China chooses to define its global role and whether the respective visions of world order on the EU, US and Chinese sides are in alignment.

It is hard to separate developments in the EU-China relationship in 2003/2004 from the "unilateral moment" in US policy, which prompted a sense in some European circles that a multipolar world might be a safer world. Similarly, the highly visible increase of China's power and presence in regions such as Central Asia and Africa in 2005/2006 has prompted serious anxieties in both the United States and Europe about the impact this is likely to have on certain key foreign policy priorities. Both share a view that democratic, well-governed states, adhering to basic international norms and a commitment to the free market, provide the best underpinning for global order. A tension remains between these different elements — the free-market and the free society — however, and what they imply for global governance.

One analysis essentially pits the forces of order against the forces of chaos. It sees those states and actors in the international system with a vital interest in the smooth functioning of international markets and the global economy ranged against a mix of rogue states, terrorists and other threatening forces, whether climate change, global pandemics or organized crime. The implication is that the forces of order — including China and a less regressively minded Russia — should combine through institutions such as the UN Security Council, an expanded G8 and the emerging regional groupings, to manage and address these problems. Democracies may be preferable, but supportive autocracies are essential allies too. The mainstay of China policy in this framework is essentially a matter of keeping economic relations on track (finding mutually beneficial ways of holding off protectionist forces) and persuading or cajoling China to take its international responsibilities seriously.

The second analysis questions whether a powerful, nuclear-armed, non-democratic state will ultimately cooperate in maintaining the western world order once it is strong enough to choose otherwise, and indeed, that it may be a security threat itself of a far higher order than avian flu. This analysis implies that it is more important to build a web of political and military relationships based on support for fundamental political values rather than just the free market. While the precise forms this could take vary, obvious models would be to include other democratic allies in existing politico-military clubs, such as NATO, to develop new global democratic alliance structures, or to develop structures similar to NATO in other parts of the world, particularly in East Asia.

At present, elements of both models — concert of Great Powers and global alliance of democracies — exist, though neither one in a fully realized state. China's behavior in the coming years will be one of the major determinants for which model assumes precedence. If China moves forward with democratic reforms of its own, it would do much to affect thinking about how its role in the new global order is likely to evolve. Alternatively, if China becomes a steadily more constructive force in the world, developing close cooperation with the United States and Europe in solving international problems, despite making only modest progress on internal reforms, the case for a global order based more closely on a concert of Great Powers model would be reinforced. At the global and regional level, China is working hard to ensure that this model emerges as the natural choice — whether through cooperation on Sudan and North Korea or through "good neighbor" and integrationist policies in East Asia — but most countries continue to hedge their bets to a greater or lesser degree, and this is likely to remain the framework within which Europeans will face its choices over which policy orientation to pursue.

Conclusion

The role of the US in EU-China relations in the future is, as this chapter has argued, going to be less about the press of Washington's thumb on Brussels and more a question of how the Europeans see China's role, the US response and the degree to which this interaction supports European interests and values. China may consciously adopt "European" positions on wedge issues, whether Iran or climate change, where Europe and the United States differ. The United States may press for closer cooperation from Europe on issues such as technology transfer to China or the shifting global role of NATO. But Europe does have the scope to make some real choices and it is entirely possible over the medium- to long-term that Europeans will be prepared to risk tensions in the Sino-European relationship — or the transatlantic relationship — for the sake of strategic influence over developments in the coming century's most important economic region. China's response to the "US factor" in the arms embargo decision has been to move more slowly on Sino-European strategic cooperation, seeing Europe as a dependent variable in the transatlantic equation. The US factor has also been blamed in China for the apparent toughening of European policy towards China in 2006, embodied in the October Commission Communication. Although understandable, there is a risk that the broader dynamics behind European thinking will be misread. If China decides that the road to Brussels runs through Washington, it is likely to become a self-fulfilling prophecy.

Andrew Small

7

Taiwan

CHINA PERSPECTIVE

In 1949, at the end of the civil war in China between the Nationalist Party led by Chiang Kai-Shek and the Communist Party led by Mao Zedong, the defeated Chiang Kai-Shek fled to Taiwan. Since then, there have been *de facto* two Chinas: the People's Republic of China (PRC) and the Republic of China (ROC). In most of the years before the 1990s, leaders from both sides intended to bring Taiwan and the mainland back together again as a complete Chinese territory. Both sides agreed that there was only one China, but disagreed as to whether the Beijing or the Taipei government should be the legitimate representative of the country. The situation has dramatically changed since Taiwan adjusted its China policy. Staying away from unification with mainland China, the current leaders in Taipei devote themselves to enhancing local identity and pursuing independence.

The changing situation across the Taiwan strait in the last decade makes the Taiwan issue an acute security problem in the post-Cold War era. On one side of the strait, the "one China" policy has eroded, with Taiwan consciousness rising. On the other side, reliance on military deterrence has been highlighted. The frequent steps towards independence taken by the Taiwan leadership test the patience of Beijing. The growing extent of the risk of war not only threatens the peace and stability of the Taiwan strait, but also worries the international community. To overcome the political and military tensions across the strait, it is necessary for the international community to work closely together with the two sides, and to exert pressure on both Taipei and Beijing that the status quo should be strictly defended.

"One China" Policy

Since the founding of the PRC, the leadership in Beijing has been following the "one China" policy steadfastly. During the five decades and more of the PRC's history, Beijing has been giving an increasing emphasis to peaceful unification, although the use of force has never been renounced. After the Korean War, China attempted to improve the relationship with the United States and to defuse the tension across the strait. On 13 May 1955, Zhou Enlai pointed out at a plenary session of the National People's Congress that, "Under possible conditions, the Chinese people would like to liberate Taiwan in a peaceful way." This was the first time that the PRC ever expressed the willingness to peacefully unite with Taiwan.

In the 1970s, the improved bilateral relations between Beijing and Washington motivated China to adjust its Taiwan policy by taking a more cautious attitude: "To liberate Taiwan is our set policy, but it depends on the development of the international situation as a whole and our own preparation. If it cannot be solved by force, peaceful liberation is the best. For the present, it is better to sustain the status quo." Later on, the "one country, two systems" model introduced by Deng Xiaoping and practised in Hong Kong and Macao strengthened Beijing's confidence in peaceful unification. Beijing expressed its willingness to strive for a peaceful resolution to the Taiwan question.

Dialogues established across the strait in the late 1980s led to the "1992 consensus" between the two sides. In comparison to the official standpoint in the past, the "one China, each with its own definitions" formula was a big step taken by the Chinese leadership. The consensus implied that while adhering to the one China policy, the Beijing government became more flexible in seeking common ground with Taipei. Rather than emphasizing Taiwan as a province of China, Beijing allowed Taipei to enjoy more freedom in defining its status. Beijing took a softer strategy: unification is the long-term goal which can be realized upon the completion of economic and cultural integration.

The emphasis on a peaceful approach by the Chinese leadership is mainly out of the following considerations. First, since the economic reform policy was carried out at the end of the 1970s, the economic achievements have not only noticeably improved the living standards of the Chinese people, but also helped legitimize the leading position of the Communist Party (CCP) in China. Maintaining economic growth is deemed an important task, which serves both the interest of the country and the CCP. Domestic economic development requires a peaceful external environment. For three decades after the PRC was founded, Mao Zedong believed that war would break out soon. A lot of national resources were consumed for the preparation of war. The focus was diverted to economic development only after Deng Xiaoping made the judgment in the 1980s that peace could possibly be maintained. Benefiting from the favorable external environment, China has been growing rapidly in its economic capacity. The experience of both war and peace motivates the Chinese to highly appreciate peace and stability.

Second, along with the improvement of external relations with the outside world, China attaches great importance to its international image-building. China tries hard to dispel the suspicions of other countries on the negative consequences of China's rise and promotes a peace-loving image globally. To counter against the "China threat" discourse, China has reached all kinds of partnerships with many other countries, solved most of the territorial disputes with its neighbors, and promoted loudly its strategy of peaceful development.

Both the military and the peaceful approaches serve Beijing's one China policy: the Chinese leadership attaches sufficient importance to both of them. The peaceful approach is the preference of the PRC. Beijing intends to keep the status quo at present and promotes the ultimate unification in the long-run. However, the initiatives taken by the Taiwanese towards independence alarm the Chinese leadership. In the absence of other effective means to restrain Taiwan's behavior, military deterrence becomes indispensable.

Taiwan Revisionist Policy

Vis-à-vis the consistent one China policy held by Beijing, Taipei has experienced salient changes in its China policy. In the diplomatic battles between the PRC and the ROC, the ROC has been a big loser. Since the PRC replaced the ROC to become a member of the UN Security Council in 1971, the diplomatic space for the ROC has been largely squeezed. The number of countries which have diplomatic ties with the ROC shrunk from well over 100 before 1971 to today's 24 (many of which are very small countries). The diplomatic pressure, the infeasibility of unification with the mainland, the rising sense of

Taiwanese identity, and the different path of economic and political development has prompted the Taiwanese to fundamentally change their policy by emphasizing their distinct identity and seeking the possibility of independence.

Chosen to be the successor of the President of the ROC in 1988, Lee Teng-Hui started to push Taiwan along the road to independence. As a native Taiwanese who was educated both in Japan and the US, Lee held a different understanding of the status of Taiwan compared to the other Nationalists who came from the mainland. Lee made his separatist policy more pronounced in July 1999 by declaring that the relations between the PRC and Taiwan should be conducted as "state-to-state" or at least "special state-to-state" relations. As President of the island, Lee promoted those who were born in Taiwan to important leading positions in the government, in order to diminish the political influence of the Nationalist mainlanders.

The Nationalists introduced a democratic system to the island in the late 1980s. The Democratic Progressive Party (DPP) came into existence against this background. The Nationalist Party lost the presidential election of 2000 and its five decade-long dominant position in the politics in Taiwan. The victory of the DPP candidate Chen Shui-Bian further pushed Taiwan on a slippery slope towards independence. A series of revisionist actions have been taken by Chen's government. Different from the standpoint of the Nationalist Party, Chen rejected the 1992 consensus. In 2002, Chen defined the cross-strait relations as "one country on each side of the Taiwan strait", implying that Taiwan is an independent sovereign state. Since the late 2003, in order to cut the historical link between Taiwan and China, the Taipei government has added "Taiwan" to the cover of local passports. In March 2004, in order to win the presidential election again, Chen called for a referendum and was in favor of a new ROC constitution. In July 2005, Chen said that the ROC and the PRC "are two separate countries with divided rule and do not exercise sovereignty over each other". In February 2006, Chen announced that the National Unification Council and its guidelines, which had committed Taiwan to unification if China adopts democracy, had ceased to function. In early 2007, the Taiwan government revised the high school history textbook with the object of "de-sinicization" by highlighting the differences between Taiwan and China, identifying Taiwan as "self" and China as "the other". The state-owned enterprises of the ROC were also asked to change their names by removing the word "China" from them.

In order to gain international support, Chen plays both the card of democracy and the card of the Taiwan people. The democracy developed in Taiwan not only enlarges the gap between Beijing and Taipei in political system, but also adds credit to Taiwan internationally. From Brussels to Washington, the western world is pleased with the democratic achievements in Taiwan, while criticizing mainland China for lack of freedom of speech and other human rights. Moreover, the rising sense of Taiwan identity gives support to Chen's policy for independence. In his new year speech of 2007, Chen pointed out that a steadily growing amount of people in Taiwan identify themselves as Taiwanese. Whereas 36.9% of the respondents of a poll identified themselves as Taiwanese and 13.1% thought themselves as Chinese in 2000, in a survey of November 2006, 60.1% identified themselves as Taiwanese while only 4.8% regarded themselves as Chinese. Chen held that in cross-strait relations, "sovereignty, democracy, peace and parity" should be emphasized; Taiwan is equal to mainland China; the fate of Taiwan should be decided by the Taiwan people. Chen's revisionist policy imposes huge pressure on Beijing, which is tensely on guard against any further movements on the island toward independence.

External Actors

The US is the most important external influential power in the Taiwan issue. Its close link with Taiwan dates back to World War II when the Chiang Kai-Shek government was a close ally of Washington. After the PRC established diplomatic relations with the US in 1979, Washington has maintained its ties with Taiwan based on the Taiwan Relations Act. In cross-strait relations, Washington carries out a policy of deterrence and reassurance with the purpose of maintaining the status quo. It does not support the use of force by the PRC to reunify the country militarily, nor is it in favor of Taiwan independence. In order to defend Taiwan from military attack, the US has not only strengthened its security cooperation with Japan, but also sells high-tech weapons to Taipei. Although President Bush pledged to do whatever it takes to defend Taiwan in 2001, the recent developments in Taipei towards separatism worry the American decision-makers. Afraid that Taipei is taking provocative maneuvers to the potential jeopardy of American interests, Washington has become hesitant to assure its Taiwanese friends of an unconditional defense commitment. In particular, it does not want to be drawn into a war if that war is in the first instance provoked by Taiwan itself. In order to curb Taiwan's further move toward independence, President Bush states that "the comments and actions made by the leader of Taiwan indicate that he may be willing to make decisions unilaterally to change the status quo, which we oppose."

Compared with US-Taiwan relations, Europe-Taiwan relations are less intensive. There are economic and cultural exchanges between the European countries and Taiwan, and 16 EU member states have offices in Taiwan. Nevertheless, none of them has military links with Taipei. Despite the support for Taiwan's democratic development, none of the EU countries has diplomatic relations with Taipei. Taiwan has so far set up offices in 19. Currently, the EU is Taiwan's fourth largest trading partner and Taiwan is the EU's 14th largest trading partner.

The issue of lifting the arms embargo has highlighted the importance of Taiwan in Sino-EU relations. The arms embargo on China has existed for nearly two decades since the Tiananmen incident. Led by France and Germany, the EU agreed to discuss the possibility of lifting the ban in 2004. Such a move was opposed by the US. In February 2005, the US House of Representatives passed a resolution by a 411–3 vote that condemned the EU's plan. Annalisa Giannella, the European envoy sent by Mr. Solana to Washington in March to explain the code of conduct to the Americans, was taken aback by the ferocity of American congressional opposition to lifting the ban. The Americans fear that the lifting of the arms embargo would shift the balance of power across the Taiwan strait. In their opinion, the lifting of the ban would lead to the cross-strait conventional military balance of power moving in Beijing's favor in the coming years. Such a shift could possibly encourage Beijing to resolve Taiwan's future through force.

The anti-secession law passed by China's National People's Congress in March 2005 made the issue more complicated. By a vote of 2,896 to 0 with two abstentions, the law, which threatens war against Taiwan if the island should declare independence, was approved. Although the law dedicates much rhetoric to ensuring peaceful reunification, the international media seemed to pay much attention to China's forthcoming military conflict with the island. Consequently in the EU, opposing voices on lifting the ban became stronger. In April 2005, the European Parliament voted 431 to 85, with 31 abstentions, in favor of a resolution urging the EU not to lift the arms embargo. Member states are not in agreement and, as a result, the lifting of arms ban has been postponed indefinitely.

Solution to the Crisis

National unification and territorial integrity are the top concerns of the Chinese leadership. Beijing will spare no pains to keep Taiwan from independence. The Chinese government adheres to the "one China" principle. After Hong Kong and Macao were taken over in the late 1990s, the unification of Taiwan has become the principal unresolved issue. Taiwan's return would symbolize the end of its humiliating history and China's rise as a Great Power. As Taiwan's future is considered as a "vital national interest" by the PRC, it is very probable that Beijing would resort to military means if the situation in Taiwan went out of control, and if there were no other alternatives left. The possibility of losing Taiwan will oblige Beijing to use force, even at the price of serious damage to the political and economic ties with the outside world.

2008 is an important year not only for Beijing and Taipei, but also for Washington. Beijing will organize the long-expected Olympic Games, whereas both Taipei and Washington will have presidential elections. During the Chinese New Year of 2007, in order to put the cherry on the cake, Chen took another step by openly asserting Taiwan's separatist policy. Chen announced, "Taiwan wants independence, Taiwan wants to change its official title, Taiwan wants a new constitution, Taiwan wants development. Taiwan does not have left or right wing politics, only the issue of reunification and independence." Reacting to Taiwan's provocative action, Beijing has taken several measures. First, the short-range missiles deployed against the island have been increased in large numbers in recent years. Second, the grandiose introduction of China's self-developed third-generation fighter J-10 to the outside world seemed to transmit a warning message to Chen. If Taiwan dared to claim sovereignty, China would launch a military offensive. Third, in order to stop Washington from intervening in the case of military clashes across the strait, Beijing revealed its anti-satellite capability in early 2007. As the US relies heavily on spy satellites for intelligence, China's possession of such technology constitutes a security threat to the US forces in case of war. On the other side of the strait, Taipei has intensified military exercises targeted at the PLA's offensive and decided to procure about 66 F-16 fighters from the US, and expressed its willingness to join the US-Japan military alliance to strengthen its defense. These developments lead to an escalation of the crisis. Pessimists are worried that war will break out across the strait before 2008.

Beijing's determination to take Taiwan back is in stark contrast to Taipei's pledged efforts for independence. However, although the positions on the sovereignty issue between the two sides are so far apart, neither is in favor of war. The gap in political understanding across the strait does not block economic and cultural exchanges. The shared cultural background and geographical vicinity facilitates economic interdependence. In 2001, the three "mini-links" were approved by Taipei which allow travel and trade between Taiwan's off-shore islets, Quemoy and Mazu, and China's Fujian province. The cross-strait trade increased from $8 billion in 1991 to $107.84 billion in 2006. The PRC has become Taiwan's largest trading partner since 2003, passing Japan and the US. The PRC is also the number one destination for investment by Taiwan residents. By 2005, the investment from Taiwan in the mainland had reached $47.32 billion and accounted for 53.28% of Taiwan's total outward invest-ment over the period since 1991. There is a large number of Taiwanese living on the mainland. It is estimated that approximately one out of 23 Taiwanese work full-time in China. In early 2005, agreement was reached to allow direct charter flights between three Chinese cities and two Taiwan cities for a lim-ited period during the Chinese New Year holiday. In mid-2006, both sides agreed to have regular charter flights between the island and the mainland dur-ing major holiday periods. Currently, the two sides are negotiating an agree-ment so that Chinese tourists can visit Taiwan. The close contact between people from the two sides helps strengthen the cultural and economic links, which may effectively help relax the political and military tension across the strait.

Apart from the economic and cultural interaction between the two sides, Hu Jintao invited both Lien Chan, the chairman of the Nationalist Party, and James Soong, the chairman of the People's First Party, from Taiwan to visit Beijing in 2005. The historical meeting of the two sides was realized after more than five decades of mutual political animosity. The ice-breaking meeting turned the Chinese Communist Party and the Nationalist Party from enemies to potential partners. Beijing looks forward to the victory of the Nationalists in the Taiwan election of 2008, as the Nationalists openly expressed that unification is one of their policy choices.

Needless to say, the solution of the Taiwan issue rests in the hands of the leaderships across the strait. How each side views itself and the other, how each side interprets the sovereignty issue, how much each side appreciates peace in the region, will to a large degree decide the future development of the situation across the strait. What is equally important is the attitude of the international community. The US, as the most influential outsider, should be cautious in its cross-strait policy by sticking to the status quo and discouraging any advance by Taipei towards independence.

Although the EU does not have a direct role to play in the Taiwan issue, its constructive participation in a peaceful solution to the regional crisis will have an undeniable impact on the situation across the strait. First, being the largest trading partner of the PRC and the fourth largest trading partner of the ROC, the EU enjoys a certain influence over cross-strait relations. Since 2002, a second track dialogue on the Taiwan issue has been developed between Brussels and Beijing. Through both informal and formal channels, the EU needs to make clear to both sides the necessity of maintaining the peace. Second, in the cross-strait-related decision-making, the EU needs to be cautious not to break the strategic balance in the region. Arms sales to either side of the strait will provoke conflicts not only between the EU and the other side, but also between Beijing and Taipei.

In the sovereign fight between the PRC and the ROC, Beijing is accepted by the international community as the official representative of China. Currently, no international governmental organizations accept Taiwan as a sovereign member. This not only discourages Taiwan's effort to seek to be recognized internationally, but also contributes to peace across the strait. If this situation changed, Beijing's confidence in peaceful unification would be shaken. To avoid losing control of the status quo, Beijing would probably go to the extremity of a war against Taiwan. In order to stabilize the cross-strait situation, international organizations should stand firm against the recognition of Taiwan as a state. Nevertheless, for those organizations where statehood is not a requirement, both China and the international community should make a gesture to Taiwan by supporting its participation. Taiwan's membership of the World Health Organization (WHO) has been in debate for several years. The arrangement on WTO memberships agreed by Beijing and Taipei may serve as a reference for the negotiation.

In the long-run, as a consequence of economic and political reform, China will possibly be more open and economically more developed. The degree of economic and cultural integration between the two sides will be further strengthened. When both economic and political conditions are mature, it is not without possibility that the PRC and the ROC will form a "Greater China". This term has already been widely used, although mainly for economic and geographical convenience. Integration across the strait would bring a political implication to this term. As former Chinese Foreign Minister Qian Qichen pointed out in 2000, there is one China, and both mainland China and Taiwan are part of China.

Despite the sovereign dispute, the leaderships from both sides seek to bring power and prosperity to their lands. The convergence of national construction objectives and the aversion to war may serve as important factors to guide the two sides out of the crisis. Beijing will be patient for the ultimate cross-strait integration and unification only on the condition that the status quo is safeguarded. Chen's revisionist policy is the biggest challenge to the regional peace and stability. The international community, while opposing Beijing's use of force, needs more wisdom and effort in maintaining the status quo across the strait.

Men Jing

EU PERSPECTIVE

Men Jing gives a clear and balanced account of the cross-strait situation, and only the rare use of expressions like "slippery slope towards independence" and "revisionist actions" by the Taiwanese government seem to betray the side which has her sympathy. A more direct comment is that she gives the impression that the cross-strait temperature is rising. I do not agree. I agree that the situation remains uncertain and may flare up at any moment. Presidential elections in Taiwan in March 2008 and the Olympic Games in Beijing may trigger events (statements or actions) that could up the temperature. However, for the moment, I see the cross-strait situation as relatively calm when considering the past 60 years or even the last 10 years. For the most part, this lucid article is very factual and initially I wondered what useful comment could be added, but then realized that there was an opportunity to elaborate on and hopefully clarify three specific points: first, the EU's policy towards Taiwan; second, the misunderstandings around the infamous arms embargo; and finally, the question as to why western democracies do not support the independence of Taiwan, a thriving democracy.

As for the first point, the EU — "Brussels" — like Washington, adheres strictly to the "one China" policy. The EU has become more vocal and visible in the region in the last few years and regularly calls on both sides to resolve the issue by "peaceful dialogue" and abstain from measures that could heighten tension across the strait. The EU has also made it its policy to welcome positive developments, such as the various series of direct flights that China and Taiwan have agreed on in the last few years. The positions of the EU and the US are very similar, although there may be differences in tone or style. The EU, for instance, adheres to the "one China" policy, whereas Washington has been more explicit in the last few years by saying that it "does not support independence".

Secondly, it is too simplistic to present it, as Men Jing does, as if it was purely Washington's intervention which stopped the embargo's lifting in the course of 2005. It is worth remembering that the European Parliament had adopted a resolution against lifting the embargo, and so had national parliaments. China adopted in March 2005 its anti-secession law, which looked ominous and threatening at the time. And, true, US pressure on the EU was increasing. These factors together created an overall climate in which it became ever more difficult to obtain the required unanimous agreement of member states to lift the embargo.

As an aside, let me recall how the heated debate on the embargo in 2004 and 2005 demonstrated how entirely wrong perceptions can prevail. EU arms, stopped from being exported to China in 2005 and today, are actually stopped by the so-called "code of conduct", a voluntary arrangement of restraint and information-sharing between EU member states. This code of conduct concerns all EU arms exports. Member states are working on strengthening this code of conduct and making it legally binding, which would make it an even more effective tool than the code of conduct in place at present. The embargo, on the other hand, has the character of a political statement, rather than of an effective ruling, and does not play a real role in stopping EU arms from being exported to China. The embargo's value is a symbolic one. But symbols count, as must be acknowledged, recalling the fierce reactions in Washington, the European Parliament and national parliaments in Europe and, not least, China, when the issue was discussed. The arms embargo was on everybody's radar screen and whatever the EU explained about the code of conduct was simply not believed.

Let me come to my last point. One of the questions frequently asked, in particular by young audiences, is: how can western democracies stick to the "one China" policy? Why do they not support Taiwan independence? Taiwan is a thriving democracy after all. This question is, I think, very clearly addressed by Michael D. Swaine in an article in *Foreign Affairs* (March/April, 2004). Swaine argues — and I agree with him — that it is "false" (or naïve) to assume or pretend that an "expression of democratic self-determination is sufficient to establish territorial sovereignty". He also makes the point that "a clear majority of Taiwanese recognizes the value of remaining pragmatic and open-minded about the future". Let us not forget that pro-independence feelings that exist in Taiwan today are in part the result of an active campaign of Taiwan's present leadership. Taiwan, and I let Swaine speak one more time, enjoys democracy and economic liberty and "the main limitation that China imposes on Taiwan is against its establishing *de jure* independence, as distinct from the *de facto* independence it currently enjoys."

It is sad and frustrating for the Taiwanese that China, while leaving them so much "domestic space" — in Taiwan — is so actively and successfully seeking to limit Taiwan's "international space", its participation in international fora. In the case of the World Health Organization, for instance, China's attitude implies a potential risk in the fight against communicable diseases, also for the rest of the world, including China itself. In this context, the EU has called on the two sides to find ways "to increase the participation of Taiwanese expertise in international fora". In the same vein, the EU has called on the WHO to improve Taiwan's "practical cooperation in technical work of the WHO", not to great avail so far. China continues to be rather unyielding on the matter. This is regrettable, but no reason to risk a devastating war.

Jan Willem Blankert

8

China and Its Neighbors

EU PERSPECTIVE

The EU and ASEAN

In its relations with the countries of the Association of South East Asian Nations (ASEAN), the European Union, as a whole, and its member countries, individually, share a number of common challenges with China, while at the same time also having a number of significant differences in approach. The common challenges spring from their shared quasi-existential status as significant players in a globalized world in which it is beholden on international actors to modulate their relations on three different levels: the multilateral, the bilateral and, increasingly, at an intermediate, regional level. A first common challenge arises from their historical legacies — in this case, differing ones — in relation to the ASEAN countries of both China and the European Union and questions of geographical proximity in the case of the former. Finally, the European Union has, unlike China, in its relations with ASEAN, the added problem of dealing with the imperious internal challenge of developing a common foreign security policy amongst its member nations, and to function itself as an international actor in a way that is more than the sum of its parts.

Both China and the European Union are perceived with a degree of wariness by ASEAN countries. Indeed, one of the challenges for both Beijing and Brussels and the EU member states is to develop forms of behavior at the multilateral, regional and bilateral levels which enhance their relations with SE Asia, are considered in a positive light within this region, yet advance national and European transnational interests. Three different challenges are addressed below, all shared by China and the EU, but the last complicated in the European case by the ostensible demands of interregionalism.

Managing a Problematic Heritage

While the independence of the nations of SE Asia is over 50 years old, in terms of the millennial history of these countries, in a sense this is only yesterday. With the exception of Siam (Thailand), all of the countries of the region were colonized and in all cases by Europeans. Five of the present 27 members of the European Union were involved in annexation of territory: chronologically Portugal, Spain, the Netherlands, Britain and France. While the colonial interregnum — with the exception of Spain in the Philippines and, incidentally, Portugal in East Timor — was relatively short, dating from the last quarter of the nineteenth century to the end of the first half of the twentieth, it had a profound impact. The borders, administrative and political structures, education systems and modern economic foundations of the countries of SE Asia date from that period. Nevertheless, it would be misleading to suggest that these were merely imposed. On the contrary, it would be more appropriate to suggest a kind of symbiosis in which assimilation of what would be described in contemporary jargon as European norms — and adaptation to local conditions — occurred concurrently.

For China, the centuries of contact with the peoples of SE Asia has left a significant legacy as attested by the major role played by communities of Chinese origin in the economic — and in certain cases — political life of ASEAN countries. Moreover, centuries of trading and tributary relations with the peoples of SE Asia continue to have an imprint within SE Asian consciousness, despite or perhaps because of the short-lived European presence. Yet, the strong anti-Chinese strand of Vietnamese nationalism — one which bundles together the northern neighbor with France and the United States as foreign aggressors from which Vietnam has managed to achieve its independence — would suggest that the rhetoric of national mobilization in a region, in which the preeminence of the national overrides the regional or multilateral, is quite indiscriminate in finding external adversaries. Throughout the twentieth century, most recently in Indonesia in 1998 in the midst of the Asian financial crisis and the fall of Suharto, periodic anti-Chinese pogroms occurred. As in the Great Depression in Siam in the 1930s, it is all too easy for cynical political manipulators to designate the overseas Chinese as a scapegoat for domestic political ills. Mentioning this politically incorrect point is not to justify racist actions in any form, but merely to point out the role of ethnicity in the political life of Southeast Asia in general and the importance of a degree of equitable economic growth as an antidote for these excesses. Europeans have no particular lessons to be offered in this regard, for the struggle against racism in all its forms (anti-Semitism, Islamaphobia, etc.) is, or should be, another of our common challenges.

In the case of Sino-ASEAN relations, a further complicating factor was one of an ideological nature, for in the early Cold War period, overseas Chinese communities were perceived of — or rather, were labelled — as some kind of fifth column. While clearly this is no longer the case, the distinction between a China, still proud to wear the Communist label, and a largely non-Communist SE Asia, is still a cause of some friction despite the acceptance of the rules of global capitalism throughout East Asia. Coming from a French intellectual tradition in which the "non dits" (the unsaid) should be examined as seriously as the "dits" (said), it would seem to be important to underline that, while the Communist/non-Communist dichotomy in Asia may be totally devoid of any real substance in terms of governmental practice, labels continue to exist. In Europe, with the exception of the rump of the French Communist Party, all of the former European Communist parties have undergone not only name changes, but also changes of political practice. One of the challenges within China — and one with consequences in relations with its southern neighbors — is to realign the Communist Party's contemporary political practice with its rhetoric and nomenclature (in both senses of the term). Basically, this will require acknowledging that, while Chiang Kai-Shek and the Kuomintang definitively lost the (civil) war, they have definitively won the battle concerning a state-directed model of capitalist development.

For Europeans, familiarity with their former colonial territories has undoubtedly been an advantage in fostering economic and political contacts today. The cases of British investment in Malaysia or that of French companies in Vietnam could be cited in this regard. Nevertheless, the impact of these "privileged relations" in today's world can be very easily exaggerated. On the one hand, European investors are merely competitors in a global market, very often finding themselves in third place after those from Japan and the United

States, as evidenced in the place of European automotive multinationals in the SE Asian market. On the other hand, the number of European countries with an historic experience in South East Asia is quite small: five out of the present 27 members of the EU, and still only one-third of the previous pre-enlargement 15-member EU.

In contemporary terms, the impact of these historical contacts is a double-edged sword. On the one hand, it clearly provides individual European countries — e.g., Britain in Malaysia and France in Vietnam — with a favorable environment for investment. Both London and Paris have sought to reinforce this position through significant investment in the education of students from these countries. Yet, "familiarity can breed contempt", to cite the old adage. To be precise, the possibility for the colonial post to be dragged up as a negative element in contemporary relations is ever present. The "Buy British Last" campaigns of former Malaysian Prime Minister Mahathir Mohamed in the early 1980s were but the most flagrant example of this tendency. Reference to the abuses of the colonial past remains clearly an element, say in Franco-Vietnamese negotiations or those between the Netherlands and Indonesia. In political terms, this makes a great deal of sense given, say, in the French case that a certain kind of discourse on the "Vietnam as France's back door to China" still has its supporters 130 years after Garnier's fruitless exploration of the Mekong to find a riverine trade route into the Middle Kingdom.

Finding a Balance between Political, Economic and Cultural Relations

Both China and the European Union are players in an international community whose contours are largely determined by other actors and a global environment which has developed its own momentum. The United States as the only remaining superpower is the only actor capable of single-handedly determining the international agenda. As the tragedy of the war in Iraq has demonstrated, while the US may have a capacity to single-handedly initiate, it does not have the capacity to single-handedly determine outcomes. Moreover, in areas where other forms of power than military ones are at play, the United States finds itself in a position of being perhaps able to block change, but not necessarily to be able alone to determine the course of change. A good example of this situation is in the negotiations of the Doha Round of the World Trade Organization. The US finds itself in a similar position to the EU, as well as to a China allied with major countries such as Brazil and India, in being able to block progress, i.e., to react, but not to be able to act alone in a proactive way. In this multilateral setting — a point to be returned to later — any hegemon finds its influence limited.

In this regard, the end of the Cold War has had two paradoxical consequences. On the one hand, it left the United States as the only remaining superpower with its military supremacy unchallenged. On the other hand, by removing the common enemy as a focus for its leadership, the ability of the US to mobilize coalitions in its favor, that is, its ability to lead, has been diminished. While the so-called war on terror did provide after 9/11 a new focus for US leadership, once again as the war in Iraq demonstrated, the US's ability to find allies in both the Asia-Pacific and Europe has been rather limited. In relation to the countries of SE Asia, while a discreet presence of the Seventh Fleet may be even more acceptable today than previously, by refusing — unlike Japan and even Australia, and now France — to sign the Treaty of Amity with ASEAN, the US finds itself, at least symbolically, estranged. Only in the case of the Philippines has a limited military presence been reaccepted, one related to dealing with ethnic/religious insurgencies in Mindanao.

The Cold War context itself was a significant factor in the economic transformation of much of SE Asia. As Richard Stubbs has demonstrated in his reappraisal of the Asian Miracle, security and economic questions were intimately related in terms of aid provision, foreign investment and access to western markets for the countries of the region. The end of the Cold War led to the diminishing of the importance of strategic and security factors in relations with the countries of the region. By the turn of the century, the economic status of most of these countries had changed from being recipients of western aid to becoming important actors in their own right in the global economy. As a result, geo-economic concerns have replaced geopolitical ones as the focus of relations with external powers. It is precisely this situation that presents a challenge for both China and the EU.

As explained above, China's ostensible peaceful rise is perceived in economic terms as both an opportunity and a threat for the countries of Southeast Asia. Over the last few years, ASEAN exports to China have grown significantly, while the tourist industry in SE Asia has benefited from a new wave of tourists from China. Suppliers of raw materials and energy, such as Indonesia, are benefiting from the enormous needs of a China with a 10% average growth rate over the last four years. On the other hand, foreign direct investment in the ASEAN countries has remained stable while FDI in China has increased substantially. In certain areas, there has clearly been a reorientation of investment away from SE Asian countries to China. Furthermore, Chinese competition has led to changes between SE Asian countries, for example in the present movement in FDI into Vietnam rather than Thailand.

In the economic sphere, Europe and China will find themselves increasingly in competition in SE Asia as more sophisticated Chinese products enter the market and Europe loses its technological lead in certain sectors. China will also become a serious competitor in supplying foreign investment in SE Asia and as a donor country in development aid. In theory, this Sino-European competition should be beneficial to the ASEAN countries. In practice, however, there is the potential for a stronger China to be to the detriment of ASEAN members or at least to the citizens of ASEAN countries. For example, by its willingness to lend and provide aid without (or with weakened) environmental and political conditionalities, a short-term gain for recipient countries could well be in the long-term a loss. In supporting the junta in Burma/Myanmar through, for example, the provision of $1 billion of weapons, the Chinese government has not only not helped the other ASEAN countries in bringing about political change through their process of constructive engagement, it has also prolonged the suffering of the Burmese people. On this question, the EU has taken a decidedly different tactic through the imposition of sanctions. A challenge for the Union in relation to ASEAN will be to find a more effective policy in dealing with the Burmese problem. Cooperation between China and the European Union in pursuing a common objective in bringing about political change in Burma/Myanmar should be a priority in EU-China cooperation.

The Burma/Myanmar conundrum is but one example of where economic, political, social and cultural relations — and increasingly questions of protecting the environment — must be pursued in a holistic way. By its responsible behavior in helping ASEAN countries deal with the Asian financial crisis of 1997, and by its willingness to pursue a China-ASEAN FTA, the Chinese government has demonstrated its ability to act as a responsible economic actor in the region. However, economic, security and other political questions are so intimately interlinked that it would be misguided to feel that economic relations can be dealt with in an isolated way. Agreement on a series of common minimum objectives in the political, social, cultural and environmental fields would open an opportunity for China and the EU to cooperate in meeting common challenges in SE Asia.

Balancing Bilateralism, Multilateralism and Interregionalism

The preeminence of the geo-economic over the geopolitical conditions the possibilities of bilateral, multilateral and interregional initiatives for both China and the European Union. With the potential failure of the Doha Round in bringing about further trade liberalization, the European Trade Commissioner Peter Mandelson announced in October 2006 that the EU would end its moratorium on negotiating preferential trade agreements and negotiate such individual agreements with China, Japan and all of ASEAN. The choice of an interregional agreement in the case of ASEAN is significant. While negotiations with Mercosur have been going on for almost a decade, these have not produced tangible results. However, Chinese — and to some extent Japanese — success in negotiating with all of ASEAN could provide a model for European action.

If a strengthened, more coherent ASEAN does eventuate, this will require the EU to develop a more interregional approach. Part of the basis for this form of action has already been laid: during the last decade, the number of European Commission delegations in SE Asia has expanded considerably with representation in virtually all of the ASEAN member countries. As well, those EU countries without an embassy in a particular ASEAN country rely on other European embassies to ensure such a presence. Finally, consultative mechanisms between European embassies ensure some minimal degree of coordinated action. This type of action within particular SE Asian countries complements EU activity on the international stage that has led to an increased visibility of the EU in Asia.

In countries which still retain some status as aid recipients (Indonesia, the Philippines and Vietnam), the profile of the EU is even greater, for aid directly from Brussels overshadows aid from individual European countries. Nevertheless, in the business sector, the EU's profile is somewhat diluted by bilateral chambers of commerce competing with EU-wide ones. Furthermore,

EU member countries with privileged bilateral links dating from the colonial period with certain SE Asian countries (Britain in Malaysia, France in Vietnam and Cambodia, Spain in the Philippines, etc.) are understandably reluctant to see these relations watered down in a larger European Union space.

Unlike China, the European Union has thus a further challenge in developing interregional relations between Europe and ASEAN, namely that of developing a common European policy towards all of SE Asia amongst its member countries. In this regard, enlargement has been detrimental to the strengthening of EU-ASEAN relations for two reasons. On the one hand, Asia in general is largely "absent from the radar screen" of many new members who lack not only an historical memory of colonial ties but also the kind of academic competence on Asian affairs to be found in the older members. More importantly, the new member country's first economic priority is integration into the European single market: not only is a concern with export to non-European markets something for the future, but they are net investment recipients rather than investors, lacking the major multinational companies that are at the forefront of European activity in Asia. The one exception to this picture is Vietnam, where countries like the Czech Republic and Poland can build on political ties established during the Cold War. Thus, a challenge for all of the European Union — one that is an integral part of the European project of an ever closer union — is to involve all its members in developing relations between a highly institutionalized Europe and an ASEAN, seeking through the establishing of an ASEAN Charter, which is at last tackling the task of establishing its own club rules.

David Camroux

CHINA PERSPECTIVE

Introduction

To maintain peace and stability and to promote economic and social development in the neighboring regions is among the main goals of China's foreign policy. Since persistent poverty and instability in the neighborhood, either caused by military conflicts or unpredictable natural forces, are going to shadow the internal stability, development and prosperity in China, a sound neighborhood policy is of critical importance for the purpose of creating a conducive environment for further economic development, as well as building an harmonious society in China. Until the present, most neighboring regions of China are still struggling with underdevelopment and various problems linked with poverty (including military conflicts) and, therefore, it is imperative for China to play an increasingly active role in promoting economic development, in solving the existing problems and in preventing potential conflicts in the neighborhood.

Though bilateral diplomacy continues to be very active in the region, China does not solely rely on bilateral diplomacy to achieve the above-mentioned goals. In parallel to strengthening traditional bilateral relations, China has made various efforts to enhance multilateral cooperation in the region. On the one hand, China fully supports existing multilateral mechanisms and seeks to strengthen them. For instance, China has stated once and again that ASEAN should play a leading role in promoting integration in East Asia, while attaching much importance to the "10 + 1" and "10 + 3" in enhancing the cooperation of East Asian countries. On the other hand, China advocates a multilateral approach in handling delicate problems. It was China that initiated the six-party dialogue on the issue of nuclear proliferation in North Korea. As a result, China's neighborhood is networked by different multilateral cooperative mechanisms with China being a hub.

Due to diversity in China's neighborhood, it is impossible to offer one menu to all guests. Therefore, a single stereotype of regional multilateral cooperation does not exist, nor does one multilateral mechanism occupy a dominant position. There are a number of multilateral mechanisms in China's neighborhood, the members, mandates and institutional structures of which are drastically different. This demonstrates on the one side that China adopts an incremental approach to promote multilateralism in the neighborhood, always seeking arrangements that make everybody feel comfortable. On the other side, these multilateral endeavors are complementary to "multiple bilateralism", dominant in the region.

China's endeavors to promote multilateralism in the neighborhood are naturally relevant to other parts of the world. It is asserted that China is seeking an "open regionalism", aiming at including as many stakeholders as possible. Consequently, the multilateral cooperation in China's neighborhood will contribute not only to a higher profile of China on the international stage, but also to the strengthening of multilateralism at a global level. Therefore, the

EU and China have common interests in enhancing multilateralism in China's neighborhood. The EU should be present in these multilateral mechanisms and should provide further encouragement to foster them.

What is to be Achieved in the Neighborhood Policy? Main Goals and the Rationale

As is demonstrated in a number of Chinese foreign policy documents, the two main goals of China's neighborhood policy are to maintain peace and stability and to promote sustainable development in the region. China's neighborhood policy is based on its understanding of the overall international circumstances. In an era of intensified globalization, the interdependence among countries is increasing. Given its size, its stage of development and cultural diversity, China is easily influenced by various events taking place beyond its borders, particularly the chaos in the neighborhood. Therefore, in order to achieve sustainable development and to build an harmonious society, China has to face the challenges both from inside and from outside. As was stated by Chinese Foreign Minister Li Zhaoxing, "China's period of strategic opportunities as we talk about is nothing but an international environment and evolutionary process where world peace is maintained and common development promoted. It is only under this strategic premise can we achieve the grand goal of building a moderately prosperous society in an all-round way."

The threats to global and regional peace and prosperity are not limited to military conflicts. Non-traditional security problems rooted in underdevelopment and isolation from the outside world are also regarded by China as a potential cause of instability. In Asia, after witnessing the financial crisis in 1997, the panic aroused by SARS and subsequently by avian flu, and the tsunami in 2004, both policymakers and the public have become increasingly aware of how urgent and difficult a task it is to work together in various fields for the sake of striving for future prosperity. As a consequence, peace and development should be linked together. Without economic development and tangible improvement of living standards, it is impossible to guarantee a secure region or a secure world. Having this in mind, China's foreign policy in the new era is summarized as striving for "peace, development and cooperation", an indispensable part of which is to promote "peace, stability and prosperity in Asia".

In general, peace and development are the stated goals of China's neighborhood policy, and cooperation is the way leading to these goals. While making all efforts to maintain, broaden and deepen bilateral cooperation, China has been making efforts to foster multilateral cooperation. One underlying reason is China's profound understanding of the prevailing challenges to regional security as explained above: it also relates to the changing situation in the region. The rise of China in terms of economic performance, political influence and military competence is transforming the economic, political and social landscape in East Asia. The huge demand for capital, resources and markets of a booming economy is a source of concern due to the possible competition and friction that it might cause. Furthermore, some by-products of expanding economic activities have a spillover effect beyond the borders, for instance, environmental degradation. Multilateral cooperation is much needed in order to keep equilibrium in the region and to cope with the negative effects of development efficiently.

Multilateral Cooperation in China's Neighborhood

Since the mid-1990s, China has played a more active role in constructing regional multilateralism in its neighborhood. A dialogue on security and political issues with three Central Asian countries and Russia was started in 1996. This regular dialogue eventually led to the establishment of the Shanghai Cooperation Organization (SCO) in 2001. Also in 1996, the first Summit of ASEM was held in Bangkok, signifying the commencement of interregional cooperation between the EU and mainly East Asia. In 1997, immediately after the establishment of ASEM, the multilateral dialogue between ASEAN and China (10 + 1), and ASEAN, and the three Northeast Asian countries of China, Japan and Korea (10 + 3) were started. These newly established multilateral mechanisms, together with former regional cooperative mechanisms such as APEC, set China and its neighbors in a network of multilateral arrangements, as is shown in Figure 1.

China claims that it "is an active participant in and staunch supporter for the regional cooperation in Asia" (Li Zhaoxing). In fact, it has become the anchor of the multilateral arrangements in the region. Firstly, the involvement

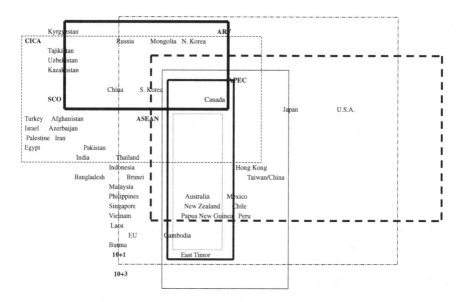

Figure 1 Main multilateral mechanisms in China's neighborhood.
Source: This figure is based on information published by the Chinese Ministry of Foreign Affairs.
Note: For technical reasons, not all regional cooperative mechanisms for which China is a member are included.

of China is necessary to make cooperation meaningful in terms of efficiency and effectiveness. For instance, China was not among the initiators of the ASEM but became one of the most important players in the ASEM process, because things would go smoothly with Chinese support and vice versa. Secondly, China provides momentum to regional cooperation. In particular, China is essential in solving existing problems that block closer relationships. For example, the Declaration on the Conduct of Parties in the South China Sea paved the way for a closer economic cooperation between China and ASEAN.

Does the Regional Multilateralism Aim at Building a "Fortress East Asia"?

As illustrated by Figure 1, there is no one dominant multilateral arrangement in China's neighborhood. China openly sticks to "open regionalism", which means the regional cooperation is not exclusive to 3rd parties, nor is it targeted against a 3rd party. This policy position responds to the fact that it is hard to formulate an "Asian" stance *vis-à-vis* the other parts of the world.

China is actively involved in multilateral cooperation in its neighborhood mainly due to political and security concerns, not out of the desire to push forward regional integration to build a "Fortress East Asia" under the shadow of China. Firstly, most of the cooperative mechanisms are based on mutual consultancy instead on binding laws, as is the case in European integration. Furthermore, European integration was started in economic fields, and gradually spilled over to other policy fields. However, most multilateral arrangements in China's neighborhood are either mainly aimed at security or political issues, are of a comprehensive nature with economic cooperation intertwined with political and security issues. In fact, China is a strong supporter of international multilateral trade arrangements framed by WTO, and only China has begun to negotiate and to sign FTA agreements with a few partners. So far, China has only signed two FTA agreements with its neighbors. One is the China-ASEAN FTA, and the other is the China-Pakistan FTA. Other measures that will result in a progress of economic integration, for instance, regional multilateral financial cooperation, are discussed by East Asian countries but still far from being realized. Without concrete economic integration, a fortress is definitely impossible.

The lagging in economic integration also explains China's flexible attitudes towards regional multilateral institutional-building. Neither does one multilateral arrangement occupy a dominant position, nor does one stereotype of regional multilateral cooperation exist. In fact, there are a number of multilateral mechanisms in China's neighborhood, the members, mandates and institutional structures of which are drastically different. On the western borders, the multilateral dialogue or cooperation aims foremost at security issues, while the economic dimension is much more important in the multilateral arrangements with the neighbors on eastern borders. Furthermore, the flexibility is also reflected in the incremental approach of China. Calling for the respect for diversity, China actually always seeks "the least common denominator" to make everybody comfortable. However, on the grounds that China and the neighboring countries share more and more common interests in the process of globalization, the multilateral cooperation would be furthered in response to the commonly faced challenges.

Implications for Other Parts of the World

China's endeavors to promote multilateral cooperation in the neighborhood deliver a signal that China is going to be proactive rather than reactive in formulating its neighborhood policy. Though to promote multilateralism is not to be viewed as a shift from multiple bilateralism, it adds some new flavor to China's neighborhood policy. It also reflects China's efforts to seek for more channels and instruments to cope with the ever complex situation in the neighborhood.

These endeavors will naturally be relevant to other parts of the world. First of all, enhanced multilateralism in the region pushed China to be further integrated into the international society. Through various multilateral cooperative mechanisms, China is increasingly closely linked not only with its neighbors, but also with other important players in the region, particularly USA and the European countries. More importantly, the efforts to build regional multilateral mechanisms are introducing internationally accepted norms and rules in various policy fields into the region, thus strengthening the basis of international order.

Secondly, the neighborhood of China is a source of instability. To the east is North Korea; to the west is Afghanistan; to the south is Myanmar. The conflicts in these countries have an impact on both regional and international peace and prosperity. Multilateral cooperation will help contain potential conflicts. Thirdly, given the unilateral behavior of USA, the multilateral cooperation in China's neighborhood would be a good counterbalance and contribute to promoting multilateralism at a global level. Therefore, China should be encouraged to make more efforts to strengthen multilateral mechanisms.

The EU actively encourages regional integration in other parts of the world. One of the intentions of the ASEM process is to provide momentum for the integration process in East Asia. China's involvement in regional multilateral cooperation is thus in line with the EU's Asian policy. The EU has so far not been sufficiently involved in the regional cooperation in China's neighborhood. There is much potential to heighten the profile of the EU and its member states in East Asia, and to deepen the interregional cooperation.

Zhang Jun

9

Japan

EU PERSPECTIVE

Japanese Prime Minister Shinzo Abe's bold action, right after his accession to power in September 2006, to take a U-turn from his predecessor Junichiro Koizumi's confrontational policy towards China and travel to Beijing for the first fully-fledged summit with the President of China in six years, would have been the top news story in the region in 2006, had it not been overshadowed by the North Korean nuclear test in early October.

While writing this chapter, during spring 2007, top-level meetings between the leaders of both countries have been fully resumed after five years of disruption during the Koizumi era (2001–2006) due to Chinese anger at the prime minister's annual pilgrimages to the Yasukuni Shrine, where Japan's war dead are symbolically enshrined, including 14 Class A convicted war criminals. Abe met Chinese President Hu Jintao for a second time at the APEC summit in Hanoi in November and Premier Wen Jiabao at the East Asia summit in Cebu, Philippines in January. Foreign Minister Li Zhaoxing was in the Japanese capital in February and Wen Jiabao visited Japan in April for another prime ministerial summit.

To paraphrase the common characterization of Sino-Japanese relations during the troubled years: *hot economics — cold politics*, one can say now that there is enough ostensible warmth at the top level, but that the temperature underneath is still somewhat volatile. This is in the first place caused by the relative weakness of the Abe administration. The decline in approval ratings — 70% in October to 37% in mid-February — not abnormal for a freshly installed Japanese prime minister, raises scepticism as to what he is likely to achieve. Now, the uncertainty is such that political commentators are wondering whether Abe will make it past the upper house election of July 2007. Unlike Koizumi, Abe belongs to the well-established central elite of the Liberal Democratic Party (LDP) and one of his first acts was, in the name of consensus building, to reinstate the rebels against Koizumi's high-handed electoral maneuvers, who had been expelled from the party by his predecessor. Abe added to the uncertainty by introducing new taxes and rolling back Koizumi's *laissez faire* reforms on encouraging economic dynamism and a growing income gap and then, in the face of too much opposition, retreated.

In foreign policy, the confusion was similar. Abe himself wants to be seen as relatively pro-American, but not as close to President George W. Bush as his predecessor. He appointed Fumio Kyuma, a long time critic of US policies from Nagasaki, to be Japan's first post-war defense minister. The Japan Defense Agency had been renamed a full ministry as of 1 January 2007 and its director-general upgraded to ministerial rank. Kyuma soon criticized the United States on two counts: its arrogant behavior in Okinawa, a Japanese island dotted with spacious "colonial" compounds for the American military, where Japanese live in little crammed houses. Kyuma also denounced the US-led war in Iraq as a mistake. In other cabinet irregularities, Health Minister Hakuo Yanagisawa had misspoken more egregiously by calling women "birth-giving machines", but had apologized profusely. Kyuma refused to do so and the State department has expressed its disapproval and warned that any more remarks critical of the Bush administration might delay the next Japan-US ministerial security talks, dubbed the "2 plus meeting", involving the foreign affairs and defense chiefs of the two countries. In February, US Vice President Dick Cheney made a three-day visit to Japan, pointedly refusing to meet with Kyuma. The latter played down this slight and said he was not of the same rank, but Cheney did meet with Foreign Minister Taro Aso, who in his own turn had criticized the American occupation of Iraq as "naïve". In the broader regional context, the most inflammatory misstep may prove to be the reopening, by Abe himself, of the debate on Japan's unique war crime of coercing hundreds of thousands of Asian and some European women into army-run brothels for Japanese soldiers. Apparently in the hope of regaining support from the hardline nationalist right wing of his own party, Abe said early March that there was no evidence that the women had been forced into sexual slavery, suggesting that they were voluntary prostitutes. Under pressure from the US Congress,

Asian politicians, NGOs and public opinion, Abe backtracked disingenuously and apologized again, seriously impairing his efforts to establish himself as a worthy new Japanese leader. Notably, China kept silent about the issue so as not to set back the positive momentum in the relationship, engendered by Abe himself.

Several other foreign policy steps of the Abe administration have caused varying degrees of concern in China. In January, Abe went to Brussels to lobby the EU to maintain the arms embargo imposed after the Chinese army's suppression of the Tiananmen demonstrations in 1989, to seek support for Japan's bid to get a permanent seat at the UNSC — which China opposes — and to forge closer ties with NATO, which is increasingly becoming a tool of American policies in Asia. One such policy is the thinly veiled containment of China by what US Secretary of State Condoleezza Rice once dubbed a "cordon of democratic nations" — Japan, Australia and India. A hybrid euphemism of containment is "congagement": containment with a shot of engagement, like a cocktail. NATO stresses that its links with Japan are only aimed at supporting "the mission" in Afghanistan, but China is sceptical about this. After some initial steps in 2002, China's dialogue with NATO has been unproductive.

More ominous for China is an impending new joint US-Japanese plan, announced in early January 2007, to coordinate military action to defend Taiwan in case of a Chinese invasion of the island. Under the plan, Japan would focus on rear area support and rescue operations of US forces, emergency aid, ship inspections and evacuation of Japanese living in affected areas. Although it is not clear yet what new policy will eventually emerge, it seems retrogressive from the policy of the Clinton and other previous American administrations all the way back to the Carter presidency. US policy towards Taiwan since the signing of the US-Republic of China Defense Treaty in 1954 until its termination — with a one-year notice — and "de-recognition" of Taiwan by President Jimmy Carter in December 1979 has always been that the US would defend "capitalist" Taiwan against Chinese "communist liberation" (of American "imperialist occupation"). Under the Taiwan Relations Act, Congress legislated that "the US should maintain the capacity to prevent that the future of Taiwan would be determined by other than peaceful means", and since China redefined its policy towards Taiwan as "peaceful reunification" without excluding the use of non-peaceful means, the US would continue to supply Taiwan with defensive arms. The Reagan and Clinton administrations practised a policy of restraint *vis-à-vis* Taiwan and would not say whether the US would intervene or not in a military conflict, because that might encourage either side to advance its reunification and its independence agenda respectively. This policy of so-called "strategic ambiguity" was abandoned by President George W. Bush early in his presidency, when he said that "the US would do whatever it takes to defend Taiwan". Bush later clarified that the US would defend Taiwan only "in case of an unprovoked attack". This statement has never been retracted nor repeated, but neither has it been spelled out what "unprovoked attack" exactly means.

Now, more than six years hence, the question of the trigger of a possible Chinese attack is no longer discussed. Considering China's growing defense expenditure and its missile deployment, it is conveniently assumed that China will sooner or later attack, regardless of the provocative politics of President Chen Shui-Bian and his possible independence-minded successor(s). Assuming that the US vows to defend Taiwan, no matter what, and the Japanese government commits itself explicitly to various types of non-combat military support, then the future of Sino-Japanese relations could be bleak indeed.

During research trips to Japan in 2005 and 2006, senior Japanese officials and academics stressed that Japan was under no obligation to participate in any way in a US-China war over Taiwan. "Our Constitution doesn't recognize the right of collective defense. Only if Japan itself is attacked will we counterattack. In practice, if China conducts a very limited operation against Taiwan, we will not come into action at all. But in the case of a massive attack, we will give rear area support to the US", said Yasuhiro Matsuda, a senior researcher in the leading think-tank for national defense.

Both experts and public opinion are deeply divided over what to do in case of a US-China war. Motofumi Asai, former director of the China bureau in the Japanese foreign ministry, expressed deep pessimism over the future of China-Japan relations: "On the subject of Taiwan, there is no room for any Japanese leader to consider the Chinese side. Even with the resumption of top-level dialogue, I am not optimistic at all about the future prospects, because the Americans will not give up Taiwan in any case and the Japanese government is now totally involved with US military strategy". A leading Japanese foreign affairs commentator, Yoichi Funabashi, disagrees. He believes that the Chinese leadership trusts Japan on the Taiwan issue: "Koizumi and Bush have actually sent a very clear message to (Taiwan president) Chen Shui-Bian: "Enough is enough, don't overstep." That has been very satisfactory to China. This is a unique plus-sum of dynamics". Funabashi emphasized that neither the US nor Japan have any interest in Chen Shui-Bian's independence politics.

But what does the US want? To maintain the status quo and keep Taiwan under its domination as an unofficial protectorate, intelligence and espionage base and market for multi-billion dollar arms deals for decades to come, with the grand strategic design to block China's rise as a naval power in the Western Pacific? And does Prime Minister Abe and his successor(s) want to go along with that and become a bigger nuisance to China than Koizumi with his offensive Yasukuni visits ever was? Koizumi in the end might become the lesser evil and China might even become nostalgic for him, because for all the bad blood his Yasukuni obsession stirred up, he never crossed the line over Taiwan policy. At the height of Sino-Japanese tensions and on the eve of violent anti-Japanese demonstrations in Chinese cities, he told the Diet in March 2005 that Japan did not anticipate providing military assistance to the US in any dispute between China and Taiwan.

The overarching question is how strong and how lasting American control over Japanese foreign policy will be. Abe is a scion from an elite right wing nationalist family, whose maternal grandfather was Nobusuke Kishi, a Class A war criminal suspect, who was never brought to trial because during the late 1940s, the Americans felt they had to abandon the purge of the right due to the rise of Communism. One of Japan's most significant post-World War II politicians, Kishi, after his release and after becoming prime minister, visited Asian countries to clear the way for improved and cordial relations with Japan's suspicious neighbors. He could not have anticipated the status of the quasi-American protectorate that Japan has slid into. Prime Minister Abe concedes in his memoirs having been much influenced by his grandfather. His father, Shintaro Abe, was one of the most successful post-war foreign ministers (in the relatively effective and outward-looking Nakasone cabinet during the 1980s) and similarly espoused a more responsible independent role for Japan. Questions have been raised about the pro-American credentials of the nationalistic Abe, because he has broken with the tradition of Japanese prime ministers to make their first foreign trip in office to Washington, DC. Abe has visited Beijing, Seoul, Hanoi, Cebu (Philippines) and Brussels, but only during the eighth month of his prime-ministership, in late April, he arrived in Washington for an uneasy, unfocused stay of two days only. His main purpose was to find out whether he could bond in the same way with Bush as his flamboyant predecessor had. The result is as yet unclear. Abe had to reiterate his half-hearted apologies on the "comfort women" issue to both the President and congressional leaders. Since Abe is a strong advocate of an enhanced Japanese role in global security as a junior partner of the United States, American criticism cooled, but the broader disenchantment with Japan's attitude towards its wartime history remains.

The US and Japan also disagree on North Korea: Japan has refused to supply its share of the fuel oil compensation that North Korea would get in exchange for abandoning its nuclear program, unless Pyongyang releases more Japanese citizens abducted by North Korean agents during the 1970s. However, the US, Russia and South Korea agree that there is no evidence that there are any more alive abductees to be released and have told Japan to settle the issue bilaterally with North Korea. Prime Minister Abe, whose climb to the pinnacle of power was aided by advocating a relentless hardline towards North Korea, is apparently unwilling to drop the issue because it would affect the support of the right wing of his party. Beijing has stepped in again and offered to help Tokyo solve the issue with Pyongyang. The *Asahi Shimbun* and the *Washington Post* have both scathingly criticized Abe's insensitivity on Japan's foreign "sex slaves" and his relentlessness regarding the Japanese abductees. The *Washington Post* commented editorially: "If Mr. Abe seeks international support in learning the fate of Japan's kidnapped citizens, he should straightforwardly accept responsibility for Japan's own crimes."

China and Japan have huge disparities in geographical and demographic size, political systems, economic development and global strategic orientation. At the same time, they have unique demographic and economic synergies for regional cooperation and integration. Japan is no different from the other developed regions of the world like North America and Western Europe, which had to import large numbers of workers from Latin America, Eastern Europe, North Africa and the Middle East to keep their economies viable. If Japan wants to remain an economic superpower, it will have to import increasing numbers of immigrants from neighboring countries, first among them China. It is already doing this to some extent, but without providing proper legal status to these guest workers. Japan will not only have to import workers, but also scientists and technicians which it no longer produces itself in sufficient numbers. Japan should stop boasting that it is an "extremely homogeneous country, historically governed by the Yamato (Great Harmonious Japanese) race" as Minister of Education Bunmei Ibuki does, with the full endorsement of Prime Minister Abe. Many observers have long held that Japan has remained extraordinarily insular, and that a strong dose of internationalism and cosmopolitanism would do it a lot of good. Business leaders and academics increasingly advocate that Japan diversify its foreign relations away from its lopsided reliance on the military power of the US, and reposition itself as part of Asia, foremost towards China for its market and low cost labor, but also towards the European Union for its model of peaceful regional integration based on international law.

Willem van Kemenade

CHINA PERSPECTIVE

Chinese Premier Wen Jiabao's Tokyo visit during 11–13 April 2007 reopened a "window of opportunity" for the two countries to revamp their torn relationship. If well-managed, Tokyo and Beijing might join hands to step into a new era of defusing tension. But it does not necessarily invite optimism for their future. The China-Japan relationship may be the most complex and quirky power dyad in world politics. Whatever way one looks at it, there is tremendous potential — actual and virtual — for rivalry and confrontation: territorial disputes over Sankaku Island, the "security dilemma", mutual distrust, suspicions and vigilance due to geographic proximity, economic competition, different national characteristics derived from distinct cultures, and perhaps most importantly, conflicting and repellent identities to each other based on the history problem, fostering nationalism in both countries. Thus, both sides appear cautious, still trying to figure out the true intentions of the other and weighing up the next step that should be taken. Notwithstanding this, the most important matter confronting Beijing and Tokyo is how to keep the thawing process going, rather than focus on how much cooperation is realistic.

Chinese Premier Wen's Visit to Japan: New Thinking Launched?

On 6 April 2007, Chinese Premier Wen Jiabao prudently defined his upcoming visit to Tokyo as an "ice-melting trip". It reads like a reasonable response to his Japanese counterpart Shinzo Abe's "ice-breaking visit" in October 2006. Such low profile discretion in China's foreign affairs, however, is quite exceptional in its history. Beijing has usually been inclined to adopt an optimistic rhetoric to describe its neighborly ties and highlight its success in its long-standing "good neighbor" strategy. Partly, it was also the need to influence the domestic audience in order to add to the CCP leaders' job approval rating. Nevertheless, there is no doubt that Wen's definition of ice-melting equates to a confession of Beijing's policy failure to deal with Japan. However, his sincerity is a big message uttered for both Japanese and Chinese that Beijing will attempt to improve its ties with Tokyo, the biggest and most significant neighbor to China in all respects.

There has been much controversy over China's Japan policy for nearly two decades. Beijing frequently hails its better ties with most of its neighbors, but is much annoyed by the recurrent tension with Japan. Strategically, Beijing has no appetite to create Japan as its enemy. Rivalry with Japan would seriously damage its national security and economic modernization. But China has been unable to prevent the deterioration of bilateral ties. Ironically, accommodating Japan is an essential Chinese strategic goal, but it has not worked well in the past decade, and this has been disturbing China's foreign relations. The past decade also witnessed Beijing's sequential push for balancing its porous approach with some "new thinking" (*xin siwei*), a specific notion referring to China's trial of new methodology to address its Japan concerns. Unfortunately, the outcome has always been lacking: either the new thinking was stifled before it blossomed, or the strong and even furious anger of Chinese people *vis-à-vis* an increasingly vigilant Japan stifled it. The Chinese leadership is aware that its Japan policy is a minefield, which can incite populist backlash and even threaten the government. But the chance has never been greater for Premier Wen Jiabao to plan his visit to Japan and exercise new thinking.

First, Abe's visit to Beijing in October 2006 was a very important fence-mending effort between the two countries. Beijing welcomed Abe without setting any precondition of a pledge to stop paying homage to the Yasukuni Shrine, a memorial to Japan's war dead, including 14 Class A war criminals from World War II. China's top leaders shunned top-level contacts between Beijing and Tokyo, protesting against the annual visits by the former Prime Minister Junichiro Koizumi to the shrine. Abe's visit to Beijing revealed a new approach. Secondly, China has recognized that raising China's history concern with Japan would increase the tension, though Beijing thinks that it has the credentials to strongly and openly express its historical concerns. Thus, the Premier has proven to be a consummate diplomat as well as a new thinking practitioner.

Wen's candour may be a good portent and he probably intended to achieve something unusual by deliberately lowering expectations in advance. His visit to Tokyo in April 2007 was more than successful. Wen played down the notable history dispute and departed from his predecessors, who often relentlessly hammered the Japanese for their historical invasion, placing an overwhelming significance on the "unforgettable and authentic history" in bilateral relations. He presented himself in a remarkably new fashion, and gently and amicably reached out to the Japanese people. In his address at Japan's Diet on 12 April, Premier Wen started with the moving words, "his coming is simply for friendship and cooperation", and was convinced that "the development of our relations has gone through tempests and twists and turns, but the foundation of our friendship is unshakeable just like Mount Tai and Mount Fuji". Such remarks with an optimistic tone and a positive color contrast sharply with the gloomy and awkward ones made by his predecessors when they came to Tokyo in 1998 and 2000. Surprisingly, he praised the Japanese politicians' remorse and apologies for the brutalities of the war and said that such statements were well-received in China. Moreover, Premier Wen expressed strong Chinese gratitude for Japan's economic assistance and contribution, and reaffirmed his appreciation of the Japanese post-war pacifist path. Wen explicitly signaled Beijing's important conceptual changes in its Japan policy. The changes purport to curb the two countries' rift about "history identification" and "history position", which mirror their profound misperceptions of each other's future and stir up malign national images. This requires that Beijing would eventually face up to the pacifist nature of post-war Japan in its discourses and no longer raise feelings about its miserable memory of militaristic Japan. His words signify that the Chinese leadership urges its people to adopt this new approach and reduce their historical animosity towards Japan.

However, Premier Wen was not blind to the history dispute between the two countries. He pledged friendship with Japan, but also cautioned that Tokyo must match its past apologies for its wartime aggression with concrete actions. But the way to address China's history concern has fundamentally changed. Chinese leaders used to ask the Japanese to look squarely at their wartime atrocities, and often criticized Japanese right wing politicians for distorting historic evidence. They also expressed China's concern that distorting history could result in a revival of Japan's militarism. Noticing the reactions in Japan, Premier Wen addressed China's history concern tactfully and subtly. He did not attack the Japanese, but warned that they should know "the untold sufferings" that the Japanese military inflicted on China. He argued that remembering history does not mean to "perpetuate hatred", but to "secure a better future" for the relationship. However, Wen also implicitly showed Beijing's discontent over some Japanese attempting to white-wash what happened during the war against China 62 years ago. But Beijing's new thinking is clearcut: it declares that Beijing has no intention to endlessly entangle with Tokyo for war responsibilities, and wishes to free the China-Japan relationship from unresolved vindication. China does not want a Japanese apology or compensation any longer. The predicament between the two countries is not about what has been done, but about what is going to be done.

China has contended for a long time that the apologies for the war brutalities which Japanese prime ministers have made since the normalization of relations in 1972 were superficial, and not "heart and soul searching". Former Prime Minister Hashimoto visited South Korea in October 1998 and openly declared "its guilt admitting" (*xie zui*). But he just mentioned "deep remorse" when he greeted Chinese former President Jiang Zemin in Tokyo one month later. Such unequal and unfair treatment enraged most Chinese, who unsurprisingly asked for more apologies. Conversely, the Japanese complain that China intentionally harasses Japanese governments for a more sincere apology, using "apology offence" to keep Japan in subordination to China. They unwittingly ask how many apologies will be enough and stress that 14 apologies have been made on the record in the past 35 years. Thus, the history problem irks both the Chinese and Japanese peoples and fuels their sentiments, turning the issue into a struggle for national prestige.

Actually, Premier Wen's remarks at Japan's Diet were favorably received in Japan. Wen's failure to directly mention the Yasukuni Shrine is likely to have come as a relief to his hosts. He raised the history problem that has been at the heart of the dispute between the two countries, but avoided the bitter tone and finger-pointing of former leader Jiang Zemin in 1998. In effect, this reflects a growing pragmatism of Beijing's Japan policy. China's softer stance on the "history problem" echoes positively in Japan. It does not make the Japanese feel comfortable, but relaxes their residual anxiety of "history psycho" by which most Japanese do not want to see their country continuously swamped in their blotted history. Furthermore, the history dispute has gone far beyond the competing evidence about historical facts. It emotionally pushed the two countries into a collision course in terms of their strategic goals and power calculations. There is hardly any room for any compromise to settle conflicts such as the Sankaku islands, East China Sea gas drilling and others. Against the backdrop of antagonistic feelings in the two societies, no politician will have a strong enough will to make a substantive concession.

Ice-Melting Trip: What Sorts of Ice is Bestowing China-Japan Relations?

Few would deny the warmth appearing in China-Japan relations after Wen's visit in April 2007. Wearing a smiling face on the visit, Chief Cabinet Secretary Yasuhisa Shiozaki declared, "We are not aware of any remaining ice." But despite the "ice-melting", the snow and ice covering the China-Japan political landscape are still so thick that they will not melt quickly.

The visit does not substantially change paradoxical situations which now plague their bilateral ties. Premier Wen Jiabao's presentation of "new thinking" is a wise but bold intiative in Chinese foreign policy. The open appraisal of Japan's economic contribution to China and the pragmatic treatment of the past do not imply a new deal between the two governments. Beijing has not abandoned its profound opposition to the Yasukuni Shrine visit by any Japanese prime minister, and meanwhile, the Abe administration still handles this issue with self-defeating ambiguity. Without a clear resolution of the Yasukuni issue, China's unilateral "new thinking" can hardly lay the solid foundation for sustainable stability and cooperation between Beijing and Tokyo. Considering the growing nationalism in Japan, expanding suspicion and worry about China's rise, and China's staunch anti-Japan sentiments, one more visit to the Yasukuni Shrine by any Japanese prime minister could easily destroy China's "new thinking" overnight. Of course, China's increasing flexibility will reduce the probability of a recurrent Yasukuni Shrine visit, and make Prime Minister Abe more hesitant, given the fact that a stable Japan-China relationship remains a key concern for most Japanese people. According to a *Ashashi Shinbun* survey, nearly 81% of Japanese respondents wish to see an improvement in their foreign relations with China.

The Koizumi administration highlighted that chasing domestic votes was a leading consideration of prime ministerial shrine pilgrimage visits. The Abe administration will be no exception as the Prime Minister's power base remains shaky. If the LDP loses control of the upper house of Japan's Diet in the July 2007 election, Abe might reroute his power consolidation attempt and again risk offending China with a visit to the Yasukuni Shrine.

So far, only a strongman in the LDP could refrain from a Yasukuni Shrine visit as Nagasone did in 1985. A strongman politician in Japan means either controlling the ruling party LDP, or controlling the popular constituency in Japan. The irony is that Abe Shinzo fails on both accounts. This is why he has stopped short of worshipping at the shrine while supporting the principle of prime ministerial visits to Yasukuni. Mr. Abe reiterates that his personal feeling "will not change", but he chose not to trouble Japan's relations with its Asian neighbors.

Wen argued in Tokyo that "We sincerely hope that Japan will show in concrete ways their expressed attitudes and promises." By saying so, he actually warned that the enshrinement of the war's top leaders at Yasukuni undermined China's baseline for the history problem: "only a handful of militarists in Japan were responsible for the war in China, and the Japanese people, like the Chinese, were victims of war". Such an interpretation is the allegedly shared foundation for the two peoples to reduce their historical resentment and keep looking forward.

During Wen's Tokyo trip, both countries appeared to make great efforts to improve ties, but there were no breakthroughs in the most contentious issues bedeviling their relations. The Japanese government had eagerly anticipated Wen's visit, particularly since Abe's initial success in defusing tensions with China has been one of his few achievements during his first six months in office. His administration pressured their Chinese counterparts to negotiate a solution to the East China Sea dispute. Tokyo made a new offer, backing down from its traditional claim of a "median line" demarcating the two countries' overlapping 200 nautical mile exclusive economic zones (EEZ), and proposing "joint development" in the more extensive overlapping area of their separate EEZ claims. But China refused to consider that offer as she considers that the entire East China Sea continental shelf is a "natural prolongation" of Chinese mainland. The notion of "joint development" is also in China's interests and not regarded as "unacceptable". But the key issue is its profound worry about

Sankaku islands. The acceptance of Japan's new offer would imply the acquiescence of Japan's Sankaku territorial claim, as it is used in the verification of Japan's EEZ demarcation point.

The two leaders emphasized that China and Japan should foster their relations based on "common strategic interests" (*zhanlue huhui guanxi*). This was regarded as "quite encouraging" in an effort to resteer the course of their relationship in the right direction. But so far, the notion of "common strategic interests" remains hollow and unsubstantiated. The Abe administration would have hoped that Beijing could publicly proclaim its support for Japan's bid for a UNSC permanent seat. But Beijing only agreed to favor UNSC reform and to say that Japan's bid was "understandable". China's passivism is disappointing for the Abe-pioneered "Japan rushing to Great Power" drive. On the North Korea nuclear issue, Beijing also expressed its understanding of Tokyo's strategy linking the abduction issue and nuclear dismantlement. But there was no indication that Wen supported this linkage.

Regarding Taiwan, the biggest concern for China is that Abe is known as a pro-Taiwan conservative. Tokyo, however, assured Beijing that it will uphold its "one China" policy and will not support Taiwan's independence. The media report about Japanese consideration of arms sales to Taiwan gravely upset Chinese leaders. In this regard, Beijing did not get any assurances. On the contrary, Abe touched on Japan's concerns over poor transparency in China's military build-up.

China-Japan Relations: What is Lying Ahead?

The Chinese Premier's visit to Japan signals a thaw in relations. What can be predicted is that a thaw in bilateral ties will continue after Mr. Abe makes a second visit to Beijing in the fall of 2007 as promised. Such visits and regular summit contacts will certainly help to stabilize bilateral relations, boosting dialogue at different levels and altering the anomaly of "chilly politics and hot economics", a snapshot of a sharply deteriorating relationship between Beijing and Tokyo in the past years. But they will do little to remodel China-Japan ties.

With China on the rise, Japan has never experienced more fear and worry that a rising China could evolve into a new regional hegemon, and in return, Japan would be marginalized in Asia. Faced with what it saw as the China threat, Japan made up her mind in the mid-1990s, along with the US, her only military ally, to contain a rising China. Reinforcing ties with the US, reactivating the military alliance commitments and restructuring Japan's defense system, strengthening its combat capability and most importantly, rewriting its pacifist constitution and restoring its right to war, are all part of a design to counter an expanding China. The main theme when discussing strategy in Japan is not rapprochement, but really containment of China in a concerted effort with the US. The notion of China "endangering" Japan is exaggerated. China has no power projection capability to touch Japan. Japan still enjoys credible superiority in conventional weapons over China. Tokyo has pursued a strategic update, relentlessly targeting China as a formidable "competitor".

Japan and US declared in the joint statement of "2 + 2" annual ministerial meeting in February 2005 that a peaceful resolution of the Taiwan Strait dispute is their common strategic concern with regard to regional security in the Asia-Pacific. The US and Japan worked out a joint military emergency plan for the Taiwan Strait in January 2007. In March 2007, Japan and Australia signed their first security cooperation treaty. A week before Wen's Tokyo visit, Japan, the US and India completed their first joint military maneuvers in East Asia.

The China card is an essential factor in Japan's domestic politics. The new diplomacy pursued by Mr. Abe's administration is meant to be a "value diplomacy", and is the first blueprint for a strategic embedment in Asia and simultaneously a long-term plan on how to allay the fear to China. It is not simply an ideological offensive that Japan wants to launch against Beijing, but also a remodeling of Japan's Asian politics based on enlarging a coalition of democracies facing the likes of China, Russia, North Korea and Iran. Tokyo fallaciously envisages an "authoritarian bloc" confronting Asian democracies. This "value diplomacy" will negatively impact on relations with China. Under the circumstances, Tokyo could be expected to speed up rearming the SDF and rivaling China openly.

The China threat is a very useful motivator for Japanese nationalistic politicians to use in order to lift their popularity, proceed with constitution mending and claim a more assertive role in the international context. Japanese conservatives often fan inflammatory rhetoric. A senior Japanese politician, Shoichi Nakagawa, the LDP's policy chief and a close ally of Mr. Abe, accused China of theft in the gas dispute with Japan in April 2007, and sensationalized that China's rise could lead to degrading Japan into "a province" of that country. Scaremongering about China is a profitable business for Japan's conservative politicians who can cash in on hawkish lines refusing to "kneel down" in the front of Communist China. This will continue to be the case as long as Japan's primary assumption of what China is about does not change, and perhaps more importantly, as long as American regional preeminence stands.

Summit contacts will not be able to dramatically change the nature and format of the complex China-Japan bilateral relationship. It is still too early to say whether both countries have taken a solid step forward towards a "post-ice period". Stopping short of visiting the Yasukuni Shrine is obviously a conciliatory gesture by Mr. Abe. But the future rests more on Japan's domestic political calculations and international power assessment, and less on its valuation of a Japan-China friendship. Despite the increasing intertwinement of their economies, China and Japan still have, in political terms, a long way to go to achieve a mature relationship of true stability and lasting cooperation.

Zhu Feng

10

North Korea

China-North Korean relations were initially one of mutual solidarity. The Korean War tempered them with pragmatism. If China was going to have to fight the US, and in the dark days of McCarthyism it looked that way, better in Korea than on Chinese soil. Then there was a kind of tug of war between the People's Republic of China (PRC) and the USSR, waxing and waning in a kind of duet between Beijing and Moscow, with over time superimposed on both a growing rapprochement with Seoul — the enemy for so long. In the 1990s, Moscow abandoned Pyongyang for the South, while China juggled both. By the time of the nuclear crises, particularly the October 2002 crisis, a new China recognized that events in the North threatened its own plans and ways had to be found both to provide security guarantees to prevent Pyongyang's nuclear ambitions from triggering a regional arms race, and to prevent an economic collapse that would have US troops on the Yalu River.

Actually, the PRC and the Democratic Republic of Korea had a relationship before either came into formal existence. In 1931 Japan invaded Manchuria, and in China's defense, strong anti-Japanese guerrilla groups were formed comprising over 200,000 Chinese and a heavy sprinkling of Koreans. Kim Il Sung, North Korea's future leader, was one.

By 1933, he was fighting with the Chinese Communist Party as part of the North East Anti-Japanese Allied Army under the banner of the Korean People's Revolutionary Army. Eventually, the weight of the Japanese offensive forced Kim and his guerrilla band to seek safe haven in the USSR, technically at peace with Japan.

Kim's partisan resistance to Japanese imperialism became the founding myth of North Korea, legitimizing his leadership, his policies and his actions.

From it, "Great Leader" Kim Il Sung emerged as philosopher-king, and for decades, the wider North Korean leadership was dominated by the legacy and personalities of this period.

The Allies decided to cut the Peninsula into two roughly equal parts at the 38th parallel, with Seoul, the capital, conveniently on the US side, while giving the Soviets enough of the cake to stop them from wanting more. Stalin's lack of ambition on the Peninsula was demonstrated by his acceptance of what was a pretty poor deal in the circumstances.

The Soviets, when they occupied the Northern Zone of Korea, brought Kim back to Pyongyang and belatedly chose him to lead, but he was "first amongst equals" as a complex set of parties and factions vied for power and influence in the aftermath of liberation.

The Korean Workers' Party (KWP) inherited four main factions: the Domestic Faction, comprising those who had remained in Korea, generally in jail or in hiding during Japanese occupation; the *Yan'an* Faction, comprising those who had spent their exile in China; the Soviet Faction, comprising Koreans from the USSR; and the *Kapsan* (Partisan) Faction led by Kim Il Sung, comprising those who had initially fought with him in China and accompanied him to the Soviet Union.

While Kim had the advantage of Soviet sponsorship, it was by no means inevitable that he would be the last man standing even amongst the Communists. The struggle for power started immediately, but the final rounds were played out long after the Soviets had withdrawn. At times, Kim's position was far from secure, particularly after the disaster of the Korean War, and many would have laid odds against his survival. But he proved a master of factional in-fighting, dividing and conquering, playing off group against group and individual against individual.

Since their collaboration against the Japanese in the 1930s and 1940s, the Chinese and Korean Communists had a close relationship, with the two working hand-in-hand exchanging men, materials and aid back and forth. There were particularly strong links in Manchuria where Kim Il Sung had fought. Tens of thousands of Koreans from both sides of the Yalu and Tumen rivers had fought against the Japanese. After August 1945, many had remained to continue the fight as part of Mao's People's Liberation Army against Chiang Kai-Shek's Nationalist Kuomintang in China's civil war, with Kim Il Sung supplying what aid and assistance he could. When Lin Biao's forces fell back before a Nationalist offensive in South Manchuria at the end of 1946, it was North Korea that provided shelter for the families of Communist troops who had been forced to flee.

The military victory of the Communists over the Nationalists on the mainland and the founding of the People's Republic of China encouraged Kim's ambitions to reunite Korea. In May 1949, as China's war wound down, Mao had returned to Kim two Korean divisions of 14,000 soldiers who had fought in the Chinese civil war. With Stalin's authorization to invade the South in his pocket, Kim Il Sung travelled to Beijing in spring 1950 to secure extra military assistance. Mao, entering the end game of the Chinese civil war with his planned final assaults on Taiwan and Tibet, was initially reluctant to become embroiled in another war, especially one where the US might get involved. This agreement was assisted by assurances from the Southern Communist leader, Pak Hon Yong — who travelled with Kim to meet Mao — that the South Korean masses would rise against the oppressors as soon as the North marched into the South. Kim swept across the 38th parallel on 25 June 1950.

International reaction to war breaking out in the Korean Peninsula was swift. The UN Security Council passed a resolution on the same day calling for "immediate cessation of hostilities". A second resolution two days later recommended member states provide "assistance to the ROK as may be necessary to repel the armed attack and to restore international peace and security in the area". The Soviet Union was boycotting the UN over its refusal to recognize the new Communist government in China and thus lost an opportunity to veto UN intervention, not that that would have stopped the US. The US used its control of the UN to internationalize the conflict. The US response was in line with domestic political concerns. The Communist victory in China had come as a profound shock to Washington. Now was a good time for a fight.

The first US troops landed on 1 July 1950, preempting the formal approval to intervene by a Security Council resolution on 7 July 1950 establishing a United Nations Command (UNC) and a UN intervention force under the leadership of General MacArthur. The initial North Korean onslaught saw the South's troops routed fleeing south to be trapped in and around the city of Pusan. They remained trapped there until the US landing at Inchon broke the North Korea supply lines and the Korean People's Army (KPA) was rapidly rolled back almost to the Yalu River. Despite grave concerns, the

US transformed the UN's commitment to restore the status quo to a war of liberation. The UN Security Council resolution of 7 October 1950 gave the UNC the green light to invade the North. Both sides were now fighting for one Korea. The tables were turned. Dispatches now talked of "liberated areas". Pyongyang fell. Just as for the KPA three months earlier, the UNC encountered little resistance and rapidly occupied almost the entire Peninsula.

This aggressive US approach was counterproductive. The Chinese were convinced that war with the US was inevitable, and they preferred to fight their battles on Korean territory rather than on their own. The Chinese People's Volunteers were ordered to cross the border, which they passed undetected on 26 October 1950. UN forces were overwhelmed and broke up in disarray. Seoul fell for the second time to the North, but supply lines again got overstretched and the North was pushed back close to where it all started at the 38th parallel where a war of attrition dragged on until an Armistice was signed on 27 July 1953, with China sacrificing 390,000 troops including Mao's son, Mao Anying, who died in a US bombing raid on Pyongyang.

There were few winners. Kim's position was under threat. But he got his retaliation in first. Pak Hon Yong was accused of being a US spy. His faction was purged long before his execution in the mid-1950s. Of the participants, China had best reason to be pleased. They had fought the US on foreign soil, fighting US-led UN troops to a standstill, proving its military was capable of holding its own with the best of the West.

After Khrushchev's denunciation of Stalin and Stalinism at the Party's 20th Congress in February 1956, Politburo members affiliated to the Soviet Group and the *Yan'an* Group attacked Kim. At the August meeting of the KWP's Central Committee, he was derided as Korea's Stalin with a second-hand personality cult and industrial policy. Leaders of the *Yan'an* faction were exiled to minor posts in the provinces or stripped of their power entirely. Some fled to China to escape the purges. Kim Tu Bong, their leader and North Korea's largely ceremonial President, who had not been directly involved in the coup attempt, survived until 1958, when he was purged and accused of being the plot's "mastermind". Relations with China and the Soviet Union cooled.

Relations with the Soviet Union remained cool although officially cordial through the 1960s and 1970s. China, on the other hand, moved closer to North Korea during this period. Zhou Enlai visited Pyongyang in 1970 and

Kim Il Sung visited Beijing in 1974, despite the shock of Nixon's 1972 visit. China even replaced the Soviet Union as the DPRK's leading supplier of military hardware. This trend was reversed at the end of the 1970s when China normalized relations with the US in January 1979. North Korea's ultimately abortive move into the Non-Aligned Movement in these years showed that it had lost faith in both the USSR and PRC.

When Deng Xiaoping came to power in China in 1978, his pragmatic approach to the economy and his implicit advocacy of market socialist reforms was summed up in his infamous aphorism: "white cat or a black cat; who cares as long as it catches mice." The Chinese Communist Party's new direction emphasized modernization and economic development at the expense of revolution and ideology. Despite this and obvious disagreements on the diplomatic front, relations between China and the DPRK saw a series of high-level visits in the early 1980s. From North Korea's standpoint, even if they did not like the trends in China, friendly relations were necessary for economic and military reasons. Pyongyang's confidence in its allies was undermined further when the Soviet Union established diplomatic relations with Seoul in 1990 and China followed two years later. But the collapse and disintegration of the Soviet Union in 1991 finally ended Pyongyang's playing one off against the other.

China and the Soviet Union had historically competed to buy influence by providing oil and other goods at "friendship" prices. With the fall of the Soviet Union, it became a seller's market. Trade between Russia and the North just stopped. For the first time since Mao's victory, China began demanding payment in hard cash. The immediate result was that the North's faltering economy collapsed. An overemphasis on heavy industry and the cannibalization of the civil sector to boost the military had created an excessively fragile situation. A series of natural disasters, including floods and drought, pushed the economy into meltdown. The consequent famine killed an estimated 3 million — one in eight of the population — as they starved in slow motion. Food was available but not enough to live on.

Triggered by the food crisis, a flood of refugees crossed into China. NGOs claim that there are up to 300,000 refugees and illegal immigrants in the border areas. The reality is that many people cross for short trips to visit relatives, buy and sell goods or search for food. During the early 1960s and the famine following the disaster of the Great Leap Forward, the traffic was the other way around with the North receiving and feeding starving Chinese.

The EU has repeatedly called upon the Chinese authorities to allow the Office of the UN High Commissioner for Refugees to investigate the situation on the Sino-DPRK border. While the majority are economic migrants, amongst them are those who have a "well-founded fear of persecution" should they be returned. On the basis of the 1953 Geneva Convention, this minority should be granted asylum by China. However, China makes no distinction between those who will merely spend a few days in detention and those who will be incarcerated for years or worse. Yet, the most significant barrier to North Korean refugees is Seoul. Constitutionally, any North Koreans are South Koreans. Neither the ROK government nor the public want the social and financial burden. They might want their relatives out, but they certainly do not want everyone else's.

Currently, the issue of refugees and asylum seekers shows Beijing torn between its anxiety not to endanger its relationship with either North or South Korea, while concerned about its own image in the run-up to the 2008 Olympic Games. China does not want to see Pyongyang collapse because any collapse threatens military adventurism by the North, together with millions of refugees and ultimately US troops directly across the Yalu River. Military conflict on the Peninsula would trigger a global economic crisis that would devastate China's growing economy. Regional stability in Northeast Asia is essential to China if it is to maintain the economic growth to enable it to meet its 2020 goal of $3,000 GDP per capita.

China is desperate not to let North Korea and Kim Jong Il threaten its long-term interests, and wants peace and stability on the Peninsula. But that requires two things at minimum — a solution to the nuclear crisis and major systemic reform in the North. Without a comprehensive solution, the knock-on effects will force China into an arms race with Japan and the US. Such an arms race would inevitably threaten continued economic and social development. However, China has had plans to intervene in place for at least five years. China's current relations with the North are driven by its desire that the North's nuclear weapons program is not used as an excuse by Japan's conservatives to rewrite Japan's peace constitution and deploy Theater Missile Defense technology that would force Beijing to multiply its own ICBMs and divert desperately needed resources away from the civilian economy into the military, and triggering a subsequent arms race in the region as Taiwan, South Korea and Japan follow suit. Equally, the North needs to embrace, "in its own style", economic reform.

As recently as 2002, Charles Kartman, then head of KEDO (Korean Peninsula Energy Development Organization), said, "the number of proven weapons is zero." Yet, a combination of ill-will and bad faith, poor crisis management and incompetence by the US has transformed that situation to one where the North now has enough plutonium for half a dozen bombs and more, and has probably become the world's ninth nuclear state after the US, UK, France, China, Russia, Israel, India and Pakistan.

North Korea's nuclear program had its origins back in the mid-1950s, following an agreement between Pyongyang and Moscow on exchanging scientists. After China's nuclear test in 1964, Kim asked China for the bomb. Presumably, Moscow had already rejected an earlier request. Mao said no.

In the early 1960s, Pyongyang had established a Nuclear Scientific Research Center near the Kuryung River at Yongbyon, 100 km northeast of the capital where, in 1965, Moscow sold North Korea an IRT-2MWe pool-type research reactor with Soviet scientists working alongside Koreans. At this stage, there was no evidence that the North was trying to produce its own nuclear weapons rather than having them gifted. It is rumoured that Kim Il Sung again requested Chinese aid for a weapons program in 1974 when South Korea was undertaking its own preliminary research, but it was not until the late 1970s that the North established its own program.

In the early 1980s, North Korean nuclear scientists with Soviet help built a 5 MW experimental graphite moderated reactor in Yongbyon. This reactor was capable of producing weapons grade plutonium and had, from a North Korean perspective, the enormous advantage of making them autonomous — it required neither heavy water nor enriched uranium.

Both the KGB and CIA believe the world came closer to a nuclear war in 1994 than at any other time since the Cuban missile crisis in 1962. Both security services informed their respective governments that the North Koreans had up to five nuclear weapons, made from diverting plutonium from their reactor at Yongbyon. In retrospect, both were wrong, massively exaggerating the North's capabilities.

International pressure grew on the DPRK to open up these sites for inspection. In March 1993, Pyongyang suddenly announced it was withdrawing from the Nuclear Proliferation Treaties (NPT). This triggered a major crisis in the US and South Korea with claims that the withdrawal proved North Korea either had or was about to obtain nuclear weapons. All it probably proved was that the North Koreans neither wanted to be caught cheating by diverting some plutonium, nor did they want the IAEA or the US intelligence community crawling all over sensitive military sites.

Inspections resumed in March 1994 only to run into yet more problems. North Korea wanted to unload fuel rods from the Yongbyon reactor without supervision, destroying evidence of any earlier plutonium reprocessing. When the IAEA confirmed that North Korea had begun to remove spent fuel in May 1994, the crisis threatened to spiral out of control as the Clinton administration threatened military action. Plans for preemptive strikes on all the North's nuclear facilities were prepared and approved by President Clinton. F-111 aircrafts in Okinawa were fuelled and ready to fly.

The situation was rescued by the maverick intervention of former President Jimmy Carter, who was invited to Pyongyang at the height of the crisis. He met at length with Kim Il Sung and negotiated an unauthorized "package deal" with the DPRK, involving direct US-DPRK talks. Announcing his deal publicly on CNN forced the Clinton administration's hand. The negotiations produced the Agreed Framework signed by both parties. This promised Pyongyang two proliferation-resistant Light Water Reactors (LWRs) by 2003 in exchange for freezing its Yongbyon reactor and halting construction of its two new reactors at Yongbyon and Taechon.

In the interim, before the LWRs were completed, North Korea would get 500,000 tonnes per annum of Heavy Fuel Oil (HFO) to compensate for the shortfall in energy supply notionally caused by the loss of energy output from the mothballed reactors. Actually, if they had gone on line, the North's rudimentary and aging electricity grid would almost certainly have been unable to cope. Washington promised to lift the economic embargo imposed after the Korean War 40 years before, and normalize relations with the North. It seemed a perfect technological fix to a political crisis.

Whether the US ever seriously intended to deliver on its promises seems unlikely. For Washington, it was just a way to buy time until North Korea collapsed. Unfortunately for the US, North Korea's resilience was much stronger than expected and it weathered the crises of the 1990s. North Korean "Communism" was not of the same brittle variety imposed by the Soviet Empire on

Central and Eastern Europe, a Communism that collapsed once Gorbachev's reforms in the Soviet Union removed the crutches that supported it. North Korea's ideological superstructure, in contrast, was deeply rooted in Korean history, experience and culture. Marxism-Leninism had metamorphosed into a version of the Japanese Emperor Cult.

The US never delivered on its 1994 promises. Economic sanctions against North Korea were never lifted. Nor did the promised normalization of relations between the US and the DPRK take place. The KEDO project, which became the operational arm of the Agreed Framework with the task of building the two LWRs by 2003, proceeded at snail's pace. HFO was delivered fitfully. The US was a serial discoverer of secret nuclear programs in North Korea, particularly when it suited them. In the late 1990s, satellite reconnaissance identified an underground chamber near the village of Kumchangri. The suspected nuclear site turned out to be secure storage in wartime to prevent the destruction of holy artefacts, namely Kim Il Sung statues and other icons. Yet, Bush was determined to find a North Korea secret nuclear weapons program. At the October 2002 meeting between James Kelly, US Assistant Secretary of State for East Asian Pacific Affairs, and Kang Suk Ju, the North Korean First Vice Foreign Minister, the latter was goaded into saying, "Of course, we have a nuclear program." This was taken as a confession of a secret Highly Enriched Uranium (HEU) nuclear weapons development program. The reality was more ambiguous. Kang's "confession" was not on record, with neither tape nor transcript. The North Koreans angrily retorted that the Vice Foreign Minister had been misinterpreted and that what he really said was that North Korea had the right to a program — not that it had one. It would be an easy interpreter's mistake. There is a subtle but crucial difference between "is entitled to have" (*kajige tui-o-itta*) and "has come to have" (*kajige tui-otta*), even for Korean speakers. The US may just have heard what they wanted to hear.

The immediate response from the US was to suspend deliveries of HFO. This suspension was the final nail in the coffin. Promises of normalization of relations, lifting of the embargo, two LWRs by 2003 and interim deliveries of HFO had finally dribbled away to nothing. It is not clear whether North Korea had the components of a nuclear weapon before the end of 2002, but now it was a dash for the bomb. North Korea believed the lesson from the US-led invasion of Iraq was that not having WMDs was the problem.

North Korea put the Yongbyon plant back on line and completed its withdrawal from the NPT in January 2003. On 10 February 2005, North Korea officially declared it had now become a nuclear-weapons state. North Korea's Head of State, Kim Young Nam, went on record saying that its "nuclear deterrent force" was for self-defense and that there would be "no first use" of nuclear weapons.

Eventually, Pyongyang tried to carry out an underground nuclear test on 9 October 2006. The blast was equivalent to an earthquake registering 4.2 on the Richter scale and radiation was detected subsequent to the test. It was a whimper rather than a bang, yielding a blast equivalent to only 1,000 tonnes of TNT, but it showed that the North has the material and the technology to build a nuclear bomb. As Beijing put it, they have a nuclear device. Any future test may prove a full, if unreliable, capability.

Putting Pyongyang's nuclear capacity in context, the US has 100,000 times more nuclear fire power in its Trident fleet alone than that which Pyongyang demonstrated with its October 2006 test. As for the nuclear crisis, when it broke, Bush argued that a peaceful resolution was possible; however, there were forces around the White House merely looking for a pause for breath after Iraq.

China has done what it can to reinforce Kim's reformism. The Chinese authorities have taken the horse to water. General Secretary Jiang Zemin visited Pyongyang in September 2001. After the 2002 crisis, both the Vice Minister of Foreign Affairs, Dai Bingguo, and the Chairman of National People's Congress, Wu Banguo, met Kim Jong Il and successfully convinced Pyongyang to participate in the proposed Six-Party Talks, joined by the US, South Korea, Japan and Russia. At the same time, they did all they could to reinforce his reformist tendencies. Kim took the train from Pyongyang to Beijing in May 2000, January 2001, April 2004 and January 2006.

During his 2001 visit, Kim undertook a "study tour" to Shanghai and Fudong, showcasing the success of China's own reforms. He was impressed and the response was instant in the *Rodong Sinmun*: "China has achieved a unique socialist development with social unity and stability under the leadership of the Communist Party, and as a result, the status of China is continuously elevating on the international stage." Kim returned to the same region in January 2006 and in March sent a 30-strong fact-finding mission, led by his brother-in-law and potential successor, Jang Sung Taek, to Wuhan, Guangzhou and Shenzhen, the heart of China's economic powerhouse. In July 2002, the

State Price Control Bureau introduced a new price and wages system that cut state subsidies, endorsed the "market" and granted greater autonomy to farmers and agricultural and craft enterprises, setting new low and easily achievable targets for delivery to the State with the surplus for private sale in the markets. In June 2004, it was announced that for 90% of industry, "The Plan" had been abandoned. As explained to the first EU-DPRK Workshop on Economic Reform in Pyongyang four months later, now that the State could no longer provide the necessary inputs of energy and raw materials, industrial enterprises had been freed to choose their own process and products and given the ability to hire and fire at will. The initial result was a lot more firing than hiring and a partial re-ruralization of the economy. Work teams from the industrial enterprises were sent out to grow food. As the Ministry of State Planning explained, the State would continue to own the means of production, but the groups entrusted with their management had the responsibility to maximize profits. The unanswered question was where this profit would go.

The slow pace of the North's reforms and its limited success outside of agriculture still worries the Chinese leadership. Recognizing that external economic inputs are vital and that direct economic assistance from South Korea — while welcome — is inadequate and not entirely reliable, Vice Minister Wu Yi signed a multi-billion dollar trade deal in Pyongyang in 2005. This was reaffirmed with President Hu Jintao's visit later in the year.

Getting the US and North Korea back to the table was never going to be easy. Neither trusted the other, and they both had valid points. The US proclaimed it would not reward "bad behavior" by engaging in bilateral talks. With the US refusal, China, whose economic successes were beginning to translate into political influence, took the initiative and proposed a multilateral framework of Six-Party Talks. The US unenthusiastically acquiesced and under enormous pressure from friends and foes alike, the North signed up to participate alongside South Korea, US, Japan, Russia, and the hosts, China. The first round of the talks was held in Beijing in August 2003. North Korea would have accepted a new freeze in exchange for a restoration of HFO deliveries. This would have stopped the flow of plutonium to the North's nuclear weapons program while a comprehensive step-by-step solution was pursued. But there was to be no deal.

The North wanted "security guarantees", a "non-aggression pact" plus assistance with its energy supply; the US demanded unconditional Complete

Verifiable Irreversible Dismantlement (CVID) without compensation. The North was not going to surrender its nuclear program without a compensating indigenous energy supply. The single most important factor contributing to the North's current economic woes was the crippling shortage of fuel and energy. The US insistence on CVID first and the North's demand for security guarantees and energy ensured a stand-off. The talks went nowhere.

It was not until the North had had two years to initiate and build its nuclear arsenal that China persuaded the US to move and the breakthrough appeared to come. In September 2005, at the end of the fourth round of talks, an outline agreement was announced.

It looked good on paper. The problem was implementation with the promise of simultaneous step-by-step progress. North Korea agreed to abandon its nuclear development program in exchange for US promises to rule out preemptive military action against it or attempts to promote regime change, accompanied by the provision "at the appropriate time" of a LWR and development aid to kick-start the economy. For the US, the "appropriate time" was closer to never than now, while for the North the "appropriate time" was prior to its final surrender of nuclear weapons. Thus, for the North, there would be no civil nuclear power for the foreseeable future, but instead, electricity would be fed in from the South with the off-switch firmly under Seoul's finger — acceptable as an interim measure, but a deeply unattractive long-term solution for a country where autonomy, self-reliance and *Juche* have been the watchwords. The reality is there is no alternative to nuclear power that gives the North any modicum of energy independence.

As it turned out, the ink was barely dry before, from Pyongyang's perspective, the US demonstrated their bad faith. They forced the North's bank of choice in Macao, Banco Delta Asia, to freeze North Korean accounts on the grounds that they were using them for money laundering, the claim being Nigerian gangs were dumping around Asia counterfeit $100 bills produced in the North. In light of the September Joint Statement, screwing it up for $25 million, small change for organized crime in any major US conurbation, was either stupidity or conspiracy. The North chose to interpret it as the latter. November's first session of the fifth round of talks saw the North walk out, to China's embarrassment.

This failure to build on the Joint Declaration did not disappoint everyone. It left the US neo-cons confident that they now had the North Koreans exactly where they wanted them — no KEDO, no nuclear power, and the country effectively embargoed by the West. Pyongyang would be bound to respond to the provocation. And, if it did — the North is notoriously bad at not responding — regime change was back on the agenda and China back where it started.

After the North Korean nuclear test, Hu Jintao sent a Special Envoy to meet Kim Jong Il, who agreed to postpone further tests and return to the talks after learning that the US had agreed to the simultaneous establishment of a bilateral Working Group that would lift the freeze on the Macao bank accounts. Talks resumed in December 2006 and the Third Session of the Fifth Round of the Six-Party Talks two months later concluded with an agreement on "Initial Actions for the Implementation of the Joint Statement".

February 2007 took the world back close to where we were when the music stopped in October 2002. The DPRK agreed to freeze plutonium production and reprocessing at Yongbyon and allow the IAEA inspectors to monitor and verify this freeze, with the provision of 50,000 tonnes of HFO within 60 days. Then, in a second phase, the DPRK will make a complete declaration of all nuclear programs and disablement of all existing nuclear facilities, including graphite-moderated reactors and reprocessing plants. In exchange, economic, energy and humanitarian assistance up to the equivalent of 1 million tonnes of HFO that includes the initial shipment will be provided to the DPRK, at a cost of approximately €210 million, plus talks on normalizing relations with the US and Japan. All fairly simple and straightforward. All conditional on, from the North Korean perspective, a lifting of the freeze of their money in the Banco Delta Asia. It seemed a done deal, although even that got complicated as the US found a most convoluted means of delivering its commitment, which to the North broke the spirit if not the letter of the Agreement. The US banned their banks from dealing with Banco Delta Asia, leaving the Chinese to unfreeze the accounts, but with the distinct hint from Washington that others might follow their example.

It is the third phase that looks tricky. Five working groups were set up, namely: (1) US-DPRK relations, (2) DPRK-Japan relations, (3) Energy and economic aid, (4) Armistice and security issues, and (5) Denuclearization of the Korean Peninsula. Within weeks, Japan refused to provide any financing without progress on its abductees and urged the US not to remove the North from its "terror state" list, with Pyongyang responding that Japan should withdraw from the whole process if it was already reneging on the agreement.

Denuclearization will be a step-by-step process where Yongbyon will be the penultimate for final demolition and Pyongyang's nuclear weapons the ultimate. To get to that final point, an institutionalization of the Working Group 4 into some permanent body may be able to provide to North Korea guarantees of the US fulfilling its intentions. Aid will be expensive, but cheaper than conflict. The EU will again be asked to contribute disproportionately. The five countries which got to go to the North to assess the energy situation did not include the EU, who will be expected to contribute, but did include Japan who said it would not. It will be a long, winding and bumpy road for China, and how it handles this offers an important example of how its future relations with the rest of the world may work. The question is whether everyone is in for the long ride, or whether, at the first hurdles, some get off. Meanwhile, progress is being made in North Korea on reform. Seoul is even beginning to worry it may be squeezed out by Beijing.

Glyn Ford

11

Iran

Whether or not Iran acquires nuclear weapons will be a defining moment for the entire Middle East region. It will also decide who will control the Middle East and its oil in the years to come. This chapter examines the underlying factors contributing to the present dispute between Iran and the West, and the context in which the PRC might determine its own policy towards Iran.

Europeans and Chinese disagree with the US policy of freezing out Iran. The big powers have broken the nuclear proliferation treaties from the outset and allowed Israel, India and Pakistan to go nuclear. If a different policy had been adopted, the Iranians might have been persuaded to enrich uranium in Russia, in return for a bankable security guarantee and reintegration into the international environment.

Ali M. Ansari (in his book, *Confronting Iran*) describes the bitter battle between the US and Iran as "the problem of Mutually Assured Paranoia, perpetuated by very similar bedfellows on either side (neocons in US and hardliners in Iran) — 'a deteriorating, absurd, vicious cycle in which the rigid obstinacy of the hawks on both sides produced a self-fulfilling prophecy and its own justification'." Iran, under Shah Mohammad Reza Pahlavi, used to be the staunchest ally of the US and Israel in the Middle East.

Both the US and Iran seem to thrive on myths about themselves and about each other. Neither appears to have a coherent strategy, with Washington probably too preoccupied with Iran's religious ideology rather than its resurgent nationalism and Tehran reactive and thriving on crises.

The "Great Satan"

The United States is naturally the "Great Satan" to the Iranian people who remember or are reminded of its role in the overthrow of the Mossadegh government in 1953, its on-going military and secret service support for the last Shah, its arms and logistical support for Iraq in the Iran-Iraq War of 1980–1988, turning a blind eye to Saddam Hussein's use of chemical warfare against Iran, its support and arms for the Taliban in the 1990s (the Taliban murdered nine Iranian diplomats in cold blood in Afghanistan and are hated by Iran), support for the Mojahedin-e-Khalq Organization (MKO) (even though a US-banned terrorist organization), and the shooting down by USS Vincennes in 1988 of an Iran Air civilian airliner with all 290 dead.

Iran does not want to appreciate the deep blow to US pride caused by the US embassy hostage crisis in 1979 and its long-term effects on US attitudes towards Iran; nor the international revulsion at President Ahmadinejad's statements about Israel.

It is as if both Tehran and Washington need a black and white enemy. The mutual lack of trust and lack of understanding make the circumstances worse. Other complicating factors include the influence of Iranian domestic politics, the Sunni-Shia schism and Iraq.

Iran has felt pathologically insecure for long periods of the last 100 years as a country exploited for its oil, and feels threatened, even when comparatively strong. Today it is surrounded by the US — in Iraq, Afghanistan, Pakistan, the Gulf states, Turkey and Central Asia. Some must genuinely feel that they are next on the list, and as former President Rafsanjani said, "had Saddam had nuclear weapons, he would still be in power."

The US stands in the way of Iran's regional ambitions. Iranians are proud of their history and know that once Persia was a huge empire, which included both Iraq and Afghanistan.

There are reports from responsible sources that the Iranian government has neglected longer-term investment in its oil industry and that this will result in lower production with obvious consequences. Its population has doubled since 1975 and is increasing by about one million per year. Iranians experience shortages, and their educational level is low (less than 80% literacy). Unfortunately, much of the international rhetoric undoubtedly serves to distract from the internal misery. The West is blamed for the people's woes. The Mullahs continue to ruin the country's economy.

Were Iran's leaders to face a determined and united international community, and to be offered a plausible mix of carrots and sticks, a solution can still be found. President Ahmadinejad has been severely criticized by other members of Iran's leadership for having so damaged international relations that UN Security Council members were able to agree a sanctions resolution in December 2006. There was also a public disagreement between him and Ali Larijani, Iran's nuclear negotiator, as to whose authority — his or Ayatollah Khamenei's — prevails in nuclear matters. But this requires everyone, Americans included, to sit down with the Iranians without pre-conditions. Washington is attending meetings on Iraq with Iranians present, but it looks unlikely that direct negotiations with Iran, with American participation, will happen under the present administration.

Compromise Package

A package which might be acceptable to Tehran would comprise a security guarantee, the lifting of all embargoes, a cessation of all US anti-régime activity within Iran, and Iran being welcomed back into the international community.

George W. Bush initially rejected the Iraq Study Group's recommendation that the US talk to Iran about Iraq, sadly confirming that a political solution to the Iranian nuclear issue is not achievable. This leaves three possible options for preventing Iran from acquiring nuclear weapons, which it seems intent on doing and which virtually no one else in the world wants: promoting domestic opposition and ultimately regime change, military action or economic sanctions.

The current Iranian regime appears stable and there is no sign that internal opposition will have any effect in the foreseeable future. The government appears to have widespread support for its current stand on the nuclear issue.

Military action by the US and/or Israel is feasible, but incapable of producing a satisfactory solution, even given the political will. However, desperate action by President Bush and/or Israel cannot be ruled out and there have been worrying noises in Washington. It is clear that the EU 27 would not support such military action.

This leaves economic sanctions. Targeted, "intelligent" sanctions are being applied, with further ones under consideration, but it is difficult to see how they will be effective — even with the support of Russia and China, which is not currently forthcoming. They risk making the Iranian regime even more stubborn, increasing popular support and enabling the mullahs to blame the West for their own economic failures. And they will cause even greater suffering — and anti-Western hostility — by the Iranian people.

Oil Embargo

One solution which should be explored is to impose a total embargo on Iran's oil exports, with the objective of persuading Iran to accept full and unfettered International Energy Agency (IEA) inspections and a commitment to not enrich uranium in Iran. Regime change would not be the objective.

This solution requires four questions to be answered: is it logistically possible to maintain such a boycott? Can the Iranian oil be replaced? Would the embargo be effective? Would Russia and China agree? Such a boycott is enforceable because the vast majority of oil is exported by ship or pipeline, which can easily be blocked. Iranian exports of about 2.7 million barrels per day can largely be replaced by increased output from willing countries — led by Saudi Arabia — which can probably provide one-half of the shortfall. According to the IEA, other OPEC members have spare capacity to meet nearly all the rest. Most of the estimated 2007 increase in demand of approx 1.5 million barrels per day would be covered by new supplies.

Such an embargo would be effective, since Iran's economy is inordinately dependent on oil, which comprises up to 90% of total export earnings. Iran imports around one-third of its petrol requirements as it has insufficient oil refining capacity. Such an embargo would therefore also cause petrol shortages.

Would Russia agree? Moscow is prepared to contemplate imposing some sanctions, but would be reluctant to go this far. But it has to answer the question: is it prepared to risk having a nuclear Iran as its neighbor? Moscow would no doubt extract a price for its cooperation with the other permanent members of the UN Security Council, but this would be manageable.

Would China agree? Iran supplies 13.6% of Chinese oil imports — around 450,000 barrels a day. China would therefore have to receive an oil security guarantee from the West to cover the shortfall. The US and Europe could provide this — the US Strategic Petroleum Reserve alone was 688.6 million barrels on 2 March 2007. China, like Russia, ultimately must answer the question: is it otherwise prepared to risk having a nuclear Iran in the region? China would not, in any case, wish to veto a Security Council resolution, nor put at risk its vast trade interests with the West. And there could be bonuses on offer, such as the US selling advanced coal gasification material to China and the EU lifting the arms embargo.

A total boycott of oil exports would bring Iran to its knees within months, and thus, the suffering of its citizens would be minimized. But could Iran's reaction be dangerous? Ultimate decision-making power lies with Ayatollah Khamenei and not with President Mahmoud Ahmadinejad. The former has been rather silent of late and a "good cop – bad cop" routine seems to be in play. Power is diffuse in Iran. The Revolutionary Guards strongly support the nuclear program, but the Supreme Leader has the final decision, and the Guards will not act without his approval. However, the President has a messianic vision and is inherently dangerous.

The Iranian leadership might be religiously extreme, but this does not mean that it would behave stupidly. There needs to be a strong western naval presence in the Persian Gulf, both to blockade the Iranian ports and to prevent Iran from retaliating by disrupting the flow of oil from other Persian Gulf countries.

Although Iran has a considerable naval and military arsenal, including submarines, Iranian-built missiles based on Russian and Chinese designs that are difficult to counter before and after launch, anti-ship missiles, sophisticated mines and aircraft procured from China, Russia and North Korea, it is still hard to believe that Iran would risk committing an act of war by blockading or mining the Strait of Hormuz, the 55 kilometer-wide passage through which Middle Eastern oil reaches the Indian Ocean (40% of the world's traded oil passes through the straits). This cannot, however, be ruled out.

A rise in oil prices caused by uncertainty must be expected, but this would be manageable with decisive action. The very threat of this common action might be sufficient to stop the current Iranian leaders in their tracks and open the way for China to work out with the Iranians a face-saving formula, including substantial benefits, not least providing the investment capital which it lacks and which has led to below-average oil production. Its 40 producing oilfields need to be modernized. And the inability to acquire the appropriate technology has impeded Iran's efforts to develop its massive natural gas reserves.

There appears to be no other choice, in the absence of a political solution. The proposed solution has its dangers, but this is less than the danger of Iran acquiring nuclear capability.

What Does Iran Want?

The foregoing analysis makes clear that there are huge risks in Iran acquiring nuclear weapons and huge risks in stopping it.

While Israel understandably sees a nuclear Iran as an existential threat, it is doubtful that it provides the motivation for Iran. More likely are two other objectives — first, as a protection against US military activity; and second, to bolster its position as the leading regional power.

A possible scenario is that, once Tehran has the capacity to produce nuclear weapons, it will then seek to negotiate a political deal from a position of strength: until then it will procrastinate. Its leaders probably also believe that its policy will lead eventually to a security guarantee, the lifting of US sanctions and its re-admittance to the international community. Also in their sights are, no doubt, full access to civil nuclear technology and support for WTO entry.

Recapitulating the elements of a political settlement:

- All embargos be lifted.
- All US anti-régime activity within Iran cease.
- Iran be welcomed back into the international community.
- Iran receive massive inward investment and other financial support.

Clearly, Iran would have to stop supporting Hizbollah, Hamas and other terrorist groups. Whether they are willing to do this depends upon whether reason or fundamentalism prevails. In the end, Iranians can be very pragmatic, when they have got what they want. Indeed, a settlement on the above lines would give Iran just the regional, and indeed international, standing that it seeks. This would be portrayed as an Islamic victory against the western crusaders. Participating in bringing peace to the region would be a prize that would be bankable by Tehran in many ways.

The United States holds the key to the political solution. But where does this leave China? It has to make a decision: is it willing to allow Iran the capacity to produce nuclear weapons? This decision should be based on geopolitical and not economic considerations (although economic commitments from the West would be needed). A nuclear Iran would be a threat to the region; it would likely result in one or two Sunni Arab countries following suit and, above all, increase the risk of nuclear weapons falling into the hands of terrorists. India and Pakistan are worries enough, but adding Iran to the nuclear cocktail could be fatal.

Considerations Affecting Beijing

What then are the considerations that Beijing needs to take into account? What are the risks of action and inaction?

The principal risk of inaction is a nuclear Iran with all the dangers that entails for China and global stability. If the PRC is seen as blocking preventative action, a groundswell of criticism from both the West and other countries will confirm the impression that Beijing is only interested in China's economic success, and any talk about wishing to play a responsible international role being merely rhetoric.

Beijing may need to be assured that double standards will not be applied. In 1998, China supported the US-led UNSC sanction mandate on India, only for the US to unilaterally enter into a nuclear cooperation agreement in 2005.

The Chinese leadership will need to balance the importance of its economic and political relations with Europe and the US against securing oil from Iran. It is submitted that, in the long-term, the former is more important. Indeed, only with a huge investment can Iran remain a major oil supplier to China, and such investment will only take place if there is an overall settlement with Iran.

The principal risk of action is Iran sabotaging oil supplies from the Middle East and promoting terrorism.

Finally, a word on the role of Russia, also holding out its potential veto in the UNSC. There is growing concern in the West as to the new forceful foreign policies being adopted by Vladimir Putin and, in particular, his use of energy as a geopolitical tool. Iran joined the Shanghai Cooperation Organization as an observer and thus is part of the Sino-Russian efforts to contain the US in Central Asia.

Thus, it is far from obvious that China could see Iran as an opportunity to work more closely with Europe and the United States, actively or passively. The western powers would need to bring very convincing arguments to the table to achieve such a repositioning of China's strategy in the Middle East.

Stanley Crossick
Wu Baiyi

12

Africa

EU PERSPECTIVE

When the Ming dynasty's Admiral Zheng He used to sail his fleet to the port of Malindi in modern day Kenya, he did so to load his "treasure ships" with gold. The gold he got there was the essential lubricant of the trade that his merchants conducted all along their route from China, at ports in the Middle East, India and Southeast Asia. It was the currency without which the Chinese would have been largely unable to buy the timber, spices and other resources that their home economy required. Sometimes, trading partners could be persuaded to take porcelain — especially the blue-and-white pieces that are still found in museums along the admiral's old route — but mostly it was African gold that drove China's first great era of seaborne commerce.

Nearly 600 years later, the continent is again the focus of China's attention, and once again, Africa is seen as a key supplier of a commodity crucial to commerce; but this time it is not gold, but oil that is the object of desire. The rapid urbanization of the world's most populous country, coupled with the energetic construction of a transport infrastructure and hundreds of thousands of factories, have created an appetite for energy that cannot be satisfied from domestic oil and gas deposits. However, the worldwide search for secure energy supplies that Beijing has conducted has led to a sobering conclusion; most oil and gas deposits in Russia, the Middle East, the US, Latin America, Canada and in neighboring Asia are — for varying reasons — not for sale to Chinese suitors. Only in Africa can the big Chinese state oil companies find country after country willing to offer up significant reserves for acquisition.

This confluence of factors — China's searing appetite, the lack of easy alternatives and the acquiescence of several African states — have propelled a pro-Africa foreign policy that eclipses anything seen during the Cold War when Beijing was keen to outdo its Communist rival, the Soviet Union, in winning kudos and client relationships across the African continent. Although oil is the main prize, it is not the only motivation behind China's mobilization: a host of other commodities and minerals — including uranium from the Republic of Niger to supply a booming nuclear energy program — and a large potential market for Chinese manufactured goods also hold considerable allure. With so much at stake, it is hardly a surprise that Beijing has expended more political and financial capital on Africa in the past five years than on any other part of the developing world.

Hu Jintao, the Chinese president, and other leaders visit regularly. Africa now supplies about one-third of China's imported oil. It took 20 years for trade between China and Africa to grow from $100 million to $1 billion, but just six years to grow from $1 billion to $50 billion, and in 2006 bilateral trade stood at $55.5 billion, up almost 40% on a year earlier, according to official Chinese statistics. Wu Bangguo, Chairman of the National People's Congress (parliament), predicted to an audience in Cairo in May 2007 that two-way trade would reach $100 billion in 2010. In a softer expression of friendship and cooperation, China has granted 20,000 scholarships to African students and built infrastructure such as roads, railways or stadiums as gifts or with concessionary loans in several key African countries. But if everything goes Beijing's way, such activity will be a mere prelude to the envisaged largesse. China, it emerged at a meeting of the African Development Bank in Shanghai in May, is planning to offer some $20 billion over the next three years in the form of concessionary trade and infrastructure loans. Much of this funding will be in exchange for oil and other commodities.

Although this amount, if it materializes, does not exceed total aid pledges from Africa's developed world donors, it is large enough to have reignited the debate surrounding China's engagement with Africa. Germany's Finance Minister, Peer Steinbruck, was among the first to criticize the $20 billion pledge, saying at a preparatory meeting of the G-8 that Beijing appeared to be "willing to relaunch what we wanted to break, with our debt relief". His comments were echoed by other European officials, who called for the formulation of a "charter for responsible lending". But initiatives such as these served to underline the contradiction it sought to correct: China is not a member of the G-8, and its policies toward Africa are not only independent of those espoused by the developed world, they are often opposed to them.

Thus emerges the contours of a classic confrontation. On one side is China, a rising power with more than $1 trillion in foreign exchange reserves and an economy that depends keenly on access to energy and resources from Africa. On the other are the developed nations, several of which are Africa's old colonial masters, who resent the arrival of a business-like new presence in their backyard. Making life more uncomfortable for the Europeans is that China does not care to spare their feelings; again and again, senior Chinese officials have blasted their history of imperial rapaciousness, while seeking to portray Beijing's own overtures as those of a sympathetic, can-do power that is not prissy over human rights or bureaucratic in the delivery of loans. Critics in Europe charge that China's involvement runs the risk of funneling funds to corrupt national elites and may presage a one-sided relationship in which Africans sell off natural treasures while opening themselves up to cheap manufactured products that threaten to cripple African industry. In China, academics counter that if the development of Africa was left to traditional donors with their strict conditionality and their regular review committees, then the continent would be condemned by inaction to a desultory rate of growth.

The lines of this confrontation appear starkly drawn, and it is possible that a new era of rivalry pitting the West against China for Africa's favor is already underway. So far, in the eyes of Africa's governing elite, at least, there appears to be considerable support for China's approach. Raphael Tuju, Kenya's Foreign Minister, accuses the West of hypocrisy, noting that the West trades openly with China, and Africa would be "crazy" not to do likewise: "It is a pity that in terms of nurturing our relationship (with the West), there is a patronizing attitude and a kind of judgment that is not always objective," Mr Tuju told the *Financial Times* in early 2007. "China respects the diplomatic etiquette and they don't bring up those issues (corruption scandals) because we don't bring up those issues."

Yet, even as China's adherence to a longstanding principle of non-interference in the internal affairs of other nations wins it friends and influence in Africa, it is finding that its involvement is also increasingly controversial. In Zambia, during national elections in 2006, an opposition candidate mobilized supporters against "Chinese exploitation" in the rich copper belt. In the

Ethiopian province of Ogaden, an area rich in oil and gas, the Ogaden National Liberation Front, an ethnic Somali independence group, attacked a Chinese-run oil field in a raid that left some 74 people dead. Public opinion in some of Africa's more developed countries, such as Kenya, may also be starting to shift. An article in *The Nation* newspaper in Nairobi in May entitled "Is the 'Dragon Empire' a Curse?" ran through a list of perceived grievances surrounding China's involvement in the continent. Most of them derived from concerns that Beijing was getting African resources at knock-down prices and the benefits of Chinese investment were staying with the elite rather than trickling down to ordinary people. In terms of reputation too, China is counting the cost. Hollywood celebrities such as Mia Farrow have begun agitating for a boycott of the 2008 Beijing Olympics in protest of China's strong commercial support for the Sudanese government and its tolerance of genocide in Darfur. The protest has helped prompt China to appoint a special envoy on Darfur and to step up the pressure on Khartoum to allow United Nations peacekeepers into Darfur.

There are signs, therefore, that the mixture of external pressure on China and growing African misgivings over the "dragon's power" may be convincing Beijing, in some respects and in some countries at least, to adopt a more conciliatory approach — and herein lies the potential for greater cooperation between the EU and China. While it is unlikely that Beijing would be willing to sign up to any "code of conduct" formulated by Africa's former colonial powers, it may be willing to consult with European powers on their experience in Africa and perhaps agree on more coordinated approaches to conditionality in lending, resource exploitation and environmental protection. It is incumbent upon European policymakers and politicians to seize opportunities to cooperate with China in Africa, and to do so in a manner that avoids *hauteur a*nd takes full account of Africa's urgent need for infrastructure and development.

James Kynge

CHINA PERSPECTIVE

Introduction

Europe has long been engaging with African countries for reasons of colonial past, economic benefits and political interests, etc. The EU and its member states have been investing substantially in economic development and political governance in Africa. China has also had a long experience of engaging with Africa, but today's Chinese activities are a new form of engagement which is very different from the existing European one and triggers controversies in the Sino-European relationship.

This contribution examines the Chinese and European approaches to Africa, with a particular consideration of Sino-European relations. Firstly, the paper begins with an analysis of the European approach labeled as "soft imperialism" (a term used by the Swedish scholar Bjorn Hettne) and the Chinese one as "pragmatism". Secondly, it discusses why China has increased greatly its political and economic activities in Africa. Thirdly, it examines why China and Europe are attractive and not attractive to Africa, with both the political elites and grassroots in Africa as agents of reference. Fourthly, the chapter goes on to discuss the contradictions between the Chinese and European approaches to Africa, and why Europe is increasingly concerned about the new Chinese engagement in Africa. In conclusion, the chapter argues that while there seem to be substantial differences between the Chinese and European approaches, they are nonetheless not irreconcilable. The European approach emphasizes good governance in Africa and seeks to build a better framework for governance on the continent, while the Chinese one stresses effective governance and wants to contribute to improving the economies in Africa. Both approaches are needed for Africa and should complement each other. More dialogue between China and Europe is needed and policy and program coordination is required.

China's Self-Identity and Role Perception

China's identity has two sides. On the one hand, the Chinese leadership and its intellectual followers see their country as a developing country in the globalization era; and on the other, they also see it as a potential world power in the international arena. The notion of China as a developing country highlights her weaknesses, in particular her pressing needs for urgent economic development and the common interests she shares with many other developing countries.

The Chinese leadership has repeatedly indicated that economic development and modernization are the highest priority for China. Deng Xiaoping, the initiator of China's economic reforms after the Cultural Revolution, proposed his argument of "development as the hard fact" (*fazhan shi yingdaoli*) and claimed that virtually all the problems China faced in contemporary time would be solved with economic development.

While stressing the centrality of economic development at home, the Chinese leadership also emphasizes the common interests China shares with many developing countries in opposing western criticisms on human rights, environmental and various other problems, exemplified, for instance, by objection to western (especially the US) proposals of criticizing the human rights record of China at the annual UN Conference on Human Rights. With many developing countries backing China, these proposals have never been passed by the conference.

The other side of the dual identity is China as a potential world power. Chinese leaders' assertion of China as the largest developing country most frequently goes together with the claim to be an influential player in the international arena. Among other attributes that emphasize China's increasing international influence is her status of permanent member on the UN Security Council, of the world's most populated country and of a nuclear power. While the Chinese leadership has never openly claimed to become a world power, China's strong appeal for creating a multipolar world order in which China herself would constitute one pole, the country's determination to oppose hegemonism, and especially its mission to become a "medium developed" country by the mid-21st century, all suggest a vision among the Chinese elites to make the country a world power in the future.

At the end of 2003, the present Chinese leadership proposed the national strategies of "rising in a peaceful way" (*hepingjueqi*) and "developing in a scientific way" (*kexuefazhan*). While the former indicates the determination of the Chinese leadership to secure the self-identity of a potential responsible world power and the consequent necessity of rising peacefully and responsibly, the latter reveals a clear understanding of Chinese leaders of the country's weaknesses and the need for development in a correct, sustainable or "scientific" way.

European Soft Imperialism and Chinese Pragmatism

The EU undertakes four different forms of foreign policy: enlargement in the core area of Europe; stabilization in the neighborhood area; bilateralism with

Great Powers; and interregionalism with other organized regions. In the last decade, interregional cooperation has become an important component of the EU's foreign policy and external relations. This form of EU foreign policy is implemented through a large number of interregional arrangements with other regions around the globe, particularly in Africa, Latin America and Asia.

As Bjorn Hettne argues, the type of power exercised by the EU is of the "soft" rather than the "hard" type, and is based on economic instruments, dialogue and diplomacy. A distinction is made between "civilian power" and "soft imperialism": the former implies power without the hard option, the latter refers to soft power applied in a hard way, that is an asymmetric form of dialogue or even the imposition or strategic use of norms and conditionalities enforced for reasons of self-interest rather than for the creation of a genuine dialogue.

Interregionalism is here understood as constructing institutionalized and formal relations between two regions. The degree of interregional cohesion is termed "interregionness", which in turn is judged by political, economic and sociocultural connections between two given regions. The main characteristics of interregionalism are interregional equality and the institutionalization of interregional cooperation. Interregional cooperation occurs on three levels, i.e., the region–region level (like Asia and Europe), the region–country level (between one region like Europe and a country in the other region such as China), and country–country level (between a country in one region and another country in the other region). The latter two levels cannot be viewed as interregional cooperation in the precise sense, but they are nonetheless promoting interregional cooperation by and large.

Both civilian power and soft imperialism are helpful in explaining the EU's interregional relations towards Africa, Latin America and Asia. It is particularly interesting to note the various ways in which the EU promotes interregionalism towards different counterpart regions. In the case of ASEM, there is a pragmatic approach based on civilian power consisting of a reasonably symmetric dialogue among "equals" in combination with a cautious emphasis on norms and good governance, at least to less significant states like Myanmar. This sharply contrasts with the EU-African relations that are more asymmetrical, dominated by strong conditionalities and imposition of norms for material self-interests. Thus, civilian power may have the most relevance in the case of ASEM and soft imperialism describes EU foreign policy relationships towards Africa, while EU-Latin American (such as Mercosur) relations lie in between.

China has long historical links with African countries, dating back to the era of independence of African states in the 1950s and 1960s. These links emphasized, among other factors, the solidarity of the developing world. Later on, China strived hard to prevent African countries' diplomatic recognition of Taiwan. During the late Cold War era, China built infrastructure for African nations, partly in competition with the Soviet Union.

The more recent Chinese engagement, or new engagement of China in Africa, concentrates more on resource extraction for fueling the growth of the Chinese economy.

Motivations of the Chinese New Engagement in Africa

At the second ministerial conference of the China-Africa Cooperation Forum held in December 2003, Prime Minister Wen Jiabao emphasized the significance of China's relations with Africa:

> China is a big country with uneven development and relatively low overall productivity level. We still have a long way to go before the goal of modernization is accomplished. Against such a background, the assistance China can provide to African countries is limited. However, we do offer our assistance with the deepest sincerity and without any political conditions. It is our firm belief that support and help between countries are mutual, and we will never forget the invaluable support China has received from African countries over the years in our endeavors to safeguard China's sovereignty and territorial integrity.

From this message, we note two important factors behind Chinese policy towards Africa: first, although China herself is a developing country with low level of productivity, China is willing to help African countries; second, the assistance that China provides to Africa is without conditionality and without selfish motivation.

However, the new Chinese engagement does have a number of motivations that are driven by Chinese national interests. First of all, gaining access to African raw materials, especially oil and natural gas, is certainly the most important reason for the renewed Chinese interest in Africa. With continuous high economic growth, China faces an increasing problem of energy shortage. Since 1993, China has become a net importer of oil, and since 2003, China is the second largest energy-consuming country in the world, second only after the United States. China accounts for 31% of global growth in demand for oil. Diversifying and increasing its energy and other raw materials sources is one of the priorities for the sustained economic growth of the country, which in turn has a profound impact on domestic well-being and social stability. Secondly, being a developing country, China shares a host of common interests with African countries. The close links between China and Africa go back to the independence movements of African countries in the 1960s and 1970s. Thirdly, as a potential world power, China needs assistance and support from Africa in a number of international institutions, such as the United Nations and World Trade Organization (WTO). Last but not least, Africa is also significant for Chinese efforts to limit the "international space" of Taiwan. If there *are* conditions attached to Chinese aid to Africa, dropping diplomatic recognition of Taiwan is probably the only one.

Attractiveness/Unattractiveness of the Chinese and European Approaches to Africa

Mandisi Mpahlwa, South African Minister of Trade and Industry, commented on the Chinese engagement in Africa in June 2006, saying:

> I believe China understands where we are coming from, as it has long been a supporter of our struggle for freedom. I believe China understands that we must redress the imbalances of our past through broad-based black economic empowerment and rapid skills development in order to be successful. I also believe that China is willing and able to assist us through investment, technology and skills transfer, and constructive partnerships.

In comparison with Europe, the Chinese attractiveness to Africa comes from the following factors. Firstly, China sets no conditionality for its aid to African countries, no matter what their political situation is, except for the requirement that recipient countries do not recognize Taiwan diplomatically. Most African elites welcome China's willingness to avoid issues such as human rights, better governance and so on. The ambassador of Sierra Leone to China, referring to the Chinese rebuilding a stadium in the country, commented that "There are no benchmarks and preconditions, no environmental impact assessment. If a G8 country had offered to rebuild the stadium, we would still be having preliminary meetings about it". Secondly, contrasting with some European countries like France and the UK, China has no colonial past in Africa and there is no problem of neocolonialism in China-Africa relations. Thirdly, China is the champion of the developing world with a seat in the UN Security Council. To some extent, China represents the interests of the developing world in the UN system. Being a developing country herself, China often has a message of Third World solidarity, which goes down well in Africa. And the Chinese engagement in Africa gives new sources of income and assistance to African countries, which provides an alternative to western aid. Africa has benefited from the dramatic rise in prices for its natural resources, not only oil, but copper, zinc, platinum and other minerals, largely due to the heavy demand from China and other fast-growing Asian countries.

Chinese engagement in Africa, while mostly viewed as very positive by African leaders, comes across as supporting corrupt regimes and damaging the interests of civil society oppressed by the ruling elites. There are also other problems regarding China's engagement in Africa. For instance, the practice of importing Chinese laborers for infrastructure projects and some industries (like textiles) limits employment opportunities for the locals in Africa. Furthermore, the intense export of its natural resources, while producing immediate cash income, might exhaust precious resources that one day will be needed for Africa's own industrialization.

European aid to Africa, with its conditions on good governance, human rights, etc., is welcomed by African civil society, but often not by African leaders. They prefer the Chinese way.

Good Governance versus Effective Governance

Two years ago, a paper published by *Survival* on China's new engagement in Africa warned that it had gone "little noticed in the West". Since then, there has been more research and policy analysis on the subject in the West, and in Europe in particular.

Are China's increasing activities a major challenge to European countries' longstanding engagement, and how competitive is the Chinese engagement in Africa?

Here we need to distinguish between "good governance" and "effective governance". The former is a value-based approach, and sometimes idealized as a vector of the western model of democracy, an objective of the foreign aid policies of Europe to Africa.

The latter (effective governance) is an end-oriented approach favored by China. In foreign aid, China much prefers the language of mutually beneficial economic cooperation to that of "aid" or development assistance. Nevertheless, there is a "Department of Foreign Aid" within the Ministry of Commerce, and each year the *China Commerce Yearbook* contains a brief report from the Director-General of this Department on "China's Aid to Foreign Countries". By contrast, the Department of Foreign Economic Cooperation is concerned both with inward investment to China and with the role of China's foreign direct investment overseas, especially engineering contracts, and with the role of China's "labor cooperation". Overall, the almost 1000-page annual volume from the Ministry of Commerce has very little that is explicitly on aid or what in OECD countries would be termed official development aid (ODA).

Two short paragraphs, which are specifically about "Aid to African Countries", are, significantly, embedded in a report on "Economic and Trade Relations between China and African Countries". And this report is just one of a series of 14 reports on these same economic and trade relations between China and different world regions or major countries. In other words, the language about aid is a very tiny element in a much more pervasive discourse about economic and trade cooperation and exchange.

When China talks about development cooperation, it avoids the language of donor and recipient. Instead, the discourse emphasizes solidarity and refers to China and Africa's shared "developing country" status, and their decades of working together. The following, taken from the earlier Beijing declaration of 2000, adopted by the first ministerial meeting of the forum on China-Africa Cooperation, typically affirms China's preference for the language of South-South cooperation and symmetry:

> We also emphasize that China and African countries are developing countries with common fundamental interests; and believe that close consultation between the two sides on international affairs is of great importance to consolidating the solidarity among developing countries and facilitating the establishment of a new international order.

African aid-recipient countries feel more comfortable with this kind of language than with the finger-pointing language used by western donors. The Chinese reengagement with Africa is a result of growing national interests and pragmatic diplomacy. One of the greatest concerns for China in Africa is energy. The existing global energy regime is largely designed by industrialized world and oil-exporting countries. As a latecomer, China does not have sufficient sources of energy supply and is therefore prepared to deal with so-called rogue states.

However, China does care about world peace and stability, and her recent initiatives in relation to the situation in Sudan should be seen in this context. As a matter of principle, China believes that the problem of Africa is more the lack of development than lack of better governance. Chinese workers build infrastructure for many African countries and help African countries to develop their own manufacturing capacity.

China believes that, with development, more effective governance might follow, but while people are starving, it is a luxury to talk about good governance.

Conclusion

Only in recent years has China pursued her new engagement policy with Africa, an engagement that largely aims at tangible economic and political gains, while it ignores to some extent problems of political stability on the continent. China seems to ignore Africa's problems such as instability and lack of good governance, although she cannot totally escape the consequences as recent cases of kidnapping and killing of Chinese nationals in Nigeria and Ethiopia attest.

There are substantial differences between the Chinese and European approaches to Africa, but they are nonetheless not irreconcilable. The European approach emphasizes good governance in Africa and seeks to build a better framework for governance, while the Chinese one stresses effective governance and tries to build an improved economic basis for political governance in Africa. Both are needed for Africa and should not be seen in confrontational terms. More dialogue between China and Europe is needed and policy and program coordination should be instituted. China is still relatively inexperienced in engaging Africa; comparing notes with the EU, learning from European successes and failures in Africa should have a place of choice on the agenda of the China-EU partnership and cooperation.

Zhang Tiejun

Part III

TRADE MATTERS

The World Trade Organization

EU PERSPECTIVE

The Protocol on the Accession of the People's Republic of China, agreed at the fourth Ministerial Conference of the WTO in Doha, Qatar, was signed on 11 December 2001. It took 15 years of protracted and tough negotiations, mainly with the US and eventually with the EU, to agree on a set of no less than 700 commitments, all binding on China. As a result, average MFN (most favored nation) tariffs — all consolidated — were brought down from 15.6% on the eve of accession to 9.7% in 2005, with 15.3% for agricultural goods and 8.8% for industrial goods. All quotas were dismantled by the end of 2004. The agricultural market became widely open to US exports of wheat, rice and cotton, while tariffs on corn were brought down to 3%. Nine out of the 12 service sectors covered by the GATS (General Agreement on Trade in Services) have been opened to trade. This brings China's protection to an intermediate level between advanced and developing countries.

This was the price to pay for accession to the WTO. Never has the entry ticket reached such a level and never again will such a price be exacted in future adhesions. Was all this justified? The future will tell, but history has taught terrible lessons about the difficulty met by latecomers in the past in their attempt to join the exclusive club of the large capitalist powers, and in that respect the conditions imposed on China were rather mild.

Remember the uphill struggle fought by Germany to gain access to international commodity sources and manufactured goods markets after its late unification in the last quarter of the nineteenth century, when Britannia still ruled the waves and when tiny Belgium had carved out the huge and rich Congo as its future colony and in the interim King Leopold II's private property. It took two world wars to integrate Germany as a fully-fledged member of the club, incidentally through the setting up of the European common market in 1957. Remember also the 1930 Smooth-Hawley prohibitive tariffs barring a transformation economy like Japan from access to the US market, thereby precipitating the overtaking of the imperial power by the military clique. At least since the setting up of the GATT (General Agreement on Tariffs and Trade) in the Bretton Woods system, room has been made for all newcomers through peaceful, if not smooth, procedures.

China's joining the WTO is, above all, the result of a thought-through decision taken by the Communist leadership once it had opted for moving from a pretty autarkic command economy to a socialist market economy: it was indeed then logical to integrate the global economy in order to gain access to the new technologies brought by the nascent IT (information technology) revolution and to foreign export markets. The Chinese leadership was the first in the Communist camp to move away from central planning and state ownership; but more remarkably, it was done in an orderly and gradual way, step by step, at a pace consistent with the depth of the change.

In that respect, it might have helped China to defer its entry into the WTO by more than a decade after its application, but just in time so as to precede Taiwan. Meanwhile, China revealed its formidable potential as the economic powerhouse of the world in such a way that its impressive performance as a manufactured goods exporter raised both expectations and fears among the WTO membership. Moreover, in the meantime, the field covered by the multilateral trading system had expanded as a result of the conclusion of the Uruguay Round, notably with regard to services, to TRIMS (trade-related investment matters) and TRIPS (trade-related intellectual protection), as well as to plurilateral deals such as government procurement and telecommunications. Time was gained but stakes were raised, and as a result, the obligations on China were heavier.

The 2001 agreement is a contract between a multilateral trading system built up upon the logic of the market on the one hand and a transition economy on the other. The system is strict and comprehensive since it has to be consistent with fair competition between market economies. Yet, it allows for enough policy space to accommodate quite different acculturations of the market capitalism ranging from harsh Wall Street capitalism to various forms of socialist market economy. Moreover, it leaves a wide flexibility to developing countries through special and differential treatment. China, though, has not been treated as a developing country, while its own version of socialist market economy might stretch WTO rules to breaking point.

The truth is that if China counted on the WTO disciplines for locking in its own reform agenda, it might get more than its taste in terms of radical transformation of its economy and, as a result, of its society. The question is not whether the deal was fair or not, nor is it whether obligations should be implemented. After all, *pacta sunt servanda* (another legal maxim, maybe worth remembering, says: *summum jus, summa injuria*) and Chinese commitments are legally binding, since they are the counterpart of a precious insurance against protectionism from advanced economies.

The interesting point is, rather, whether the main trading partners of China will stick to their legal rights and use them in full for commercial or strategic reasons, the latter consisting of pressing for more reforms or for more rapid reforms, whatever China's social concerns and implementation capacity. Or will they see the wood from the trees and take a long-term view of what is good for China and of what is good for the world economy, using their assessment margin to give China more policy space to carry out its formidable task?

It would be a mistake to list all distortions or obstacles to trade and foreign investment caused by public policies as deliberate ways to crowd out foreign business for the benefit of local firms. China is a complex society undergoing very fast economic and social change. It is, therefore, subject to major dysfunctions and tensions which hinder foreign companies operating in China. First, the central government is steering a route towards a set of different strategic objectives, while trying to avoid some serious pitfalls. Maintaining growth at a high level is a condition of political stability; but at the same time it generates rising inequalities and causes serious environmental damages. China's "Gini coefficient" (a measure of inequality of distribution) of 0.49 makes it one of the most unequalitarian countries in the world, despite the fact that at the same time it holds by far the best record in terms of taking people out of extreme poverty. With regard to the environment, the World Bank estimates annual environmental costs at approximately 7.7% of GDP, partly nullifying the high growth performance. Both social and environmental problems are the source of a growing number of public demonstrations of discontent among ordinary Chinese.

Second, China might be ruled by a single-party system with a strong central government; at the same time, it is a vast country made up of large provinces and autonomous regions and territories which enjoy their own policy space for implementing the directives issued by Beijing. Political and regional balances are complex and put effective constraints on the translation of central directives into local implementation measures. The degree of control exerted by the central authorities is sometimes complicated by the lack of proper statistical and factual information.

Third, China is both an advanced and a developing country: an elite bureaucracy at the top often sees its instructions poorly enforced by rivalling agencies and by incompetent local officials. Finally, but importantly, the complexity of the political and economic system, in particular when the frontiers between business and government are unclear, allows many opportunities for corruption. The gap between the low wages of officials and the extravagant profits made by a fast growing class of well-connected businessmen is increasing so quickly that only a strong ethic can contain this dreadful scourge which might prove in the long-run to be China's Achille's heel.

China's record with regard to its WTO obligations is usually considered as satisfactory and even impressive, taking into account the formidable magnitude of the task of undertaking and carrying out reforms while building up an enforcement capacity over such a short time span. China's trade policy review conducted by the WTO in 2006 provides a balanced assessment of the implementation of China's commitments and obligations.

But as the saying goes, "good news is no news", and at the risk of not doing justice to China's image, one has to highlight what foreign business sees as bad news. Reports from foreign chambers of commerce and international consultants operating in China depict a contrasting situation with regard to China's respect for its WTO obligations. It would be unfair to finger China as a particularly unreliable or unfaithful WTO member. But its size and its success expose its shortcomings or failures to more attention and concern from the international community. On 7 July 2006, the European Commission ordered an extensive, in-depth analysis of the mix of challenges, opportunities and risks inherent to doing business with and in China. Reviews by the Japanese trade authorities and by the US General Accounting Office provide a somewhat similar picture.

Only detailed sector and sub-sector analyses can account for the realities of the numerous types of non-tariff barriers and policies which affect the conduct of business in China because the problems are essentially microeconomic in nature. On the one hand, some non-tariff barriers hurt in one sector and prove harmless in another; on the other, Chinese authorities genuinely welcome and support foreign companies more in some industries or regions than in others. Foreign companies can thrive even when confronted with severe discriminations and distortions, partly because the fast expanding Chinese market offers tremendous profit opportunities, and partly because of their own capacity to cope with the real difficulties they are confronted with. Therefore, only an in-depth review can secure an accurate picture of what goes wrong in China and in what respects foreign companies, particularly the EU ones, are being discriminated against or see their development hampered by infringements to the national treatment WTO precept.

The rationale for deliberate discriminatory practices varies according to the sector and to the level — national or sub-national — of government. First, as should not be surprising in a socialist market economy, authorities often pay more attention to production than to consumption, a vision which incidentally finds its parallel in the Colbertist or Saint-Simonian traditions which live on in some EU countries; therefore, local firms and local jobs matter more than the consumer.

Second, many officials, particularly at the local level, are imbued with the idea that foreign companies' technological and managerial capacities put them at an advantage over their Chinese competitors and that a balance should be restored by public support. They perceive a level playing field as unfair for a developing economy.

Third, bureaucracies tend to assert their power by using it in a discretionary way which often means a discriminatory one. Competition among provinces goes both ways, sometimes attracting FDI (foreign direct investment), sometimes for giving preferential treatment to large state-owned enterprises as main job suppliers, and this provides another explanation for intended discrimination.

The policy instruments and administrative practices used as discrimination tools are countless.

With regard to market access, although on average tariffs are low, effective access might be limited or biased through different channels ranging from sheer denial to higher transactions costs, eroding the foreign firms' competitiveness. First, public procurement is in China a grey area which in fact extends to a large share of governmental public spending, going far beyond the definition of the WTO Government Procurement Agreement where China is still only an observer. Second, although SOE (state-owned enterprises) are supposed to conduct their operations on strictly commercial terms, they have actually the possibility to give a preference to the local suppliers in their purchasing policies; local content requirements are a widespread practice either in bidding for government projects or for supplying SOEs. Third, in a sector like telecommunications services, the legislation has established the ground rules for competition including cost-oriented network interconnection charges; but the legal and regulatory framework has not been completed yet in a way that national treatment, for example with regard to equal access to radio spectrum, is guaranteed to all players, while licences for value-added services are lacking and the choice of a joint venture partner is imposed on the foreign operator.

An endless list of non-tariff barriers make life more difficult for foreign operators: product certification, labelling standards, import approval requirements and customs clearance delays; uneven application of Chinese laws in provinces and regional variations in customs procedures; unreasonable sanitary and health requirements on imports and differentiation between local and foreign investors in environmental standards; and specific Chinese standards versus international standards. When talking of market access, China's preferential and bilateral trade policy cannot be ignored, in particular the RTA (regional trade agreement) deals concluded with Hong Kong and Macao or with its ASEAN neighbors and Chile or, under negotiation, with New Zealand, Australia and the Gulf Cooperation Council. Barter trade deals with energy- and commodity-exporting countries from Africa and Latin America cannot be ignored either, since they are also growing sources of potential discrimination both in the Chinese and in third country markets, at the expense of China's MFN partners.

Foreign investment is welcome in China and it is, like in every country, subject to prior registration and, according to the size or the sector, to a set of conditions. In many cases these conditions are rather restrictive because foreign investment is above all perceived and handled as a contribution to China's own industrial capacity building: on the one hand, FDI is first and foremost a source of technology, of know-how and of best management practices including quality control, which should be tapped abundantly at the best conditions; on the other hand, foreign companies' development in China is not allowed to put at risk the emergence of national champions striving to climb quickly up the value ladder and set up global brands and global networks of their own. Several instruments are used either to force technology transfer, or to restrict foreign operations to less lucrative or less strategic business: joint ventures, limited equity ownership, excessive capital requirements in the financial sector, local content requirements, geographic or branch restrictions, and import restrictions on inputs. It is not unusual that in sectors where overcapacity exists partly in account of lax lending policies from the public banking sector or partly because of local subsidies, foreign investment is either prohibited or limited, regardless of the technological advance and the competitiveness of its planned equipment.

Yet, unsurprisingly, the most contentious area is the protection of intellectual property rights where the lack of effective enforcement is the main problem. China has opted for moving up the value chain by building up a robust and dynamic technology basis. But China is here confronted with a dilemma and it is standing at a crossroads: on the one hand, it badly needs technology transfer and a multitude of Chinese firms operating in hundreds of sectors are determined to get it by all legal and illegal means, sometimes unaware of the criminal character of their copying practices; on the other, China is itself investing massively in advancing a technology of its own and therefore is very keen not to shoot itself in the foot by indulging in lax IPR protection policies.

The fact is that IP violations have been growing in recent years, both in patent and technology secret and in counterfeiting and piracy. Technology transfer takes abusive forms ranging from refusing to pay royalties on essential patents and forcing disclosure of secret data, to using joint ventures and government procurement for acquiring technology at a price under its actual value. Fake trademarks and names, counterfeited designs and patterns and pirating of protected works through industrial reproduction, broadcasting and online diffusion are common. The legislation is there, but the deterrence for IP infringers is weak because of burdensome administrative and judiciary procedures by understaffed agencies and courts. The pressure is growing from China's main partners, first among them the USA and the EU, to move from the dialogue towards a WTO trade dispute settlement procedure.

Conclusion

China's entry into the WTO is the hallmark of a tectonic shift of greater magnitude: the beginning of a — too long delayed — real convergence between North and South, which originated in East Asia with the surge of the Asian tigers triggered off by the "wild flying geese pattern" initiated by Japanese multinational companies. Hopefully, India will follow on a track of its own through services exports and behind higher tariffs for industrial and agricultural goods. A train whose China is now the main steam engine has set off and it should not slow down, but keep a steady speed. What all those countries are trying to achieve is unprecedented, and our own industrialization experience cannot provide them with a benchmark. There are very few genuine success stories worldwide and they can hardly be replicated, for each country has to find its own path out of poverty and towards industrialization.

The responsibility of the West is to allow the governments of the emerging economies to catch up in their own way, provided they aim at equitable and sustainable development and that they do not harm our long-term legitimate interests. The quick rise of "Chindia" will force radical changes in the allocation of resources worldwide, both with regard to sustainability patterns and to social adjustment costs. The global economy is heading for unchartered waters. Pressures on the multilateral trading and financial systems will be as severe as those on natural resources and climate. Dialogue among the large economies — China, Japan, the US, EU, Russia, India and Brazil — must become a permanent feature of economic governance in order to achieve consistency between the three pillars of the system: trade, finance and mandatory multilateral norms-setting. Common rules and disciplines as well as financial solidarity will contribute to make domestic policies converge towards sustainable development and North-South convergence on the basis of open markets. China and Europe should join their forces to stir up the thinking over such an agenda. But this long march begins now with a positive conclusion of the Doha Round. China has here a responsibility to share with regard to the credibility of the WTO which remains for the Chinese exporters the most effective shelter against protectionism.

Pierre Defraigne

CHINA PERSPECTIVE

In assessing China's commitments resulting from its entry into the WTO, international public opinion is often astonished by the resolution of the Chinese government to abide by these commitments, or in other words, to agree to pay the price for gaining access to the world free trade club.

While analyzing the central government's intention to push forward China's economic reform by its international commitments, Pierre Defraigne highlights the complexity of China's social reform and its implications. Actually, Chinese society is as complicated as that of the European Union, if not more intertwined with problems of a transitional society. Certainly, problems of social inequality and environment pollution are worsening, as China's growth accelerates. But if we look at these problems more cautiously, we may find that the opening to outside players could be a very important source of enlarging social inequality and worsening environment pollution.

For a relatively long period between the founding of the People's Republic in 1949 and the reform and opening up to the outside world in 1979, the Chinese government implemented economic policies giving top priority to equality. But when equality is absolute in an economy, it tends to swamp private incentive and overall growth may stagnate for lack of initiative. Egalitarianism in China was not favorable to economic growth. For example, in 1950 there was a gap of $2,265 between China's per capita gross national product (GNP) and that of developed countries. By 1975, this gap had enlarged to $4,818. At that time, China's Gini coefficient (a measure of income distribution or inequality of wealth distribution) was 0.16, among the lowest in the world. Since the 1980s, China has had a much higher growth rate and Chinese GNP is catching up with that of developed countries; however, income inequality also began to increase, with the Gini coefficient rising to 0.38 in 1995 and up to 0.49 nowadays. Income inequalities between rural and city dwellers, the coast and inland areas, and between men and women are increasing with growth. Although income inequality is greater now in China than before, the nation undertook reform and decided to open to the outside world. Absolute poverty has been reduced, and poor people have a better living standard than in the past.

There is some mechanical transmission between opening to the outside economy and enlarging disparity between urban and rural areas, coastal and inland areas, etc. When foreign firms invest in China, they mostly choose coastal cities because they have easier access to maritime transport to ship their products to their home country or to a third market. Chinese major markets are there as well. Foreign direct investments contribute to local economic growth, thus pushing up local salaries. The average income increases more rapidly in sectors related to the world economy and globalization has become the vector of wealth in China. The closer people get to the globalization process, the greater their chance to see their revenues increase rapidly. Within China, there is an internal dislocation of production which helped to transplant some old-fashioned industries from coastal regions towards inland regions, contributing to local economic growth, creating a sort of ladder production chain. This trend allows inland areas to benefit from growth by a trickle-down mechanism, so that absolute poverty has been reduced even in poorer regions in China. However, as more low-income activities are transferred to inland regions, the average income between inland and coastal regions is increasing logically.

With respect to environment pollution, a similar logic also applies. As China has been involved in globalization, more foreign firms take the China factor into account in their global strategy. As these firms seek to add value to their production, they transfer less lucrative parts of production to China. That is the case for the heavy industry such as coke, metallurgy of iron and steel, and petrochemicals. Those industries are far from being environmentally friendly. When prices on the international market are very attractive, some Chinese firms respond to market demands using all the means they have at their disposal, including rudimentary means that aggravate environmental pollution.

Therefore, when westerners criticize China for worsening environment pollution, they should also keep in mind that China is making some sacrifice to ensure the world supply of necessary materials and goods, thus improving world living standards. That is also a price China is paying for joining the process of globalization. Talk about the somehow discretionary powers of Chinese local authorities leading to discriminatory practices means that their credibility is questioned. It is undeniable that while the Chinese market is on its way to unification, some provincial authorities are still trying to protect their firms and interests against competition from the outside world, including from other Chinese provinces. That is why keeping its WTO commitments is also a way for the Chinese government to enhance competition in a unified Chinese market, in order to raise efficiency and competitiveness. Nevertheless, we should not forget that since the beginning of the reform and opening up policies, foreign firms have been privileged in terms of taxation compared to Chinese firms, so that the latter complained to the authorities about their being discriminated against. The Chinese National People's Congress adopted a new law this year, unifying profits taxation at a relatively low level. That means that national treatment will apply to all firms, and both foreign and domestic firms will compete on equal grounds.

On the IPR protection policy issue, the Chinese government's attitude is clear and firm. It will use this policy to promote national innovation and encourage Chinese firms to create their own technologies. However, this kind of macroeconomic concern is not shared by some local authorities, because their major concern is to earn quick money, no matter whether these profits are obtained by fraud or counterfeiting. Chinese WTO commitments are in line with Chinese government policy orientation. Some European firms have tried to make joint efforts with Chinese firms to protect their trademarks by special packaging, in order to check and discover counterfeit products in the Chinese market. Their efforts have been successful and that kind of approach, although very pragmatic and empirical, is nevertheless a useful expedient for China's transitional period.

Overall, although some sacrifices by China are considered unjustified by Chinese public opinion, such as the denial of market economy status, China's WTO accession gives it access to a larger market across the world. Thus, China will rise to the WTO challenges and take this opportunity to render the Chinese economy more competitive in the future.

Ding Yifan

14

Market Economy Status

Under the terms of China's 2001 accession to the World Trade Organization, members of the trade body can treat China as a "non-market economy" until 2016.

So far, 69 nations have recognized China as a full market economy, but the country's major trade partners including the United States, the European Union and Japan have yet to do so.

The non-market economy status has left China a victim of rampant anti-dumping measures imposed by other WTO members, which often use production costs in other countries as a reference to evaluate whether Chinese exports are dumped or unfairly priced.

At the heart of the so-called market economy status (MES) is the issue of anti-dumping measures, the most frequently used trade safeguard method. Market economy status is a different concept from that of "market economy". Even under the terms of China's 2001 accession to the World Trade Organization, members of the trade body did not define Chinese economy as a non-market system. In fact, "market economy status" should only be considered in the context of anti-dumping, but generally the issue has become much wider. Moreover, China's trade affected by anti-dumping represented only 0.51% of trade volume in 2006 — China encountered anti-dumping in 2006 in 70 cases from 23 countries and regions from January to October, and during this period, China's trade volume was US$1,593 billion; though, as in the year

2003, anti-dumping cases of WTO member states *vis-à-vis* China represented 21.6% of total anti-dumping cases in the world, affecting US$4 billion of China's exporting value, 1% of China's trading value, and directly and indirectly affecting RMB60 billion to the economy.

The MES might seem to be a marginal issue for the Chinese economy, but it goes to the heart of how the Chinese government views its position in the world trading system and underpins its fears about western protectionism. MES would change how anti-dumping actions against Chinese firms are judged. Granting of MES by the WTO members, particularly the major players, has become a matter of national pride for Beijing. As a result, a huge diplomatic offensive was launched to gain MES, since the WTO itself does not classify countries as market economy or non-market economy.

Origin of Non-Market Economy Country Issue

The term "non-market economy state" originally appeared in the 1930 Tariff Act of the United States, as opposed to "state-controlled economy". For the US, socialist countries totally monopolized the national economy and controlled prices of all merchandises. Hence, the prices of exported goods were untrue, and importing countries needed to seek a third country's data to be a reference to calculate the market price for anti-dumping investigations and for determining anti-dumping duties on goods from the socialist countries.

This Act and its amendments determined six criteria to judge "market economy status": degree of currency convertibility; degree of salary determination by negotiation between employers and employees; degree of freedom for foreign companies' investment; degree of ownership or production methods of enterprises controlled by government; degree of government control over distribution, prices and quantities; and other adequate factors that US investigation authorities should consider.

In accordance with these criteria, all socialist countries were listed as "non-market economy states". The EU, Canada and other WTO members followed the US in defining the concept of "non-market economy" and relevant criteria in their anti-dumping laws.

Before China became a member of the WTO, countries could do whatever they wanted. When she became a member of the organization, however, the picture changed dramatically. The members of the WTO are in fact obliged to apply the normal anti-dumping rules of the WTO in respect of their trade relations with China. There is one temporary exception. The exception is a limited one and applies exclusively to the methodologies that are permissible — under limited circumstances — for determining "normal value", the price that a product under investigation should ideally be selling for on the market of the country in which it is produced. That clause dates from the mid-1950s and applies only in the case of countries that have a complete or substantially complete government monopoly over international trade and where all domestic prices are fixed by the state. This definition would have fitted China two or three decades ago, but it certainly does not characterize China's economy today. Since all members of the organization already agree that China does not fit the GATT definition of the 1950s, members have in effect made a determination that China is a market economy deserving non-discriminatory treatment under the anti-dumping laws.

With such a logic, when a WTO member launches an anti-dumping investigation into a Chinese product, it has to calculate the "normal value" in terms of Chinese production cost of the similar good, but not with the surrogate country's cost and price. In China, the fact is that the competitiveness of its goods is mainly based on low cost and productive labor rather than subsidies, easy finance or controlled prices.

Market Economy Status and the Anti-Dumping Framework

In its WTO accession agreement, China agreed that other WTO members could treat it as a non-market economy until 2015. This classification was agreed in the US-China 1999 bilateral agreement and was multilateralized as part of China's WTO entry protocol. This classification is vital to one area of trade policy: dealing with dumping allegations against Chinese firms. The GATT Article VI, which lays down rules on anti-dumping, provides some discretion for WTO members on how these rules are interpreted. When a firm from the EU or from any other WTO member believes that a Chinese exporter is dumping its goods in its market, it can complain to its trade authorities. The home and export prices of the goods might be compared. This is the normal methodology for market economies, where home price reflects the true costs of production. If the overseas prices are below domestic prices, it is likely that they will be found to be "less than fair value".

Anti-dumping has been by far the most important commercial instrument used by the EU and, since the late 1960s, implemented at European level.

An anti-dumping complaint is generally triggered by a claim from EU manufacturers that an exporter has caused them damage. The Commission has to establish, after consulting the member governments, if dumping has occurred, whether the industry concerned has been injured and where the "community interest" lies. The community interest test requires an assessment of the costs to consumers and other industries and the benefits for the injured industry of imposing anti-dumping duties. The Commission can impose preliminary anti-dumping duties, which now means that a Commission proposal is upheld, unless there is a negative vote in the Council by simple majority. The Council must approve definitive duties, which can run for up to five years.

On 9 June 2006, EU Trade Commissioner Peter Mandelson told a press conference in Beijing, "In the respect of the criteria (of market economy status), I believe China is heading in the right direction." The EU criteria on full market economy status includes markers on the level of state intervention, bankruptcy legislation and accountancy law. The EU says that China has not yet met all the criteria. The lack of market economy status has become the Achilles' heel of Chinese exporters involved in anti-dumping investigations, because their production costs are not accepted.

A statement from the European Commission in 2004 said the EU was committed to granting China the status as soon as certain conditions are fulfilled (2004–2006). They are:

- State influence: Ensuring equal treatment of all companies by reducing state interference which takes place on an *ad hoc* basis or as a result of industrial policies, as well as through export and pricing restrictions on raw materials.
- Corporate governance: Increasing the level of compliance with existing accounting law in order to ensure the usability of accounting information for the purpose of trade defense investigations.
- Property and bankruptcy law: Ensuring equal treatment of all companies in bankruptcy procedures and in respect of property and intellectual property rights.
- Financial sector: Bringing the banking sector under market rules by removing discriminatory barriers, in order to ensure rational allocation of capital by financial institutions.

But EU officials failed to elaborate how these conclusions about the shortcomings were reached since the assessment report is confidential.

China is the most targeted country of anti-dumping measures in the world. The success rate of cases brought against it is 35%. The non-market economy status is generally seen as encouraging countries to use the anti-dumping instrument against Chinese exports. This is the major reason for China lodging its request for market economy status in June 2003 and providing supporting documentation from September 2003.

In the case of China, an economy in which some input prices might be below real market cost, its trade authorities agreed that other WTO members could use the "surrogate country" approach. Investigators find a comparable firm in India or Japan to see what the "real" market costs of producing those goods are. If the Chinese firm is selling its exports for less than the Indian or Japanese firm's costs suggest it should, then it can be found to be selling goods for less than fair value. It is worth noting here that finding a surrogate firm is not easy. Those firms in developing countries are likely to be direct competitors of the firm under investigation and tend to refuse to be the surrogates, forcing investigators to look for firms in developed countries, since the latter's costs are evidently higher. This increases the chance of dumping being found.

Not only the Chinese government and companies, but also most Chinese people, believe that the treatment of China as a "non-market economy" by developed countries, especially the EU and the US, to China, is unfair. Firstly, China's private sector is booming, the Party oversees one of the most liberal trade regimes of any developing country, and provinces are privatizing their assets at a rate that would cause Margaret Thatcher to blush.

Secondly and most importantly, most Chinese see the treatment as a political rather than an economic or trading issue for the EU or US. The explanation is simple: Russia and other countries of Eastern Europe have got the MES, but China, with a much higher degree of market economy, does not. The framework is as shown in Figure 1.

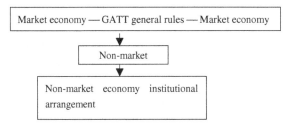

Figure 1

Weak rules are cited in Table 1.

Table 1

Non-MES Special Terms	Reasons	Relation with Relevant Terms of Multilateral Trading Regime
Import promise	Lack of efficient tariff system	In accordance with Article 28 of ITO
Quantity limit	Market disturbances	Violation of Article 11 of GATT of 1947
Selected special safeguard terms	Market disturbances	Diversified from the GATT's principle of non-discrimination of Article 19
Surrogate price for anti-dumping	Lack of efficient price mechanism	Article 6 of GATT appendix, footnote for domestic implementation
Special trading relation in WTO accession agreement	Regular review and dialogue	Non-relevant stipulation of 1947 GATT

Super rules are cited as follows:

- Economic policy: non-discriminatory treatment, foreign exchange and payment, international balance, investment system, state-owned system and privatization, price policy
- Policy-making and reality: administration, legislation and justice, power of local government
- Polices affecting trade of goods and management of imports
- Intellectual property relevant to trading
- Policies affecting trade of service
- Transparency: domestic laws and regulations (relevant to trade) reporting system
- Trading agreements

The changing attitude of the EU regarding these two kinds of rules *vis-à-vis* China and Eastern European countries is totally different, as we can see in Figure 2.

The reason for the changing attitude of EU to the Eastern European countries on the issue of MES, is that they were candidates for EU membership. The case for Russia did not provide enough formal arguments for the Chinese

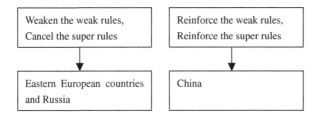

Figure 2

government, since Russia is hardly known for its transparency and openness, but still, was recognized by Europe as a market economy in 2005.

We may easily reach some conclusions from the above analysis regarding MES for China:

(1) The essence of the non-market economy status issue is the conflict between political and economic institutions.
(2) The non-market economy status issue is about the conflict between major trading partners.
(3) The power to make the rules is on the side of market economies, particularly big market economies.

The right policy, however, is to encourage China's economic development and integration into the world economy and an international system based on fair rules. By extending MES to China, Europe would make it hard for the anti-dumping framework to be abused for protectionist ends, and so would support this broader objective. Such a move might also nudge the United States away from its current protectionist instincts when it comes to China.

Li Jinshan

15

The RMB in the Global Currency Market*

This paper assesses the likely impact of a rapid major appreciation of the RMB *vis-à-vis* the major global currencies, especially the dollar, euro, yen and sterling, for China as well as for the rest of the world. The main effects would be a shift away from Chinese imports to alternative suppliers, primarily elsewhere in Asia. The RMB appreciation would only have minor effect on global trade and savings imbalances, although the negative effects on China itself would be quite important and would inevitably limit its buoyant export growth.

The likely responses from China to a "unilateral" tariff increase imposed by the US would be to "retaliate" in both import as well as financial markets, reducing the demand for US goods and its treasury bonds. Although the US-China trade deficit would still be reduced, the net reduction after substitute imports from elsewhere should be expected to be small. Moreover, the reduced demand for dollar assets would itself lead to a fall of the dollar *vis-à-vis* the yuan as well as relative to other currencies including the Euro. If the Federal Reserve Bank were to increase its interest rates, it should be expected to contribute to better managing global imbalances. However, a reluctance to do so, for reasons of domestic demand management, could sharply lower the international value of the dollar.

* The author would like to acknowledge his useful exchanges with Dr He Fan of the Chinese Academy of Social Sciences, Beijing; Dr Gao Shiji of the Development Research Center and the PRC State Council; and Director-General Liu Jieyi of the Ministry of Foreign Affairs, PR China, on this subject. All errors and shortcomings are the sole responsibility of the author. The views expressed are his own only.

This paper therefore also looks into the scenario of a significant realignment of the US dollar *vis-à-vis* the Euro — a dollar crash. This would leave the Euro zone weak on trade, but strong on outward direct foreign investment. In extremis, the scenario might mean deflation in Europe, whereas a milder version, reflecting a more likely scenario, might nevertheless mean that the EU's external competitiveness erodes significantly. In addition to having to address the thorny issues of domestic adjustment and increased labor market flexibility, the question of international cooperation in exchange rates would become much more important than it is today. Hence, global and regional monetary cooperation would have to include the Chinese authorities, already holding the largest foreign exchange reserves.

Appreciation of the RMB *vis-à-vis* the Global Currencies

The "simple" or "naïve" case to consider first would be the one in which the RMB appreciates in a major way *vis-à-vis* the US dollar, the Euro and the Japanese yen. One would here use the adjective "major" primarily as a qualitative indicator, but it may be useful to imagine a Euro-RMB exchange rate change from its 2005 level of € 1 purchasing 10.22 yuan down to a level where € 1 would fetch approximately 7.1 yuan, in effect an appreciation of the Chinese currency by 30%.

The exchange rate between the Euro and the yuan has of course been identical to that between the Euro and the dollar, given the dollar-yuan peg (until a 2.1% adjustment took place in July 2005). The Euro-yuan exchange rate has moved very significantly over the years, with the Euro initially below the dollar during 2000 and 2001, but after this appreciating quite sharply. Therefore, a 30% appreciation of the yuan would merely reverse the appreciation of the Euro *vis-à-vis* the dollar and yuan that has taken place during the period 2002–2005 and return to the value of the "early days" of the Euro in 2000.

An adjustment of this magnitude can only be expected if it were brought about as a response to intense US *and* EU *and* Japanese pressure on the People's Bank of China to appreciate its currency. The EU-US-Japan arguments in favor of such an adjustment would point to the ever-increasing foreign exchange reserves of China and the persistence of high levels of trade surpluses globally, and in particular with the United States and the member states of the European Union. It would of course only be accepted by the Chinese

Table 1   RMB/Euro and US exchange rates, 1999–2006.

	Average Exchange Rate RMB/€ (daily, unweighted, ask rates)	Highest Bid Rates (during the period)	Lowest Bid Rates (during the period)	Average Exchange Rate RMB/US$ (daily, unweighted)
2006 (1 Jul.–21 Sep.)	10.1798	10.2882	10.029	8.0204
2006 (1 Jan.–30 Jun.)	9.885	10.399	9.538	8.0392
2005	10.220	11.244	9.436	8.2033
2004	10.308	11.306	9.797	8.2872
2003	9.382	10.406	8.587	8.2772
2002	7.838	8.687	7.114	8.2869
2001	7.424	7.933	6.935	8.2804
2000	7.657	8.558	6.859	8.2792
1999 (from 15 Dec.)	8.828	9.776	8.252	8.2796

Source: http://www.oanda.com

monetary authorities in the context of an effective threat at least as severe as that which the Schumer–Graham bill posed. The threat of the US senators to table a bill for imposing a tariff of 27.5% on all Chinese exports to the United States was *not* backed up by credible action. Nevertheless, the Chinese authorities responded by changing its currency basket rule as well as a revaluation from 8.28 to 8.11 yuan per dollar.

Undoubtedly, a voluntary move from the Chinese authorities of this order of magnitude implied by Schumer–Graham is extremely unlikely as it is entirely contrary to the country's short- and long-term growth and development objectives. Indeed, any US trade policy initiative is likely to be challenged at the WTO. Therefore, a non-committal attitude from the EU and Japan, and hence pressure from the US alone, is *unlikely* to lead to any adjustment of this magnitude.

Impact of a Major RMB Realignment

In response to such a significant realignment, the relative exchange rates between the US, the Euro zone and China, but also between China and its competitor countries, would change markedly. A price shock of this magnitude would affect international trade flows very significantly. Net gainers are likely to include suppliers in countries which have a similar export basket as China, i.e., characterized by undifferentiated products or by differentiated products targeted at lower market segments. China's competitive export advantages *vis-à-vis* these countries would erode. These are likely to include countries such as Indonesia, Korea, Taiwan, Thailand and Vietnam. However, for example, India and China have a 75% *dissimilar* export basket and hence, India should not be expected to gain significantly in the short-to-medium term.

A significant realignment, way beyond the 3% of today, would cause a decline of demand for Chinese products (in the short-run), but simultaneously increase the demand for similar substitute products from other countries in the region. Hence, the impact of a revaluation of the yuan on the US trade deficit may be quite limited at the aggregate level, provided that the competing countries have adequate supply capabilities to fill the gaps which China has left.

During 2005, the level of the EU trade deficit was estimated at €106 billion by EU sources, whereas for the US the trade deficit with China amounted to $202 billion. Chinese statistics indicate lower bilateral trade deficits, partly due to transhipments through Hong Kong and partly due to statistical discrepancies, in particular in the field of trade of services. For the EU-25, the Chinese customs report a trade surplus of $70 billion, with the US trade deficit reported at $114.2 billion. According to the same source, out of Chinese export of goods and services of $779.8 billion during 2005, 21.4% went to the US, 18.9% to the EU and 11.0% to Japan. The total value of exports during 2007 is expected to reach $961.1 billion, assuming an export slowdown and a slow or gradual devaluation.

Estimates prepared by the OECD Secretariat about the short- and long-run price elasticities of import demand of manufactured products help to gain some insight as to the possible impact which a major revaluation of the yuan might have on the trade deficits which the EU and the US are presently running with China. The price elasticity estimates are as summarized in Table 2. The "back-of-the-envelope" partial equilibrium calculation would indicate that a 30% RMB appreciation would reduce Chinese exports to the US, Japan and the major EU importing countries by approximately 10% in the short-run, and this may rise more than 20% if all adjustments are fully passed through over a ten-year adjustment period.

Table 2 Short- and long-run price elasticities of import demand in selected OECD countries.

Country	Short-Run Price Elasticities	Long-Run Price Elasticities
United States	−0.36	−0.84
Japan	−0.36	−1.18
Germany	−0.60	−0.84
France	−0.21	−0.45
United Kingdom	−0.06	−0.45
Italy	−0.36	−0.45
Netherlands	−0.15	−0.36

Source: OECD, 2001, "Modelling import responsiveness of OECD manufacturers' trade", Economics Department Working Paper No. 311, Organization for Economic Cooperation and Development, Paris, p. 22, Table 4.

At the same time, China would be able to purchase goods from the international markets at much reduced prices, which would, in principle, boost OECD exports to the Chinese markets. However, even without targeted retaliatory action from the Chinese side, the increased demand for EU and US goods can only be expected to be quite small — price elasticities of China's import demand are estimated to be quite low at values below −0.2 (if not even below −0.1). This reflects, amongst other factors, that for the Chinese production networks the import intensity of exports remains quite high, especially because of intra-firm and intra-industry trade between the OECD and China. Hence, a reduction of exports would quite directly result in a reduced level of imports. More importantly, any revaluation would have significant negative income effects in China — depressing demand for imported goods from the US and elsewhere including the EU.

McKibbin and Stoeckel (2005) have analyzed the impact of punitive US tariffs (with and without retaliation) as well as a self-induced appreciation of the yuan, using a multisectoral general equilibrium model. The key results are summarized below.

US tariffs on Chinese imports. Total Chinese exports will fall, but China would seek to make up rapidly by sending its exports elsewhere, including the EU, increasing the EU-China bilateral trade deficit. The GDP may fall by as much as 3% initially, but recover to −1% within one to two years.

The impact on US GDP is negative too, though very small, while trade and current deficits are only reduced by less than 0.1% of GDP. This reflects that US buyers will switch to alternative sources of import, as well as increased domestic production. However, fiscal effects are positive, due to greater revenue collection, reducing US public deficits.

Chinese retaliation. If China were to retaliate with a general tariff on US goods, it would cause US exports to fall, but since China is not a significant destination, the real US GDP effects will be small, estimated at merely −0.05%.

Chinese revaluation. McKibbin and Stoeckel estimate that a 27.5% revaluation would reduce exports by 11% in the short-run, working with a short-run price elasticity of −0.4, quite similar to the OECD estimates noted previously. The initial shock, amplified by rising real interest rates, could lead to a fall of as much as −10% of GDP in the first year, recovering to −4% in following years — a veritable recession in China. This would have significant negative income effects. The authors estimate that these would exceed the positive import price effects, thus *reducing* China's aggregate import demand from the rest of the world.

In conclusion, the aggregate trade surpluses which China presently accumulates with the rest of the world might be reduced, but certainly would not disappear. The net effects on the EU trade deficit, using crude partial equilibrium estimation methods, could be estimated to amount to a lowering of the deficit in the order of approximately 11% for 2005. Thus, the hypothetical revaluation of the yuan by some 30% might have reduced the 2005 EU deficit by approximately 11% (from €106 billion to €94 billion). However, this would not have changed the overall scenario of large deficits between China on the one hand and the US and the EU on the other hand very much.

The economic reasons for expecting these rather limited effects are quite well-rehearsed. The trade deficits of the United States reflect the excess of investment over savings. These are financed through the issuing of bonds and fiscal deficits and appear as an excess of aggregate domestic demand over domestic supply — in effect, as imports. Textbook economics would therefore recommend domestic adjustment through higher savings, requiring higher relative interest rates on savings as well as direct fiscal measures to reduce the public deficits.

The solution for the United States savings-investment imbalance lies in reducing its growing fiscal deficit and increasing the domestic private savings rate. This would require the monetary authorities to raise the real interest rates beyond the present levels, already increased significantly from its 2004 level. A further interest rate rise would slow down the US housing markets further and therewith negatively affect macroeconomic growth in the US.

If China were to reduce its purchases of US bonds, the US treasury would be forced to raise interest rates, as well as introduce measures to cut the fiscal deficit. To the extent that alternative buyers are readily found, e.g., from countries with high reserves and trade and current account surpluses such as Japan, South Korea, Russia, Saudi Arabia or Brazil, this would affect US growth only to a limited extent. However, if dollar exchange rates are perceived as likely to depreciate in the short- or medium-term, the negative impact on US growth could be quite considerable.

Implications for EU-China Relations

Over recent years, the RMB has depreciated significantly with respect to the strong Euro (which was less than one dollar at the time of its introduction) and hence, exports to the Euro zone have been particularly attractive for China-based exporters. The share of China's exports destined for the EU-25 has increased faster than that of the US (see Table 3).

Hence, there is genuine case for concern from the EU side, but there are diverging views, reflecting diverging interests. The EU concerns would be greatly amplified if the current Euro-dollar exchange rate were to change significantly through a steep further appreciation of the Euro.

In particular, a reduced demand for dollar assets would itself lead to a fall of the dollar *vis-à-vis* the yuan as well as relative to other currencies, including the Euro. If the Federal Reserve Bank were to increase its interest rates, it should be expected to contribute to better managing global imbalances. However, a reluctance to do so, for reasons of domestic demand management, could sharply lower the international value of the dollar. A further significant appreciation of the Euro *vis-à-vis* the dollar, for example to a level of €1 trading at a level of $1.50 or above, would also mean that the €-yuan rate would still rise to a level approximately 12–13 RMB/€. This is a distinct possibility during 2006–2010, in view of the steadily increasing twin deficits of the United States.

Table 3 Chinese export shares to the United States and the European Union.

	1998	1999	2000	2001	2002	2003	2004	2005
Total Chinese Exports (US$ billion)	183,809.1	194,930.9	249,202.6	266,098.2	325,596.0	438,227.8	593,325.6	761,999.1
United States (%)	20.7	21.5	20.9	20.4	21.5	21.1	21.1	21.4
RMB/US$		8.28	8.28	8.28	8.28	8.28	8.28	8.20
EU-25(%)	16.2	16.4	16.4	16.6	16.1	17.9	18.1	18.9
RMB/€		8.828	7.657	7.424	7.838	9.382	10.308	10.22

Source: WTO, 2006, "Trade policy review: China", WTO-Geneva, Table A.3.1.

Appropriate Policy Response for the EU

First, as discussed above, any "unilateral" US tariff on Chinese imports would achieve preciously few of the US objectives, while hurting not only the Chinese economy (through a sharp slowdown of growth), but also fuelling further the already large trade deficit which the EU runs with China. Hence, it is in the EU's interest to lobby against any such unilateral move. Fortunately, in such an endeavor, the EU would have significant allies within the United States, most notably the US-China Business Council which opposed the Schumer–Graham bill.

Second, the likelihood of China introducing a significant revaluation of its currency on its own initiative is very low indeed. Chinese economic analysts are fully aware of the problem of "overheating", in particular through its manifestation in the Chinese context as overinvestment in the manufacturing sector. Hence, they are fully aware of the need for greater exchange rate flexibility. However, their preferred option is to introduce greater flexibility in the exchange rate regime gradually. They favor: (i) increasing the volume of foreign exchange trading; (ii) developing instruments for managing currency risks through hedging; and (iii) strengthening financial sector regulations. The Chinese are fully aware of the costs of a substantive revaluation. The unsolved problem of a very high fragility of the Chinese banking sector (in terms of non-performing loans) remains an important background factor.

Third, the EU might join the US and Japan in urging the Chinese to revalue — concerted action would strengthen the chorus. In view of the arguments outlined above, this is unlikely to yield a positive response from China, beyond the slow and gradual path engaged upon by the Chinese monetary authorities.

Any "threat" of taking the issue to the International Monetary Fund, as advocated by Morris Goldstein (2004), is unlikely to yield the desired results. The Treasury Department reported in May 2005 (prior to the announcement of the Chinese change to a basket rule) that "China was not manipulating its exchange rate in violation of its obligations under Article IV of the IMF charter."

US Treasury Secretary John W. Snow welcomed the commitment to exchange rate flexibility after the July 2005 announcement. In his 2006 statement before the Senate on International Economic and Exchange Rate Policies, Mr Snow reiterated the same position, saying:

> ... China's international economic and exchange rate policies are deeply concerning. The United States has been joined by the international community, including the G-7, the IMF and Asian Development Bank, in vigorously encouraging China to implement greater exchange rate flexibility. In the final analysis, though, the Treasury Department is unable to conclude that China's intent has been to manage its exchange rate regime for the purposes of preventing effective balance of payment adjustment, or gaining unfair competitive advantage in international trade (18 May 2006).

The US position may be summarized as expressing its concern and dissatisfaction, but stops short of seeking an intervention from the International Monetary Fund. At the recent Singapore meeting of the IMF, there was no statement to indicate that China's exchange rate regime will receive any attention beyond the normal surveillance. Hence, the US policy approach may be characterized as one of continued public pressure, while pursuing a policy of restraint. The rather more drastic options of (i) restricting exports to the US, or (ii) taking it to the IMF, are not presently pursued. Instead, the present Treasury Secretary, Mr Hank Paulson, in September 2006 met with the Chinese leadership and agreed on a bilateral US-China dialogue at the level of the Vice President to "lock in economic liberalization".

Fourthly, and perhaps most promisingly from the EU perspective, would be to encourage and assist China towards regional monetary cooperation, including an exchange rate mechanism (an Asian ERM). The strongest argument against revaluation from the Chinese side is that a revaluation only involving their currency would simply hand a windfall gain to the neighboring competitors. At the global level, the revaluation would perhaps only yield small positive gains because it does not address the underlying problem of global imbalances. However, from a Chinese perspective, the revaluation might be perceived as a negative sum-game in a regional context, creating competitive advantages for other countries in the region, including Vietnam, Taiwan, Indonesia, the Philippines, South Korea, etc. An exchange rate mechanism to coordinate responses within the region could address this concern at least to some extent.

Willem van der Geest

16

The Arms Embargo

EU PERSPECTIVE

The debates on both sides of the Atlantic in early 2005 on the lifting of the arms embargo on China generated much heat and little light. The issue is a case study in diplomatic bungling.

History

The ban was imposed in 1989 following the Tiananmen Square massacre by a Declaration of the European Council, meeting in Madrid on 26–27 June, in the following terms:

> In the present circumstances the European Council thinks it necessary to adopt the following measures: . . . interruption by the member states of the community of military cooperation and an embargo on trade in arms with China.

And that was all. The declaration is not legally binding.

Currently, EU arms embargoes are in force against al-Qaeda, Osama bin Laden and the Taliban; Bosnia & Herzegovina; Burma/Myanmar; China; Congo (DRC); Iraq; Ivory Coast; Liberia; Sierra Leone; Somalia; Sudan; and Zimbabwe. Note that Cuba, Iran and Syria are not on the list.

The 1998 EU Code of Conduct on Arms Exports controls arms exports generally, although it too is not legally binding. It *(inter alia)* precludes sales to countries which might use the weapons to abuse human rights. But the code is not mandatory and cannot, in itself, prevent member states from selling weapons to Beijing. There are substantial arms sales to the PRC by EU member states.

Lifting the Embargo

China has been calling for the lifting of the ban since 2003. Its "Policy Paper on the EU" of October 2003 urged the EU to do so in order to "remove barriers to greater bilateral cooperation in defense industries and technology". President Chirac and Chancellor Schröder both repeated this call when they visited Beijing in October and early December, respectively. The EU began reexamining the arms embargo in early 2004.

The arms embargo was discussed at a PRC-EU summit in The Hague on 7–9 December 2004. In the run-up to the summit, the PRC had attempted to increase pressure on the EU Council to lift the ban by warning that the ban could hurt PRC-EU relations. PRC Vice Foreign Minister Zhang Yesui called the ban "outdated", and he told reporters, "If the ban is maintained, bilateral relations will definitely be affected." In the end, the EU Council did not lift the ban. An EU spokeswoman said there were still concerns about the PRC's commitment to human rights. But at the time, the EU did state its commitment to work towards lifting the ban. Bernard Bot, the Dutch Foreign Minister, who held the EU's rotating presidency at that time, said, "We are working assiduously but . . . the time is not right to lift the embargo."

The joint EU-China summit declaration of 8 December 2004 stated that the Union "confirmed its political will to continue to work towards lifting the arms embargo". Javier Solana, High Representative for the EU Common Foreign and Security Policy, stated immediately after the summit that the embargo might be removed in the first six months of 2005. The European Council on 17 December 2004 confirmed this "political will to continue to work towards lifting the arms embargo", while at the same time it "underlined that the result of any decision should not be an increase of arms exports from EU member states to China, neither in quantitative nor qualitative terms".

The PRC continued to press for the embargo to be lifted, and some member states began to drop their opposition. Jacques Chirac pledged to have the ban lifted by mid-2005. However, in March 2005, China's National People's Congress unexpectedly passed an "Anti-Secession Law" which, while stressing the objective of peaceful reunification, threatens war against Taiwan if the island should declare independence. Unfortunately, there was no public explanation from Beijing. This played into the hands of United States and European elements opposing the ending of the ban.

A European Parliament resolution in April 2005 opposed the lifting of the ban by 431 to 85 votes. The EU Council failed to reach a consensus and although France and Germany pushed to have the embargo lifted, no decision was agreed upon in subsequent meetings. Since then, Schröder has been replaced by Angela Merkel, who strongly opposes lifting the ban. The European Commission, under President José Manuel Durão Barroso, has also made a lifting of the ban more difficult. At a meeting with Chinese leaders in mid-July 2005, he said that China's poor record on human rights would slow any changes to the EU's ban on arms sales to China.

Various conditions have been discussed in relation to the lifting of the embargo, including an improved EU code of conduct for arms exports, Chinese ratification of the UN International Covenant on Civil and Political Rights and the release of the remaining Tiananmen Square prisoners. China acknowledged in 2004 that it was studying how to ratify the covenant, but nothing has been said since.

US Opposition

US President George W. Bush appeared resigned to the likely EU decision during his February 2005 visit to Brussels, leaving it to the US Congress to threaten retaliatory measures. However, after he returned to Washington, pressure was stepped up on the Union. The reactions of Congress — and many Americans outside Congress, and then the administration itself — were tough and uncompromising. The House of Representatives voted 411–3 against the EU's intention. Voices in Congress threatened an arms technology ban on the EU. The issue is particularly sensitive in the US because of its commitment to Taiwan. There were several concerns in Washington. These included a fear that the military balance of power across the Taiwan Straits would be upset. The American concerns center round high-tech and dual-use arms. A further concern was that China's human rights violations that formed the basis for the embargo still existed. Whether the EU's arms embargo is significant or symbolic, lifting it is seen in the West as reducing the leverage of the United States and Europe over China to improve its human rights situation. From a US viewpoint, a relaxation would send a signal to China that it can continue to violate international standards of human rights and that the United States, rather than China, is increasingly isolated in its views.

The debate was emotive — "They're talking about helping the Chinese kill Americans more effectively"; "It is not at all in the EU's interest to lift the arms embargo"; "Efforts we've made to open, widen, deepen transatlantic defense industrial trade are going to be circumscribed." These were the terms in which the American defense community talked about the EU's moves towards lifting the embargo. The Pentagon warned that lifting the embargo could lead to a curtailment of military technology cooperation between the US and Europe.

Members of the US Congress also proposed restrictions on the transfer of military technology to the EU if they lifted the ban.

Lessons to be Learned

The diplomacy was mishandled from the outset. First, President Chirac initiated the lifting of the ban without sufficient prior consultation and for commercial reasons. Gerhard Schröder then supported him. The EU leaders made a commitment to the PRC to lift the ban without proper consultation with the US and without first ensuring that Congress knew the facts. Thus, it was not understood that the ban was only of symbolic value and arms exports were controlled by the code, which is also not legally binding.

No one is suggesting that China's current human rights record meets EU standards. EU leaders continue to stress that Beijing must respect human rights. But the situation has improved during the last 15 years and the reason for imposing the embargo has disappeared. China resents being included on the US or European embargo lists. Exerting pressure on China with a view to establishing the rule of law, in accordance with China's World Trade Organization commitments, is likely to be more effective than keeping it on the blacklist.

Respect for human rights should be presented as an issue of national interest for China and not as external pressure. As European Trade Commissioner Peter Mandelson put it: "Human rights should increasingly be seen as the way to release the full potential of the Chinese people, as well as an important political pressure valve, and therefore a national interest." Restrictions on freedom of expression affect the individual's ability to innovate.

The US human rights policy is riddled with hypocrisy. Leaving aside its Guantanamo Bay and Abu Ghraib prison practices, the US — and Europe too — continue to supply arms to several countries with poor human rights records. As for Taiwan, the Union has a duty under the existing arms export code to ensure that sales do not lead to regional instability in general or to strengthening China's military position *vis-à-vis* Taiwan in particular. EU leaders recalled the importance of the criteria of a new EU code of conduct on arms exports, "in particular criteria regarding human rights, stability and security in the region and the national security of friendly and allied countries".

The ban has not prevented China from building up its military strength by buying from Russia and Israel, but also from France, Italy, the UK and the US, for some arms components. The PRC's official annual defense budget for 2006 was Yuan 283.8 billion (nearly €28 billion), a figure which Washington considers substantially understated. It will therefore be seen that the ban is pointless and it is also hard to see how the EU can enter into a strategic partnership with China without lifting the embargo.

There are problems in Europe connected with technology transfer and "dual-use" technology. However, public pressure put on the EU by the US could backfire. Members of Congress are seeking to restrict transfers of US military technology to European countries selling arms to China and to forbid Pentagon purchases from such countries. This could affect current US efforts to make American forces inter-operable with the forces of its European allies. The UK would be the hardest hit from US retaliation over such a move, both because of its increased reliance on American military technology and because two of its companies are major suppliers to the Pentagon. Heavy-handed pressure from Washington could in fact help the EU-27 reach agreement on lifting the embargo. But it should only be lifted once the code of conduct on arms exports is strengthened and after China has signed the International Covenant on Civil and Political Rights.

Efforts are continuing to strengthen the EU's rules on arms exports. The revised Code of Conduct, which sets out common criteria for approving arms exports, is set to include tougher measures on arms brokerage in third countries and exports of "intangible" high-tech exports such as jet aircraft. Experts are still discussing the contents of a separate "toolbox" for dealing with countries that are coming out of an embargo. It would include five safeguard measures including compulsory reporting of accepted and denied export licence requests, and introduce periodic reviews of past exports and consultation on policy changes. Member states will also be expected to issue a declaration stating that the overall level of their exports will not increase. There is no agreement yet on all aspects of the package, but with political will (at present lacking) the few reservations can be resolved.

The European Parliament has consistently opposed the lifting of the arms embargo to the PRC. Though its agreement is not necessary for lifting the ban, as a directly elected European body, its voice is relevant. The PRC is perceived to have been slowing its progress in the human rights field. In particular, worries are being felt over new restrictions, particularly on freedom of expression, e.g., the foreign press agencies issue.

It is recommended that China, irrespective of and not linked to the ban, now ratifies the UN International Covenant which it signed in 1998.

Stanley Crossick

CHINA PERSPECTIVE

Arms Embargo in Transformation from Tactical Linkage to Strategic Embargo

In "Economic Containment: COCOM [Coordinating Committee for Multilateral Export Control] and the Politics of East-West Trade", Mastunduno divided export controls into four categories according to their purposes and scope, namely: (1) economic warfare: to weaken the economy of a state by restricting all kinds of international trade; (2) strategic embargo: to delay military developments of an adversary by prohibiting the export of items that "could make direct and specific contribution to target military capabilities"; (3) structural linkage: to induce desirable changes in the target state by economic engagement; and (4) tactical linkage: to expand or restrict trade according to changes in the target state.

When the EU arms embargo on China was first imposed, it was a move of tactical linkage. The EU tried to punish China for its domestic political behavior. As the situation in China significantly changed, "the reason for imposing the embargo ... disappeared", and it was natural for it to be lifted. That was what the EU tried to do in early 2004. But when the US intervened in February 2005, this approach was reversed and the embargo was gradually transformed from a tool of tactical linkage into a weapon of strategic embargo.

First, the purpose of the embargo is no longer limited to the improvement of China's human rights situation. The US opposition to lifting the ban is related to its military catch-all initiative. In December 2003, the Wassenaar Arrangements approved a "Statement of Understanding on Control of Non-Listed Dual-Use Items", which is also known as the "Military Catch-All Agreement". According to this agreement, all members agreed to control non-listed dual-use items destined for nations subject to an arms embargo. If the EU lifts the ban, this document will become pointless. The US worried about such a result and stepped up its efforts to strengthen its export control towards China. In July 2006, the US Commerce Department published a new "China Rule" forbidding any exports that may make "a material contribution" to China's military capability. The US is now trying to persuade its European NATO partners to follow suit. Once it succeeds, a COCOM-style coalition aimed at containing China's military development will be in place.

Second, introduction of the "no-undercut" principle will allow the US to revive its veto privilege. One major difference between COCOM and its successor, the Wassenaar Arrangements, is that the latter is a loosely organized regime. The US can no longer veto the other partners' contracts with any nation it does not like. But the US is trying to introduce a so called "no-undercut" principle into all international export control regimes. According to this principle, parties to the regime should not approve licences for any items already denied by another member state to a particular target state. The no-undercut principle will entitle the US to stop any dual-use transactions between Europe and China. The UK, France and Germany will not be able to independently determine whether they can export a high-tech item, whether on the list or not, to China.

Third, the door to some international export control regimes is closed to China. The most notable example is MTCR (Missile Technology Control Regime) membership. In the late 1990s, President Clinton tried to induce China to join the organization. Out of suspicion of this multilateral regime, China declined the invitation. Now China has become more open-minded, but the door has been closed by the US. It seems that Washington is determined to turn such export control regimes into an exclusive western club in spite of China's consistent efforts to strengthen its national export control regime.

In fact, the Cold War warriors on Capitol Hill have never given up their dream of reviving the COCOM. In October 1999, the 106th US Congress directed the Department of Defense to "develop a new effective, COCOM-like agreement" on a multilateral basis. The discussion over the EU arms ban on China just gave them an opportunity to garner domestic support and bully EU allies.

Potential Dangers Brought by a Revived COCOM

The development of the EU arms embargo into some kind of strategic embargo will have three negative implications.

First, it will be a "scarlet letter" that may alienate a rising China. Living in an era of grand transformation, Chinese people are very sensitive to outside perceptions and comments. Negative symbols like the arms ban will nurture suspicion about the intent of the West. Stanley Crossick correctly points out that it is hard to "see how the EU can enter into a strategic partnership with China without lifting the embargo". The composition of the Wassenaar Arrangements will make the case worse because some of its member states were part of the notorious Joint Army of the Eight Powers (UK, France, US, Germany, Italy, Japan, Austria and Russia) that invaded China at the beginning of the last century during the Boxer Rebellion. New leftists and nationalists in China may interpret such embargoes as new attempts by old western powers to hold back China's development.

Second, as far as regional stability is concerned, the embargo will worsen rather than enhance the security in East Asia. Stability is based upon the balance of power. But this formula does not work in the most dangerous regional flashpoint, the Taiwan Strait. Here, we should take domestic politics into consideration. Preoccupied with economic development and political regime transformation, Beijing wants most to maintain stability across the strait. The source of instability is on the other side of the strait. The Democratic Progressive Party (DPP), Taiwan's ruling party, always tries to shift voters' focus from its corrupt and impotent performance to its independence course by challenging the status quo. To sell advanced weapons to such a "troublemaker" while maintaining an embargo against Beijing will make the DPP overconfident in its own force and western support, and encourage it to take more provocative actions.

Third, EU countries will suffer heavy business loss as a result of the embargo. Restricted by the obsolete arms ban, the European defense industry, unlike its American counterpart supported by a huge domestic defense budget, will find it more difficult to maintain economies of scale and a competitive edge. And, as mentioned above, the new COCOM-style coalition against China will also seriously affect dual-use goods producers.

It is dangerous to underestimate the potential damages of a new COCOM-style regime, a platform of strategic embargo. As COCOM in the Cold War, it will disrupt the economic links between Europe and China and cause a vicious cycle of distrust and misperception. In that process, the arms ban may play an essential role in connecting European national export control regimes, multilateral regimes and US trade disincentives.

No More Linkage between Arms and Human Rights

We should also be cautious about the tactical linkage between the arms embargo and human rights issues such as the ratification of the International Covenant on Civil and Political Rights. First, it would be impossible for Chinese leaders to be seen to show weakness for such a symbolic step. Second, dialogue and communication instead of pressure and embargo, are more effective in trying to persuade a proud nation to change its own way of thinking. China is not a closed-mind society, which is clearly demonstrated by her history as the first republic in Asia (a fact usually ignored by most historians) and Deng's reforms. But coercion and force does not help change her mind. Stanley Crossick suggests that "respect for human rights should be presented as an issue of national interest for China and not as external pressure". I think that this is a better promotion tactic.

Guo Xiaobin

Part IV

CULTURAL AND SOCIAL REFLECTIONS

Mutuality: Confucius and Monnet

This short chapter suggests that historical commonalities exist in current Chinese and European thinking, and also therefore in the attitudes towards the relationship between the two polities. That common approach may best be summed up in the word "mutuality".

Confucius

The fundamental impact of Confucius (551BC–479BC) and Confucianism on modern Chinese thinking and ways of doing things has been rediscovered and discussed lately, after decades of criticism for the sake of revolutionary thinking. The call for harmony by the Chinese leader Hu Jintao reveals a revitalization of Chinese tradition in social philosophy and rethinking of human relations in a fast transforming and evolving modern world.

The basic "virtues" of Confucianism are: proper behavior (*li*), humanity (*ren*), doing one's duty (*yi*), knowing what is right (*shi*), reciprocal care of others (*shu*), and respect, fulfilling the obligations of a child (*xiao*). Confucius is recorded as saying that one word is enough to serve as a rule of practice for all one's life and that that word was mutuality (*shu*). *Shu* also means tolerance and reciprocity. Mutuality teaches humans to respect each other and their different roles in society, thus helping to restore or establish peace and tranquillity.

The inclusion of mutuality appears to be contradictory to the authoritarianism which prevailed in Confucian society and indeed teaching: the son must render total obedience to the father's exercise of arbitrary authority. To understand this, it is necessary to think in historical terms. When Confucianism was practised as a political ideology, the society was pre-modern and the father functioned not only as head of the family; he was also in charge of family business based on his farming experiences, labor and skills, and was duly respected and obeyed. Of greater interest for us, however, is that its core values of respecting different human roles in societies have survived and remain relevant in East Asian societies, after over 2,000 years. For that reason itself, Confucianism as a moral and social teaching merits re-reading and careful scrutiny.

Like other great thinkers around the world, Confucius, living through wars and turmoil, yearned for peace and order. When his calling met with deaf ears among the kings and princes, he devoted his time and efforts to developing his theory for order, and to teaching. In Confucianism, we find harmonious orders in all human relations and that harmony requires reciprocal efforts. Thus, the father should be loving and caring, as this encourages the son to be filial, which in turn encourages the father to be loving — relationships are not one-dimensional, but based on the concept of mutuality. A similar relationship should also be established beyond the family, at the state level, as for Confucius the state resembled the structure of the family and thus, the relations demonstrated in the family should also be reflected in the state and vice versa. In other words, an ideal state or polity should function as an extended family, with fathers and sons, lords and subordinates, all fulfilling their own duties and showing mutual love and respect. If states are structured with mutual responsibility, the world will be governed with order, with humans and human groups living in harmony. Mutuality is thus a prerequisite to peace, order and harmony.

Mutuality, not isolated autonomy or some personal autocracy, provides the circumstances in which we are to flourish or to struggle against whatever opposes our will and self-interest. According to Confucius, it is the context that must guide our use of power and position. Central to that context is our humaneness (*ren*) and the advantages of reciprocity (*shu*). Confucius observed that the lordly man (*jun zi*) sought for success in that which was inside him, and did not seek to exploit others. Inside the person is the power of virtue (*de*), the mind of humaneness (*ren*) and the ability to reciprocate (*shu*). The mean person (*xiao ren*) seeks one-sided relationships of personal profit. Put simply, what you do not wish for yourself, do not do to others.

Confucius taught that when everyone observed this mutuality of respect and obligation, there would be harmony on earth. We are still waiting for this. It is obvious that Confucius — like Buddhists — had a higher opinion and deeper trust of human nature than the realistic European, Jean Monnet (see below).

What may be more relevant in today's world is Confucius' judgment of humans not only as equal, but as equally different. He teaches that the lordly men (*jun zi*) are supposed to consist of people with different characteristics and identities, yet who can still live in harmony, whereas mean persons (*xiao ren*) are identical, yet discord all the time. An ideal society for Confucius, therefore, should be made up of different people living in harmony and order, people respecting each other, serving each other in their own ways.

China failed to modernize herself in the eighteenth and nineteenth centuries under Confucianism. The country, with its static human relations, could not adjust to the fast-changing outside world. The traditional goals of harmony and virtue tended to be displaced by competition for supremacy and the "rule of the jungle". For the last century or so, Confucianism was severely attacked as a predominant ideology for failing to lead China along the road of modernization. It is only recently, when the process of modernization is seen to threaten an harmonious society, that a revaluation of Confucius' teaching is taking place.

Monnet

It seems far-fetched to compare Jean Monnet, a modern statesman who travelled extensively including working and living in China and took upon himself many tasks such as businessman and statesman, with a thinker like Confucius. However, when we study the insights of these two historic figures and their understanding of human societies, we do find that mutuality and diversity cross ages.

The starting point of Jean Monnet (1888–1979) was equality, and this equality stems from Monnet's belief in human rationality and ability to follow the logic of nature and events. According to him, a group carrying out joint tasks must accept common responsibility for the effects of the collective decisions on each member. If the parties are to trust one another to accept a common view, they must feel equal, and they are equal because they have equal capacity to comprehend the context in which they are working and living.

But Monnet never idealistically believed that human nature can be changed, only human behavior.

Monnet spent his life persuading people to work together to seek common solutions to common problems or, in today's parlance, seeking "win-wins" rather than playing "zero-sum games".

Monnet's thinking (he would not want us to say "philosophy") was that lasting peace is only possible if based on equality between peoples and organized solidarity. His post-World War II objective was to organize the peace, which required countries to cooperate closely, based on shared sovereignty and without individual national vetoes.

Monnet did not speak in terms of "mutuality" as such, but clearly this was present at all times in his thinking. However, mutuality was not enough for him as sharing sovereignty was essential to achieve his objectives. "Solidarity" was also recognized as a necessity.

He was Kantian by nature and Immanuel Kant emphasized the mutuality principle by pointing out that the right course of action is the one we would *wish* that all other persons would take in a similar situation. 200 years after Kant, we are perhaps beginning to accustom ourselves to the fact that the mutuality principle has to be applied to the relationship between rich and poor countries, as well as between regions in countries. It must also govern the relationship between generations. This requires a concerted effort by all the political, economic and social players and, where appropriate, government-directed income redistribution program. Kant's central thesis was mutuality of self and world, according to which self and world are "correlarities mediated by the activity of representation".

Lee Kuan Yew and Mahathir Mohamed argued in the early 1990s that Asia's economic success was rooted in distinctive Asian values — a combination of Confucianism and Buddhism. Authoritarian government was different there, as it promoted economic and social welfare, as Confucius advocated, and overrode interest groups that would obstruct the general good. Democracy, they argued, impedes the disciplined mobilization of resources. Belief in the family reduced the need for welfare spending. The Confucian work ethic and belief in self-development meant first, be educated and trained, and then work hard. The Asian model was low taxes, low welfare, high education, high savings, high investment, business-building and entrepreneurialism, all under an authoritarian, Confucius-minded government. This justification has tended not to be heard after the 1997–1998 Asian financial crisis. Obviously, Monnet would not have agreed with this argument, as he believed deeply in western-style democracy.

Conclusion

We conclude from this quick review of Confucius and Monnet's thinking the following:

- Both Confucius and Monnet represent the best spirit of their respective civilizations, and behind their thinking, a fundamental commonality is to be found in their deep belief in a peaceful, orderly and righteous human society. Confucius devoted his life-long teaching to this belief, whereas Monnet labored to invent a working model that realized his ideal.
- Confucius believed in mutuality and peaceful order within a hierarchical society where people, though different in their positions and roles, share equal responsibility in maintaining peace and harmony.
- Monnet believed in mutuality, which he extended to building institutions guaranteeing solidarity and peace — which is only achievable through equality and sharing of sovereignty.
- China has inherited from Confucius a sense and appreciation of mutuality and responsibility. Starting from respecting different roles of human society, the Chinese civilization tends to settle differences and disputes by peaceful means, and this tendency suits multilateralism rather than unilateralism in an international environment.
- Europe has inherited from Monnet an institutionalized supranational system, in which the mutuality of nations and multilateral processes are embedded.
- Despite their different political systems, therefore, China and Europe both believe in mutuality and practise multilateralism.
- They disagree, however, on sharing sovereignty.

Stanley Crossick
Zhou Hong

18

Similarities and Differences

Introduction

China and the European Union have gone through dramatic changes since the end of the Cold War. They have had to adapt to the new international situation and to the accelerated speed of globalization, the latter challenging traditional notions of the nation-state. While 20 years ago, one could have argued that China and Europe do not sit in the same boat or share the same bed, today there is no doubt that the world has shrunk and that the line between domestic and international issues has become blurred. Do China and the EU and its member states have a similar view of the world? Do they share a common understanding of concepts like sovereignty and non-interference? Do they have compatible visions of a world order as it should be and the means and instruments that can be used to get there?

Strictly speaking, to compare China and the EU with respect to sovereignty, national power, etc., is like comparing an apple and a pear tree: the EU is a unique entity quite different from a nation-state like the United States or China. Europe might have come a long way in integrating a group of states on the basis of common standards and common values into a single market and community in terms of economic, social and environmental policies, but in terms of foreign and security policy it is not a unitary actor and will not be for quite a while. As Hanns Maull put it, the EU is a "force" rather than a "power", since it lacks the necessary feature of an independent power center. China, in contrast, definitely is such a power and has more in common with the United States or India in terms of national power, decision-making, ambitions and framework of authority than with the EU.

It has to be noted, moreover, that the issues addressed here are not static, but have been undergoing dynamic change — in the US, the EU and in China. Until well into the 1990s, for example, Chinese officials and academics were hardly willing to talk about issues like human rights, rule of law or democracy (at least not western forms of democracy with multiparty systems, etc.). But over the last ten years, there has been more and more readiness to participate in a national and international discourse on all these concepts.

Sovereignty

National sovereignty is a concept that originally developed in Europe in the sixteenth and seventeenth centuries. The concept acknowledged that a state has full power and jurisdiction domestically over its territory and is independent of external authorities (Keohane). "Westphalian sovereignty" dominated European understanding of the state until well into the twentieth century. It was only against the background of two devastating wars in the first half of the twentieth century that European states started to go on their journey of building a community that would pool national sovereignty on the supranational level.

So far, Europe is the only example of such an endeavor to transfer sovereignty and build a common economic and political space. However, the European Union is not a super-state. The field of external relations — of foreign and security policy — has turned out to be a bastion of national sovereignty. All member states have their own foreign ministries, foreign services and their own armies. While integration with respect to trade and economic matters is very deep and the Commission can negotiate on trade issues on behalf of the member states, this is clearly not the case with respect to foreign policy. On many issues and conflicts outside the EU, there is no common position of the 27. The former colonial powers (e.g., UK, France, Germany, Spain) often consider certain parts of the world for historical reasons as in their particular, if not exclusive, sphere of interest.

China, on the rhetorical level at least, still upholds the classical Westphalian sovereignty. For a country that has perceived herself as a victim of colonialism and imperialism for more than 100 years, it is hardly surprising to come up with a very strong notion of national sovereignty and the right of self-determination. In general, countries in the Asia-Pacific region that won independence from colonial rule only after World War II have very strong feelings about the principles of sovereignty and of non-interference in each other's internal affairs. From the Chinese perspective, the "Five Principles of Peaceful Coexistence" which go back to agreements between China and India and to the Bandung Conference — a meeting of Asian and African states in 1955 — are still the best foundation for states to get along with each other, especially if they belong to different ideological and/or systemic camps. These five principles are:

- mutual respect for each other's territorial integrity and sovereignty,
- mutual non-aggression,
- mutual non-interference in each other's internal affairs,
- equality and mutual benefit, and
- peaceful coexistence.

National sovereignty and independence are identified as primary objectives of China's foreign policy in all major foreign policy documents. For example, the Ministry of Foreign Affairs stated in a document titled "China's Independent Foreign Policy of Peace" in 2003: "China unswervingly pursues an independent foreign policy of peace. The fundamental goals of this policy are to preserve China's independence, sovereignty and territorial integrity . . .".

Mutuality is central in the five principles, and this is arguably also where we can observe a big difference between China and the United States. While both countries are very strict in defending their sovereignty against interference from other countries or from international institutions, China wants to see this principle basically applied to every country, no matter whether big or small, powerful or weak: every state is entitled to the same kind of sovereignty. All countries are entitled to make their own choices with respect to political, social and economic system and with respect to their development path.

The United States, for its part, defends mainly its own sovereignty against outside interference. With respect to other states, however, the US is much less opposed to interference, e.g., through sanctions and even military interventions. Actually, this higher readiness to intervene abroad and the alliances and security commitments the US has around the globe, are exactly the reason why it rejects being subjected to any outside jurisdiction. The United States has been less willing than members of the EU to limit its external sovereignty. It is reluctant to make binding commitments that it cannot veto.

However, the US and China have made one important exception by becoming members of the World Trade Organization — as a founding member of the General Agreement on Tariffs and Trade (GATT), the United States accepted the WTO charter in 1994, while China, after many years of negotiations, finally became a member in 2002. As for the European Union, it is exactly in the trade area where it is seen as defending its (supranational) sovereignty and interests. Within the dispute settlement provisions of the WTO, there exists no veto power and all three players have accepted this rule of the game.

Non-Interference in Domestic Affairs

On the rhetorical level, China advocates the principle of non-interference in domestic affairs. This is, of course, closely linked to the Chinese understanding of national sovereignty. In reality, however, the Chinese government has adopted a more flexible stance over the years. Through economic reforms and the opening up to the outside world, China has become more and more integrated in the global economy. With a growing stake in the existing international system, Beijing's attitude to the United Nations and other international organizations and regimes has changed from downright opposition to cautious support and to active engagement. Beijing has become more active as a contributor to UN mandated peacekeeping operations since the late 1980s. Of the P-5, the five countries with a permanent seat in the UN Security Council, China has over the years become the strongest provider of personnel, albeit mostly technical (medical and technical teams).

However, China consistently argues in favor of peaceful solutions for conflicts and is still very reluctant to vote in favor of sanctions, especially if they hold the danger/risk of leading automatically to (military) intervention. The condition for Chinese participation in peacekeeping operations is the assent of all involved parties.

China has come closer to western (European) positions concerning the nuclear issue in North Korea and Iran's nuclear program and is cooperating with the West, even though China's bilateral relations with both countries have a long tradition and China has energy interests in Iran. Beijing has even voted in favor of the 2005 World Summit Outcome resolution (A/RES/60/1) at the UN General Assembly, which endorsed the "responsibility to protect". But despite this, China normally still does not approve of sanctions and interventions in the name of human rights. Recent examples of this attitude are Sudan and Burma/Myanmar: in the latter case, China argues that the human rights situation there is mainly a domestic affair which has no implications for regional security and stability. Together with Russia, China vetoed a resolution against Burma in the Security Council — the first joint veto since 1972. With respect to Sudan and the situation in Darfur, Beijing has taken a slightly different stance. Behind the scenes, Chinese leaders have appealed to Khartoum to cooperate with the UN and strive to end the humanitarian crisis in Darfur.

Within the European Union, intervention and interference by the European institutions in the domestic affairs of the member states has become the norm: these countries no longer set rules and regulations, nor do they make sure that these norms are respected and implemented. With respect to other countries and regions, the EU, by declaring the promotion of democracy, good governance and the rule of law as one of its policy objectives, seems to be more prepared than China to interfere in domestic affairs. However, the instruments implemented by the EU to reach these goals consist in offering economic cooperation and partnership. The prospect of becoming a member of the EU has been one important incentive for adhering to EU standards, and "neighborhood policy" has become the standard instrument, e.g., *vis-à-vis* countries in North Africa and the Middle East.

The EU is quite reluctant to use military force. The idea of preemptive or preventive strikes which emerged in the United States in response to 9/11 is not widely shared and supported by Europeans. This reluctance to use military means has been attributed to the relative weakness of the EU. But even if there is some truth in this explanation, it is only part of the story. The institutional setting and the complicated decision-making process also plays a role. And since the very existence of the EU is rooted in the experience of war and integration is seen as a way to prevent it, it would also be considered as acting against the "nature" of the European community.

Hard Power and Soft Power

The concept of soft power was originally introduced by Joseph Nye. He defined it in 1990 as the ability of a state to influence others through the attractiveness of its culture, its values, institutions and political system. In China, the understanding of "soft power" is somewhat broader — it comprises basically everything except military or "hard" power, i.e., it includes the whole range of economic and diplomatic means as well. Since the early 1990s, China tried to project a peaceful image of herself to counter the "China threat" theory. On the rhetorical level, this image is reflected in the phrases "peace and development" and "peaceful development", which have been officially used to describe the main trend in international politics during the 1990s and even today. The term "peaceful rise" of China was only briefly used in official speeches, but can still be found in academic articles. China's leaders nowadays describe China's — especially economic — dealings with other countries as "win-win", and since 2006 the vision of building a "harmonious world" has become dominant in speeches of Chinese politicians.

China did not propagate herself as a model to be emulated by other developing countries. But her success in reforming the economy, achieving high growth rates, and at the same time preventing political instability started to attract the attention of other countries, at least in developing states and among the ruling elites of non-democratic countries. If China now takes a more proactive stance in foreign policy, this is also the result of and the response to growing expectations from the outside.

Of course, the peaceful image China tries to project does not mean that hard or military power does not play a role in her modernization efforts. China's military spending since the early 1990s has witnessed double digit growth rates. This military modernization is mainly directed at deterring Taiwan from declaring independence. In view of her long borders with other states, China's leaders are convinced that a strong and modern military is necessary to safeguard independence and territorial integrity.

In Europe, the term "soft power" has not been widely used to describe the influence of the European Union. Instead, the EU sees itself as a civilian or civil power. The success of the European model seems to have suffered a few setbacks, however, in recent years. Low economic growth rates and low birth rates, the failure of the referendums on the constitutional treaty in France and the Netherlands, disunity among member states over important foreign policy issues like the war in Iraq — all this has contributed to disappointment about the progress and the capabilities of the EU. Some countries that had expected the EU to become and act as a real counterweight to the United States were especially disillusioned over these developments.

Multipolarity, Multilateralism, Bilateralism

Since the late 1980s, many academic articles and political speeches in China spoke of a "multipolar" world with several "poles" in terms of economic, political and military power. Multipolarity contrasted with a unipolar world order dominated by the single superpower, the United States. However, whether this multipolar world would come about automatically or not was never really clear. In Europe, only a few countries used the term multipolarity, foremost France and, for a brief while, also Germany. Multipolarity, however, does not describe a structure or world order; it rather describes the distribution of (economic, political and military) power.

Due to its own emergence and characteristics, the European Union propagates multilateralism, and now "effective" multilateralism as the best way to tackle the challenges of today's world. For the same reason, the EU supports regional integration and regional organizations everywhere.

With respect to multilateralism, China underwent a far-reaching transformation. With the beginning of the reform process, China became more integrated not only in the global economy, but also in the international system. She became a member in most important international organizations and regimes, especially during the 1990s. While China might originally have intended just not to be excluded from organizations like the ASEAN Regional Forum and to have a say in what would or would not be discussed, membership convinced China that multilateralism has some advantages by lowering transaction costs. Moreover, the Asian financial crisis in 1997–1998 demonstrated growing interdependence and the vulnerability of individual states in a globalizing world. Obviously, the most important step with the most dramatic implications was China's accession to the WTO in 2001.

That China is also pursuing her national interests bilaterally where she is in a strong position to do so, should not surprise anybody, even EU member states.

Conclusion

In today's globalizing world of growing interdependence, China and Europe truly share the same bed. They sometimes even share the same dreams or at least believe to do so. However, a closer analysis of their respective visions reveals that there are substantial differences in concepts, ambitions and approaches. Moreover, concepts have been undergoing dynamic changes.

In terms of sovereignty, the EU remains the exception — no other group of states in the world has gone so far in transferring authority to a supranational level. Globalization might have eroded national sovereignty to a certain degree, but the nation-state is still the central international actor. Whether the EU will become a model to be emulated by others is not at all clear — and will depend, to a degree, on how successful the EU will be in the future, economically as well as politically.

If we look at the developments in the last 15 years, China is now integrated much deeper in the global economy and in the international system. She has turned from a revolutionary into a status quo power (with the notable exception of the Taiwan issue).

Gudrun Wacker

19

Governance

EU PERSPECTIVE

The EU-China strategic partnership has strengthened considerably since the drafting of the last cooperation agreement. The new agreement is, however, being negotiated during a period of growing calls for protectionism, a questioning of the global governance structure that has supported globalization (e.g., the failure of the 2005 Doha Round) and a growing Chinese confidence signalled by its sojourns into African aid. The argument in this paper is that the European Union should avoid approaching the issue of governance as if it is simply a case of cloning a European model of governance onto China as though it were grafting Dolly the sheep (although I am sure this was not a simple matter); and that China should avoid the all-too-simplistic rhetoric of home-grown conservatives that "China's so different that it can learn nothing from European examples". The key to a real strategic partnership is continued engagement around a process of intercultural dialogue surrounding political, economic and social systems that produce long-term sustainable benefits for all. This long-term agenda will require a greater openness and broader dialogue, debate and public diplomacy than has hitherto been the case.

EU-China Historical Paths: Substantively Not That Different?

Acknowledging that this is at the risk of simplifying the different historical paths of EU member states and 5,000 years of Chinese civilization, it is argued here that Europe and China have both developed from feudalistic historical paths to what are now modern economies requiring a complex set of relationships between citizens and the state. Hence, the process of globalization will continue to push towards convergent future paths of better institutional governance, both soft and hard, through a process of exploration, experimentation and learning. The EU is in an ideal position to undertake this strategic challenge with China, given that it has been the most successful multilateral institution in history, providing post-war peace in Europe and a model that does not undermine the national sovereignty of member states but insists on a minimum set of rules by which members must abide. In his book *Why Europe Will Run the 21st Century*, Mark Leonard equates joining the EU to joining a club, with a minimum acceptance of club rules (good governance across the board), but with the acknowledgment of the need for national sovereignty.

This chapter argues that for EU-China relations to become of strategic significance, there needs to be a common approach to thinking around what our societies want to achieve over the next 50 years. China has experienced fantastic economic growth since the late 1980s and has experienced in that period a level of change unprecedented in social history, with the largest migration from the rural countryside to urban centers that the world has ever seen. During the previous 25 years under Deng Xiaoping's Hayekian "let a few get rich first" formula, economic growth has been miraculous but not surprisingly it has produced growing inequality, not only between rich eastern seaboard provinces and the less wealthy inland and western provinces, but between rural and urban residents. Equally, however, as Will Hutton documents in his new book *The Writing on the Wall*, growing inequality has risen in the western democracies of the US and UK since the late 1980s, despite reasonable economic growth and, in the UK, relatively low unemployment compared to France and Germany. Hutton's prescription is that the UK and US need to rediscover the soft infrastructures of good governance that are necessary to sustain a harmonious society. In the UK's case, this may be a process of initial discovery as although the independent institutional framework exists, the enlightenment ideas that were developed anew in the US to underpin its political economy never took hold in the UK, due to the *laissez faire* approach of 19th-century UK governments. In the UK, increased government intervention into the lives of people only really took hold after the Second World War, and with hindsight, the nationalization of key strategic industries, the welfare state, the national health service and universal basic education were a temporary response to rebuilding the state, not a process of constitution-building despite the efforts of Beveridge and Keynes.

A prosperous Europe has taken much longer to emerge, and managing equality issues has been relatively peaceful after 1945 through the development of institutions that provide the necessary infrastructure for a harmonious political economy. Hutton contests this in the US as since the era of Reaganomics, the soft institutional infrastructures of democracy have been in decline including "accountability, representativity, respect for the rule of law and the capacity, through free speech, for debate, and exchange and deliberation".

China's economy has developed rapidly and impressively and like Europe, but for different reasons, social harmony is moving up the agenda. In the UK, modern social writers such as Richard Layward and Geoff Mulgan are conscious that for all the economic progress that has been made in the UK, there does not appear to be an increase in the level of happiness which one might expect. The United Kingdom experienced massive economic restructuring during the 1980s and 1990s and with it a changing pattern of social relationships. GDP growth has been steady and employment relatively high, but recent research suggests that social capital has not moved in the same direction.

Government

The Chinese government, headed by the CCP, has presided over a period of peace and stability for sustained economic growth in China since the 1980s. China has averaged a GDP growth rate of 8%–12% since 1989, whilst the majority of the EU's largest economies has remained stagnant. To date, much of China's economic success has been export-driven with a plentiful supply of cheap rural labor to make it the manufacturing workshop of the world.

The free market model followed by China is not dissimilar to the successful economies developed in Europe in the 19th century, except that it has achieved success in a mere 20 years rather than 100 years. Hence, there has been little time or inclination for western-style domestic institution-building or Huttonian-style reflection of the enlightenment kind, as energies have been targeted towards export-led growth. However, with growing incidences of social unrest stemming from rapid economic growth, the CCP needs a new injection of social ideology to overcome flawed models of economic growth that may inhibit long-term social cohesion and stability. The European Union therefore, with its diverse array of social democracies, provides China with a potentially valuable source of political options from which to engineer a more harmonious model of socioeconomic development.

Political Economy

Recent publications variously discuss the Chinese economic miracle as having a negative effect on certain localized economies of Europe and America (e.g., James Kynge), and other analyses suggest that China's economic rise is exaggerated and should not lead Europe or the US towards protectionism (e.g., Will Hutton). China's 11th five-year plan could be interpreted as a break from the Deng Xiaoping formula of letting a few get rich first, to focus more on a balanced economic growth strategy to address rising social instability. Traditionally, Chinese governance is characterized by a social contract between leaders and citizens that is tautological. In short, leaders govern according to the mandate of heaven and citizens expect that leaders provide for them. When things go wrong, it is because the mandate of heaven has been withdrawn and a new leadership is required.

This is a traditional view and it is unlikely that the urban population in a modern Chinese society would believe in the mandate theory, but in a still largely rural dominated population, old-style expectations of the government/citizen social contract still persists, as evidenced by the "petition" system whereby individual grievances are presented to Beijing government departments for resolution. Hence, Chinese leaders, like their European counterparts, have the task of satisfying an ever increasing set of public expectations and dissatisfactions and scarce resources to meet those expectations.

Arguably, 17th–18th century Europe was governed in a similar manner to that of traditional China. Simply put, legitimacy of governance was accorded to the leadership (kings and queens) as a perceived mandate of heaven through Christian belief. This is what is meant by the historical paths of European nations being similar to that of pre-Communist China, whereby empires were governed by a mandate of heaven rather than a mandate of the people.

The UK is a case in point. Firstly, power in the UK was fundamentally lodged with a ruling elite dominated by a monarch and a feudal system of landed gentry and agricultural production. Land was the sole source of power on which taxes were levied. The taxes were then used to finance overseas adventures and gradually, trade developed. Later, during the industrial revolution, commodities were transformed into manufactured goods, requiring the movement of people from rural to urban production. Much of this can be found in any Marxist account of economic development in Europe and the Karl Marx study of 19th-century Manchester. If one accepts this potted account of economic development in Europe, it is also essential to understand the trajectory of political development. Again, focusing on the UK, firstly, the monarchy had to develop a parliament so that landowners and merchants could settle economic disputes through dialogue and realized that they could only secure economic power through political power. Without this, trade would be affected and economic growth stultified by growing social instability. Parliament was therefore set up as a talking place whereby economic objectives could be achieved by agreement, supported by the rule of law and a system of independent courts. Today's political parties of the Conservatives and Liberal Democrats stem from this time. In the late 19th century, social disputes occurred as workers in manufacturing production were organized so that their route to social and economic justice came through their political representation in parliament. If rich landowners, merchants and businessmen had their economic interests protected through laws passed by parliament, then it was only right that the interests of workers should be protected too.

China's greatest challenge therefore is to develop a system of governance that maintains unitary power within the ruling party elite, whilst allowing for more diverse modes of supervision and accountability that act as a source of real political legitimacy, assuming that direct multiparty elections are not on the foreseeable agenda.

Civil Society

The role of civil society is contested, but it is an area where a good deal of work can be done between Europe and China. For example, in the UK, many civil society organizations are used by the government in the provision of social services. In return and through accepting public finance, civil society organizations are expected to have transparent systems of financial accountability, not to engage in political activity and to safeguard the public interest.

Social Innovation and 21st-Century Philanthropy

Social innovation describes the processes, dynamics and methods through which social needs are met and scaled-up via government, business and civil society. In its institutional form, social innovation should continue to be a key area for European and Chinese cooperation since the concept and, indeed, practice of social innovation requires a strong partnership orientation between government, business and civil society. Social innovation can be driven by any actor and does not therefore carry the political baggage associated with many civil society agendas that seek to make such organizations anti-state and to some extent anti-business. In the institutional form, such organizations are known as "social enterprises", operating commercially but for social benefit as opposed to private gain. Social enterprises trade in goods or services, and link that trade to a social mission. The need to deliver on financial, social and environmental performance targets is often referred to as having a triple bottom line. They are generally held to comprise the more business-like end of the spectrum of organizations that make up the third sector or social economy. Many social enterprises receive finance from government or a private benefactor, but without the 19th-century paternalism associated with the giving of charity. This 21st century form of philanthropy requires that an organization has a strong business vision and plan for the future, including financial sustainability. Such organizations are emerging in China and are attractive to the government because they can provide services to groups of disadvantaged persons which the government finds it difficult to reach. There are institutional challenges which need overcoming, not least the legal framework which frequently mitigates against the emergence of social enterprises and the need for a well-formed political will to support such initiatives.

A New Enlightenment for China-Europe?

In his recent book *The Writing on the Wall*, Will Hutton admirably reminds us that neoclassical economics offer societies little in the long-run, even if it can kickstart or shake an economy out of stagnation in the short-term through a period of painful economic restructuring as happened in the US in the 1970s and the UK in the 1980s. The first problem with neoclassical thought is that it treats all individuals as self-interested, atomized economic actors, when humans also aspire to Maslow's higher order social needs, including happiness and self-esteem. The second problem with the neoclassical approach is that it is tautological. It allows government to say that it has minimal responsibility covering macroeconomic management and a few functions of law and order and defense; takes a minimum tax to pay for this and leaves the market to deliver the rest, including health, education and other public services. The problem with this 19th-century *laissez faire* approach is that the Hayekian trickle-down effect does not work; inequality rises even further over time and government has to intervene ever more to overcome social instability.

Marxism therefore can be seen as a European political economy experiment introduced as a reaction to the social instability, inequality and injustices brought about by a lack of government intervention, to challenge inequality and injustice. The ideals of Marxist thinking cannot be disputed, but unfortunately the practice, wherever it has occurred, has failed to deliver anything other than poverty because it cannot deal with the real need of individual economic incentives that coexist with Maslow's higher order social needs.

The argument here, however, is that because of the fast pace of Chinese economic reform, it has not been possible to develop a set of enlightenment principles or institutions that underpinned industrialization in Europe and America. The concepts and institutions of freedom of association and speech, transparency and accountability, the rule of law and a free press, took time to develop and embed (but, according to Hutton, unravelling in the UK and US since the 1980s). China's 11th five-year plan does, however, signal a move in the direction of greater concerns over equality, and it is time that China and Europe worked jointly to investigate openly and honestly a new enlightenment model of good governance. On the one hand, Europe should not listen to Europeans who assume Europe has all the answers for China as though it was somehow cloning Dolly the sheep, because it does not; on the other hand, China should not listen to those Chinese conservatives who believe that China is so different that it can only learn from within. China is and does need to go through a process of enlightenment-style thinking to underpin its future political, economic and social trajectory and to rationalize the current contradictions of Marxist-Leninist thought with a freewheeling economy. It would be a shame, however, if this happens behind closed doors as with any new thinking, debate, dialogue and deliberation from challenging opposites makes for more coherent thought. Hence, EU-China relations need to foster intercultural dialogue based on enlightenment principles as well as technical cooperation around trade.

Gary Hallsworth

CHINA PERSPECTIVE

Building a strategic partnership is a new milestone in the EU-China relationship. In light of the experience of economic restructuring in developed countries, an important part of cooperation between the EU and China is the coordination of structural policy. The EU has proposed to China to promote "good governance", which embraces both government and society. The reform of government and enterprise is a major task in the restructuring of the economic system in China. The central government wants to promote "scientific development" and " harmonious society". Governance is relevant in two respects. One is to rationalize public governance, and the other is to socialize enterprise governance. Cooperation between China and the EU on governance has much to offer. This paper briefly introduces the objectives, contents and measures of China's governance and makes suggestions for cooperation between China and the EU.

Knowledge Economy: Building an Harmonious World

The UN's "Agenda 21" of 1992 contains a global consensus on the road map towards achieving sustainable development. The assessment in *The UN Millennium Development Goals* sees China as one of the countries most likely to reach the goals, thus confirming the relevance of its "harmonious society and world strategy".

Before the new millennium, we entered a new industrial revolution with the arrival of the knowledge economy, which is based on technology and human resources. Compared to natural resources, knowledge resource cannot be captured by armed forces. It is no accident that the knowledge economy developed at the end of the Cold War. Peace and development are its goals.

In the industrial economy, people create tools that substitute and amplify the physical power of mankind; in the knowledge economy, people create tools that substitute and amplify the mental power of mankind. These intellectual tools are made up of information technology. The computer is one of the most popularly used tools that changes the way we live and work. Firstly, it partly replaces mental work, which forces people to do more advanced mental work beyond the capability of the computer. Innovative ability is thereby further improved and economic power derived from this intellectual work. Secondly, computers through the internet enlarge the connection between people. Computers are used not only for personal work, but also to interact with others. The internet not only provides new channels of knowledge distribution, but also opens up new means of commercial transactions.

In physical production, information technology reduces the limitations of individual firms and produces a new organizational mode of inter-firm cooperation. This new mode includes the intra-firm production chains between multinational corporations and their subsidiary companies, the inter-firm production chains among producers, suppliers, dealers and retailers, and the intra-firm and inter-firm production chains of industrial clusters made up of SMEs (small and medium enterprises). These chains interact with each other and form the global production system.

In such a knowledge economy, knowledge-sharing becomes more important in order to promote man's dynamic role. It results in a new way of knowledge production and organization, namely a common peer-to-peer production mode, whose characteristics are inter-firm research & development alliances, consumer innovation by producers and the openness of technology innovation. In the 1990s, the internet connected personal computers in place of high performance computers. By means of the internet, the capability of dispersed personal computers was integrated to carry out a huge amount of calculation work. Many research projects in electronic technology, biological technology and space exploration, which need a large amount of computing work, bring computer subscribers from all over the world to participate. The services they provide are free and the behavior of participants is not guided by the price, the firm's management or any time constraint. This new way of knowledge production and organization provides opportunities to fully exert human capability.

In order to adapt to the development of the knowledge economy, China proposes to construct an "innovative society", which will contribute to global technological innovation. The science and technology cooperation between China and EU helps not only the economic and technical development of each other, but also the construction of an harmonious world. Hence, there is a common base for cooperation in governance.

The Science of Public Governance in the Harmonious World

In China, market reform was initiated by the government. Because of the existence of SOEs (state-owned enterprises) as the main economic force, the government acts as the owner of the resources and promoter of economic growth. Thus, the Chinese government has its own special role in promoting economic development. After more than 20 years of rapid growth, China should change its goals to harmonious and sustainable development, and transform its intensive material input growth into intensive technical input growth The major challenge China encounters is to further improve the market mechanism and achieve a better balance between efficiency and equity.

In terms of traditional economic theory, the goal of economic development is the growth of GDP. From the macroeconomic theory of Keynes to the stages of economic growth theory of Kuznets and to the economic growth theory of Lewis, economic growth is considered to be the core objective of economic development. The index of measuring economic development is GDP, which every nation uses. However, the growth of material wealth does not bring corresponding development. Although Kuznets has put forward the "trickle-down theory", which argues that economic growth will alleviate poverty, the crucial problem people face is still the increasing inequality and poverty accompanying economic growth.

For more than 20 years, China has strived to establish a prosperous society, with economic growth being the primary aim of development — growth and development thus being synonymous. In terms of "development is the absolute principle", as stated by Deng Xiaoping, growth is misleading as the "absolute principle". Because of the lack of clarity of development goals, the growth rate of real income is far behind the growth rate of GDP, and consumption lags behind investment. From the perspective of economic theories, economic growth is not an ultimate target but a means of human development, an instrument of social welfare improvement, which should be the most important objective of economic growth. Many developed countries, in their road to development, have realized the necessity of social welfare improvement together with economic growth. Sustainable development includes sustainable development for humans, which has multiple objectives. Raising per capita income to improve living standards is just one of the objectives. There are other objectives such as establishing education and healthcare, providing opportunities for ordinary people to take part in public affairs, ensuring a clean environment and promoting inter-generation equality.

Throughout history, there have been two trends of economic and social development. First, with the development of technology, economic development is becoming more and more difficult because of the complex production structure, methods and organization led by technical invention. Economic development cannot be monitored by the market system in which price is the sole signal, but must be coordinated with social organization. For example, we cannot use the price signal of the market to protect the environment in order to ensure sustainable development. Second, with the rising level of economic development, the task of social development is becoming more and more difficult. However, the complicated social and economic activities may cause government interventions to fail. Therefore, we need both market and government to achieve harmonious and sustainable development.

The World Bank argues that "the development dominated by the government will doom to failure, while the development without government will not be successful. . . . It is impossible to have a sustainable social and economic development without an efficient government." Hence, "development not only means economic and technical input, but also concerns the institutional environment"; "Understanding the role government plays in institutional environment . . . is far more important to efficiently promote the economic development by the government." Development requires various kinds of capital, which may be classified as: (1) physical capital, including production and other material capital; (2) human capital, including labor, knowledge and health; (3) social capital, or in other words, social network relations, such as the institutional environment. Social capital encourages mutual trust and benefit among people and the sharing of social welfare; and (4) ecological capital.

Quality of public governance depends on social capital. China has emphasized the importance of reinforcing social construction and governance. The Chinese government takes these concrete targets further: "We should further improve the function and quality of social governance and public service, upgrade the management according to the law and form a comprehensive governance system covering the entire society. We should also pay more attention to exert the effects of self-governance of villagers, community autonomous organizations, social communities and social agents. We should also fully exert the effects of the serving function of the Communist Party, coordinative role of urban-rural autonomous organization and normative role of industrial and social agent organization, and form the composition of forces of social governance and social service."

Socialization Trend of Corporate Governance in the Harmonious World

The Corporation Law of the PRC clearly states that enterprises must meet their social responsibility obligations. The global production system requires businesses to take care of the relationship with their shareholders, challenges the modern company's hierarchical structure and urges a new mode of governance. For these legislative and market requirements, Chinese enterprises must make social responsibility their main content of governance.

Global production systems use "standards" or "norms" as a means of governance for production and management activities. In recent years, Chinese manufacturing companies have participated actively in international norms certification and followed these norms in the production process, such as quality and corporate social responsibility standards. As for sustainable development, international environmental protection standards are much higher than in the Republic. The Chinese government is bringing forward the implementation of the "concept of scientific development" so that Chinese firms have to follow the new international standards.

Since 2005, the EU has implemented a series of technical standards in the production and reuse of finished products. For example, raising the recycle and reuse rate of discarded electronic and electric products; minimizing harmful residues such as plumbum, hydrargyrum and cadmium; strictly limiting the usage of chemicals by industry; designing ecological and energy-conserving products; and minimizing energy waste during production. Chinese companies have done a great deal in order to implement these standards. Thus, a mechanical firm in Zhejiang province was banned from exporting to Germany because of a poisonous printing ink on the symbol of its machine. In order to solve the problem, several printing ink factories began improving their products and finally developed a substitute for the poisonous printing ink. Since then, Zhejiang province has developed technical cooperation between electric firms and painting firms to research and develop innocuous printing materials.

The cooperation between China and the EU is based on mutual benefit. The two sides should coordinate their macroeconomic policies in economic and trade cooperation, as well as cooperate at the technical level in establishing and implementing international standards. China's governance experience may also be relevant for the Eastern European EU members that face similar problems in transforming from planned economies to market economies.

Li Jinshan

20

Developing a Chinese Civil Society

CHINA PERSPECTIVE

Ten years ago, talking about *gongmin shehui* (公民社会 or civil society) was a very sensitive issue. Now, it is a hot discourse among Chinese intellectuals and a very popular term in Chinese academic circles. The English term "civil society" is translated into Chinese by three different terms: *shimin shehui* (市民社会), *gongmin shehui* (公民社会) and *minjian shehui* (民间社会). Although the uses of these terms overlap, their meanings are not completely identical; there are subtle differences among them. The term *shimin shehui* is the one most widely used and is the standard translation for "civil society". Its origin lies in Chinese translations of the classical texts of Marxism. However, in its traditional usage, it has to some degree a negative connotation and many people equate it with the term "bourgeois society". Moreover, it is easy to misinterpret it to mean "urban residents". The earliest use of *minjian shehui* to translate "civil society" was by scholars in Taiwan. This usage was embraced by mainland historians and widely adopted in research on non-governmental organizations in modern China. It has a neutral connotation, but many government officials and scholars feel it conveys the sense of being marginalized. The term *gongmin shehui* was adopted as a translation for "civil society" after the beginning of reform and opening up. It has a positive connotation and emphasizes the political science aspect of the term, i.e., both citizens' participation in public affairs and citizens' restraints on state power. More and more young scholars prefer this term.

We define civil society as being comprised of all civil organizations and civil relations that are outside the state, the government system, the market and the commercial system. It is a civil public sphere outside the spheres of government and the market economy. It is constituted of all kinds of civil organizations not affiliated with the government or businesses, including organizations for safe-guarding citizens' rights, all kinds of trade associations, public interest orga-nizations, community organizations, interest groups, collegial groups, mutual assistance organizations, recreational groups, voluntary organizations and asso-ciations spontaneously created by citizens. Therefore, we can view them as the third sector intermediary between the government and enterprises.

The process of the reform and opening up is a process of fundamental social change in China. One such change is the rise of a relatively independent civil society. The reform with orientation towards market economic system and democratic governance has led to the emergence of civil society organiza-tions (CSOs) in great numbers and civil society with Chinese characteristics is rapidly emerging, whose influence on China's social and political life is deep-ening by the day.

After the CCP came to power in 1949, it implemented socialist public ownership of property and mandatory planned economy in the economic sphere and a highly centralized system of political power under the monolithic leadership of the Party in the political sphere, and it abolished nearly all of the CSOs. At the end of the 1980s, China began reforms to reorient the economic system to the market. It gradually abandoned the former planned economy and introduced a socialist market economy. It also transformed the monolithic system of ownership by collectives and the state to a diverse system that complemented ownership by the state and collectives by various forms of private ownership such as single proprietorship, joint venture and foreign investment. Meanwhile, China's political system also underwent great reforms, many of which either directly or indirectly stimulated the development of civil society. For example, revising the Constitution, separating the Party from the government and the government from business, transforming government functions and placing the country under the rule of law. It has also produced a series of laws, regulations and policies to encourage and standardize CSOs and transformed its attitude toward civil society. All these reforms laid the foundation upon which China's civil society depends.

The above stated changes in the economic and political environment brought about by reform and opening up set off a rapid expansion in CSOs beginning in the late 1980s. By 1989, there were 1,600 national mass orga-nizations and more than 200,000 local ones. After the political turbulence in

Beijing in 1989, the Chinese government required all mass organizations to be reapproved and to re-register. This led to a temporary reduction in their number, and in 1992, there were 1,200 national mass organizations and 180,000 local ones. However, the number soon began climbing again. By 1997, the number of county-level or higher social associations reached 180,000, of which 21,404 were provincial-level and 1,848 were national-level, and in 1998, there were more than 700,000 civilian-run non-enterprise units. It is difficult to get an accurate count of civil organizations because there is a relatively large fluctuation in the number registered. According to the most recent statistics, there were a total of 147,937 social associations of all kinds, 131,322 civilian-run non-enterprise units and 714 foundations in China on 31 March 2005.

There is no official data on CSOs below the county level. A number of scholars have made general estimates of the number based on their own research data. According to some recent investigations, there are at least around three million civil society organizations of all kinds at the different levels across the country. Some scholars have noted that at the end of 2003, China had 142,000 registered social associations, 124,000 registered civilian-run non-enterprise units, 40,000 unregistered social associations and 250,000 unregistered civilian-run non-enterprise units (the numbers for unregistered units are estimates made by officials of the Bureau for Supervising Civil Organizations of the Ministry of Civil Affairs). At that time, there were also estimated to be 5,378,424 primary-level organizations of the eight major types of mass organizations (including trade unions, the Communist Youth League, and women's federations, students' federations, peasants' associations, literary federations, friendship associations and professional associations); 1,338,220 quasi-governmental, primary-level social associations, such as disabled persons' federations, family planning associations, and art and literature federations; and 758,700 grassroots organizations, such as students' groups, community recreational groups, homeowners' committees and Internet groups. Thus, the total number of social associations is estimated to be 8,031,344.

The rise of China's civil society is an important manifestation of China's overall social progress. Our case studies prove that the emergence of civil society exerted a great influence on social politics and economic activities, changing governance to a large extent and effectively promoting good governance in China. It is of particular significance to citizens' political participation, political transparency, government innovations, high quality of public service, citizens' self-governance, government's cleanness and efficiency, and government's democratic and scientific policy-making. It also helps promote the healthy development of the market economy, raise the governing capacity of the CCP and build a harmonious society in China.

One of the big debates on civil society among Chinese intellectuals is whether there is a real civil society in China. A few scholars argue that there is no civil society in China at present in western terms. A real civil society in China does, however, exist because Chinese CSOs as the elements of civil society more or less share the following common features with western ones: non-governmental, non-profit and relatively independent, and voluntary. However, CSOs in China are also quite different from those in the West. Thus, compared with western countries, China's civil society has its own characteristics.

First, China's civil society is led by the government, and it obviously has both official and unofficial aspects. The vast majority of China's CSOs was established by the government and is led by the government, especially the most influential CSOs that are legally registered, such as professional organizations, academic associations and interest groups. Governmental dominance of CSOs has always been a prominent feature of China's civil society. The government-led civil society is manifested in the following three ways. First, government regulations concerning the registration and supervision of CSOs require that when CSOs register, they must affiliate themselves with a Party or government body authorized by the state, which serves as its regulatory body. Second, the vast majority of CSOs that have considerable influence in society were established by the government itself. Third, the central government published a document in 1998 that Party and government officials at the section chief level and above may not have leadership positions in CSOs; however, most of the key leaders of important social associations are people who have retired from leadership positions in the Party or government or transferred to the organizations during restructuring. Fourth, according to government regulations, CSOs should in principle raise money themselves to pay their expenses, but in fact the government appropriates funds to pay for the activities of a number of important NGOs and they are completely economically dependent on it.

Second, China's CSOs are in the process of being formed and have a transitional nature. Compared with their counterparts in western countries, China's CSOs are still very immature, and they are not clearly independent, voluntary and non-governmental, typical characteristics of their western counterparts.

The vast majority of China's CSOs began maturing after the mid-1980s, a period of less than 20 years. They are in the process of change and growth, and neither their structure nor functions have taken a set form. For example, the latest government regulations require all CSOs to separate themselves from the government, yet the government guides their important activities through the government bodies to which they are attached. In addition, a number of CSOs are guided and controlled by the government and are not as independent, voluntary and non-governmental as CSOs need to be; whereas other CSOs are at the other extreme — their formation is completely due to the spontaneous initiative of the people, they are not even registered with government departments, and they receive no leadership or guidance from the government. This kind of transitional nature of CSOs is just one aspect of similar changes taking place throughout the whole of Chinese society and it is the specific manifestation in CSOs of these more general social changes.

Third, in accordance with the above stated characteristics, China's CSOs have not yet been normalized. Although the Ministry of Civil Affairs promulgated revised supervision regulations in the attempt to standardize CSOs in 1998, this standardization process has just begun and has a long way to go. In terms of organizational systems, China presently has at least the following kinds of CSOs: (1) Social associations with high administrative degree, such as trade unions, the Communist Youth League and women's federations; (2) Social organizations with significant administrative functions, such as all kinds of professional supervision associations like associations of commerce and consumers' organizations; (3) Academic associations, which have become essentially unofficial, such as scientific and research associations; and (4) Civilian-run non-enterprise units, which constitute a unique kind of civil organization. They do not have administrative rank and perform few administrative functions. Some of them engage in research and exchanges, and others provide specialized services to society.

Fourth, the development of China's CSOs is very uneven at present, and there are great disparities between the social, political and economic influence of different organizations and their position in society. Among primary-level rural and neighborhood CSOs, those with the greatest influence and prestige are villagers' committees, neighborhood committees, and some community organizations, such as retirees' associations. Organizations that were previously very influential, such as Communist Youth League branches, women's conferences and militia battalions, have lost much of their influence. At the central and provincial levels, the influence of professional, management, charitable, professional and civilian-run non-enterprise units is, in general, growing.

After more than 20 years of development, China's civil society has shown that it is crucial for Chinese democracy, market economy and harmonious society. A new stage has been reached in which many aspects of China's present institutional environment are no longer conducive to its further growth, and some institutional factors have already become a bottleneck restricting its growth, making it necessary to undertake reforms. This should prevent CSOs from becoming adversaries of the government and promote cooperation between CSOs and the government, so that they work together towards a society with democratic governance and harmony.

Yu Keping

EU PERSPECTIVE

There is no general, uniform or single-definition concept or framework of civil society. As Yu Keping correctly argues, the term refers to the domain between the state, the market and the private sphere and is concerned with a public sphere of society autonomous from the state. As the concept was developed in Europe and North America (the "West"), there was and still is a widespread assumption that it is strongly related to democracy and democratic systems. In recent years, western scholars have explicitly challenged this standpoint and argued that on a global scale and due to various historical and sociocultural contexts, not only different and multiple forms of modernity had emerged but also various types of civil society development. Key patterns of such a society — it is argued — could also evolve under different political systems. Accordingly, the question arises whether this concept is also applicable to states like China, where the political sphere is strongly controlled by the party-state.

Yu Keping's paper is organized around three principle issues. First, he defines civil society as "being comprised of all civil organizations and civil relations that are outside the state, the government system, the market and the commercial system" which is "constituted of all kinds of civil organizations"; secondly, he describes the development of social associations and an associational life in China; and thirdly, he argues that in China, civil society development is led by the government.

Since the early 1990s there has been an on-going discussion among western academics on whether the term "civil society" is appropriate with regard to China. So what are the pros and contras of applying the term to countries like China?

The pros are:

- structures of a civil society evolve prior to democratization and not afterwards,
- Chinese scholars have already adopted the term and are arguing with it,
- structural preconditions of a civil society are gradually emerging.

The contras are:

- civil society refers to democratic systems only,
- it requires a separation of state and society which currently does not exist,
- the party-state tightly controls and curbs civil society's development.

As Yu Keping argues, since the 1990s, a broad discourse on civil society and on the application of this concept has arisen. Chinese scholars are intensively debating the features, patterns, conceptions and functions of such a society in the current context of China. We should, therefore, seriously take into account the arguments of Chinese proponents of the civil society concept, even if it could be argued that in the Chinese case, state and society are closely cooperating and do not constitute separate spheres.

Concerning the Chinese discussion, the understanding and perception of the civil society concept differs significantly from western notions. Even its conceptuality is distinct from western concepts. Yu Keping illustrates that the Chinese terms used for civil society are *shimin shehui* referring to the urban sphere only, and *gongmin shehui* which means "society of public people" and focuses upon the responsibility of citizens in terms of public goods and good behavior. It is, therefore, not concerned with the issue of political power. Accordingly, civil society is perceived as a non-confrontative model that should not pose a challenge to the state. This is also related to China's traditional political culture and approach to authority, according to which even a social or politically-motivated organization ought to respect government and seeks to work with it (as opposed so often in the West to working against it).

In China we find strong interweavings between state and society. The party-state, for instance, integrates the existing associations into bargaining processes, though strictly controlling them. It bans associations which apparently attempt to act autonomously from the government. Yet, sociologist Ding Xueliang is right in that via social associations, society infiltrates the party-state and thus initiates processes of change. This Janus-faced nature of associations, which Ding called "institutional amphibiousness", can be seen in the fact that, on the one hand, associations through countless threads are closely connected to party and state structures even to the point of "institutional parasitism" (i.e., their interests and financial means frequently are bound to the party-state), while, on the other hand, party and state institutions can be infiltrated and changed by these associations ("institutional manipulation and conversion"). That party members and cadres are represented in all social institutions finally leads to mutual interweaving and penetration. Ding is right in arguing that the western concept of civil society does not match this dual character, as it is based upon a state-society antagonism and thus is unable to figure out the interconnections between both.

Differences of political systems are not the only reason for the existence of diverging conceptions. China is still in a process of both state- and institution-building. Institutions governing the coexistence of people and providing certainty of expectations are only gradually evolving (for instance, in terms of rationalization, juridification and creating a legal system). There is a strong lack of civilizational competence, i.e., a deficiency of a complex set of rules, norms, values, of a law system, law security and civic liberties. Among people, groups and organizations, there is a lack of respect of law, a distrust *vis-à-vis* authorities, deficiencies in terms of institutionalized rules, and double standards with regards to speaking and conduct. In China's rapidly changing society, new rules of social behavior will have to be learned and internalized. A public sphere which controls the state bodies, a process of "civilizing" the behavior of authorities and citizens has still to emerge. In China, where institution-building is still in progress, the state exerts an overpowering control and subsequently monitors and restricts the activities of its citizens. We can, therefore, not yet speak of the existence of an *autonomous* civil society.

Yet, such a society does not simply emerge right after a successful realization of democratization. Even under authoritarian conditions, a gradual development of civil society structures is feasible and desirable so as to facilitate the evolving of a democracy. Accordingly, what is crucial here is the issue of whether fields are emerging which first are not yet fully autonomous, secondly are not congruent with the party-state, and thirdly out of which nuclei of autonomous social fields beyond that state might occur.

Professor Yu is absolutely right in that social associations and associational life are core characteristics of civil society. Undoubtably, in the past decade we were witnessing a tremendous increase of associations and associational life in China. Yet, as the civil society concept is multidimensional, we have to include further domains in the analysis. Accordingly, four further and crucial fields need to be understood: (a) the rise of a private economy and a private entrepreneurship (in contrast to the dominant state sector until the 1980s); (b) an increase in citizens' participation in the public sphere (individually or collectively, e.g., in villages and urban neighborhood communities); (c) the development of an intellectual debate on political and social issues and problems (among intellectuals, think-tanks, and NGOs and also via the Internet); and (d) the evolving of civilized patterns of individual and group behavior.

Since the 1980s, a private economy and private entrepreneurship have rapidly emerged. Secondly, proto-citizens are gradually emerging (civic culture). Thirdly, both an intellectual debate on social and political issues (discourse culture) and the promoting of a civilized way of behavior towards co-citizens (everyday culture) are gradually developing.

Undoubtedly, as Yu Keping argues, in terms of autonomy, associations and NGOs in China differ from those in western societies. Yet, in a society like China, interconnections and interweavings between social associations and the party-state are helpful as they contribute to solving problems through informal channels and by informal bargaining. The Chinese "bargaining society" in which interests of social groups are negotiated in an indirect way in fact requires such interweavings in order to enforce interests more easily. Concurrently, such half-autonomous associations might function as precursors of genuine autonomous economic and political associations. At the moment, associations have a rather ambiguous character: on the one side, they are subject to the supervision and control of the party-state; on the other side, they may exhibit certain elements of independence as long as this independency does not challenge the party-state.

Furthermore, the significance of the Internet as another field of public space and discourse is constantly growing. In recent years, the Internet has spawned new forms of publicness. Many relevant social and political issues are exhaustively discussed here. Western social scientists have, therefore, argued that the Internet would facilitate and favor the emergence of a civil society.

Undoubtedly, the Internet affects three social fields: the public space, the development of (virtual) social organizations and of Internet social movements. It encourages public debates and the articulation of problems and thus functions as a tool of social transparency. Undoubtedly, in recent years the number of Internet portals with news, up-to-date information and of virtual communities has significantly increased. Particularly, people in urban areas participate in public debates in the public space of the Internet, thus redefining the interrelationship between state and society. The anonymity of the Internet has spawned a new critical public. Proactive users, in China called *wangmin*, cyber-citizens or netizens (deduced from the term *citizen*), take up information on social injustice, hush up local disasters, criminal or corruption cases, provide information on the latter and put it up for discussion. Yet, recent research findings underpin that the Internet does not necessarily develop into a tool of political change. The majority of the *wangmin* do not oppose the political system. We have, therefore, to make a distinction between Internet contributions opposing the political system and those only critical of specific social developments.

In fact, the political leadership has a certain interest that young people adopt a critical attitude and are concerned with social matters. Internet users are primarily younger people with a higher educational level and members of the new middle-classes who are not concerned with a change of the political system, but rather to make the system more efficient — in the sense of good governance.

While the role of society is certainly increasing, the party-state still plays a decisive and paramount role. For instance, with the beginning of the reform process at the end of the 1970s, developed market structures and a strong, proactive and participating society did not yet exist. Therefore in the 1980s and 1990s the state took over the task of creating the institutional frames and preconditions for their development. As entrepreneurs who could have taken over this role did not yet exist, local officials had to fill the function of local developing agents. They established or took over enterprises and thus accomplished entrepreneurial functions. Correspondingly, the party-state created an incentive system. As a result, an entrepreneurship was emerging and thus an enterprise culture. In the 1990s, the party-state established grassroots elections in villages and urban neighborhood communities, thus initiating a rudimentary civic culture. Meanwhile, the administrative bodies of villages and neighborhood communities have to be elected at fixed intervals. The party-state has also established many social associations as well as intellectual think-tanks, thus engendering a discursive culture.

As Yu Keping's analysis has shown, a public sphere beyond the party-state is gradually evolving and therefore initial fields of civil society structures. Yet on the whole, further institutional alterations are necessary so as to convert the current top-down process initiated by the party-state into a bottom-up process. Greater autonomy for associations and interest organizations, the implementation of direct elections in neighborhood communities, increased electoral competition, etc., could certainly conduce to such a conversion.

On the other side, Yu Keping rightly argues that "China's civil society is a typical case of a civil society led by the government". In China, the institutional preconditions for a civil society are widely lacking, and the party-state conceives its role in initiating them. Its intention is to generate the structures of such a society top-down. As mentioned above, Migdal has pointed out that under conditions of both weakly developed structures of a civil society and of a strong state facing a weak society, a state may function as a political architect. Accordingly, the Chinese state is not a "developmental dictatorship" but rather a development agency. The latter requires more than pure authoritarian mechanisms of enforcement, i.e., an increasing involvement of social groups in processes of bargaining with the state, participation in community affairs and a corresponding institutional setting.

It is precisely the combination of mobilized participation and volunteers, the top-down implementation of grassroots elections, the top-down establishing of neighborhood communities so as to establish structures of a (illiberal and controlled) civil society. Yet, already the 1997 *World Development Report* ("The state in a changing world") has underscored that in developing societies, the state has to initiate development processes to function as an activating state. This is exactly what is happening in China.

Clearly, the opportunity to establish social associations or to participate in social issues are not yet markers of a lively civil society in the sense of the western conception. Genuine public spheres between the state and the private sphere have developed only in a limited way. On the other side, the various fields briefly touched upon in the foregoing sections are strongly impacting upon both the party-state and the Chinese society. A public sphere is gradually emerging and, accordingly, elementary structures of a civil society which reinforce society *vis-à-vis* the party-state. Citizens in the sense of western "citoyens" do not yet exist. The principles of legal security, constitutional reality, major prerequisites for a free public space are still strongly underdeveloped. Involvement of major social groups is still constrained by the existence of large socially weak groups on the one side which are primarily concerned with the issue of daily survival; and of socially strong groups (middle stratum) enjoying material wealth and a stronger level of individual autonomy *vis-à-vis* the party-state.

Yet finally, the cases of Japan, South Korea or Taiwan have proved that authoritarian regimes can successfully initiate and accomplish economic and then political modernization, top-down. So why should it be impossible to do the same with civil society? Perhaps China might successfully demonstrate that by enforcing economic modernization, an authoritarian state is capable of engineering civil society structures top-down. The latter could give rise and stimulate bottom-up reactions which could facilitate the emerging and development of a civil society in a not too far-off future.

Thomas Heberer

21

Knowledge, Economic Development and Democracy in China

Knowledge is information or the accumulation of useful human experiences that people are aware of. The role of knowledge in the development of any society is heavily shaped by its historical and cultural conditions. How knowledge is acquired and applied in the development of East Asian societies offers some unique experiences, and this can be discussed from three angles: social, economic and political.

Historical and Social Background

Historically, the social aspects of this relationship are more important. To the extent that China, Japan, Korea, Taiwan, Hong Kong and Singapore share the mainstream Chinese philosophies as manifested in Confucianism, the discussion of knowledge and development in the context of Confucian learning and teaching is the best starting point.

Within the highly humanistic and moralistic Confucian curriculum, knowledge is learning, which means "self-cultivation for one's self", as dictated by *Analects*, *Mencius*, *The Great Learning* and *The Doctrine of the Mean*. But learning is not just for self-serving literary pursuit, because the learned people or the educated class (who comprised a very tiny segment of the population) is understood to carry a larger social responsibility. The Confucian cultural elite or *junzi* (gentleman) is supposed to fulfill his moral obligation to his family first and then work for the state.

241

In other words, self-cultivation is a precondition for regulating the family, which in turn is a necessary condition for governing the state. Ultimately, a good Confucian scholar must also be a successful Mandarin at the service of the Emperor to maintain stability and prosperity in his kingdom. Furthermore, self-cultivation of Confucian ethics will inevitably strengthen one's moral character. He will be at harmony with his fellow human beings, with society and ultimately with nature ("harmony of man with heaven or nature").

Viewed from today's standpoint, Confucianism represents a highly conservative force operating to maintain social stability and the existing political and social status quo. Everybody in the Confucian society is supposed to know his own place in the world, his role, his functions and obligations. There are implicit ethical standards (*li* or etiquette), not codified law, to regulate the behavior of both the common people and the ruling class. The Emperor, too, has to observe certain ethical behavior. He is supposed to rule by moral authority, while the Confucian cultural elite will help him govern the country in order to achieve stability and prosperity. The people have the right to basic needs and expect to be treated in a reasonably decent way as required by the Confucian moral standards. If the Emperor should neglect his duties as a ruler and make his subjects too miserable, his Mandate from Heaven would be withdrawn and the people would have the right to rebel.

It is sufficiently clear that under the Confucian order, knowledge is basically created for and by the ruling elites. In China, however, the rise of the ruling elite is not always by birth, but sometimes by merit. A bright peasant's son can acquire the Confucian learning to become an official, hence joining the ruling elite. Such is a form of upward social mobility in old China. Knowledge plays an important role in economic and social development, especially in terms of providing basic needs to the common people. But knowledge is also applied to maintain political and social stability, i.e., for the status quo. There is limited democracy in the old system. But then, this also helps explain the unique continuity or the long lasting of the Chinese civilization through the centuries.

Economic Aspects

Under the impact of western intrusion in the 19th century, East Asian societies started to respond to the challenges of economic modernization, first in Japan in the late 19th century and then in the four East Asian societies of Korea,

Taiwan, Hong Kong and Singapore in the later part of the 20th century. Suddenly, the world was shown that a Confucian society is also capable of initiating industrialization. Much like the "Protestant ethic" as portrayed by Max Weber, many aspects of the Confucian ethic could provide the right value orientation and attitude for modern industrialism.

Most East Asian economies are land scarce and resource poor, with their economic growth largely the result of intensification of their human resources. Confucian values, in holding education and learning at high social esteem, have undoubtedly contributed a great deal towards human capital formation in East Asia, most critical for successful economic development. It is widely recognized that on account of their great penchant for learning and skills upgrading, East Asian societies have all along been highly successful in education and manpower development, particularly compared to many developed countries elsewhere. In short, East Asia offers one of the best examples of successful application of knowledge for economic development.

Economic Development in East Asia

Historically speaking, the East Asian growth process is marked by three waves. Japan was the first non-western Asian country to become industrialized. Its high growth, at double or near-double digit rates, dated back to the 1950s after it had achieved rapid post-war recovery, and the growth momentum was carried over to the 1960s and much of the 1970s.

Japan's economic growth engine was initially based on the export of labor-intensive manufactured products; but it was soon forced by rising wages and increasing costs to shed its comparative advantage for labor-intensive manufacturing in favor of the four NIEs (newly industrialized economies) of South Korea, Hong Kong, Taiwan and Singapore, which started their industrial takeoff in the 1960s. These four NIEs, once dubbed "Asia's Four Little Dragons", were arguably the most dynamic economies in Asia, as they had sustained near-double digit rates of growth for more than three decades, from the early 1960s to the 1980s. The rise of the NIEs constituted the second wave of the East Asian region's growth and integration.

By the early 1980s, high costs and high wages had also caught up with these four NIEs, which had to restructure their economies towards more capital-intensive and higher value-added activities by passing their comparative advantage in labor-intensive products to the latecomers of China and the four ASEAN economies of Indonesia, Malaysia, the Philippines and Thailand, thereby spreading economic growth to the latter. In this way, China and some ASEAN economies were able to register high growth through the 1980s and the 1990s. Many Japanese scholars used to depict this pattern of development in Asia as the "Flying Geese" model, which still provides a highly intuitive explanation for the East Asian development process, albeit with a lot of oversimplications.

Development First, Democracy Later

One distinctive characteristic of the East Asian development process, from the political angle, is its sequence of "economic development first, democratization later". The Confucian ethic, highly worldly and practical in nature, has shaped a pragmatic outlook for the East Asian governments and people. Thus initially, East Asian societies had all mobilized their institutional and human resources for their single-minded pursuit of economic growth. Knowledge was to serve purely GDP growth first, but not political development like democratization, which was to come later.

Broadly speaking, East Asian political development has, interestingly, also followed a broadly similar "flying geese" model, with Japan taking the lead in democratization. This was later followed by the NIEs of South Korea, Taiwan and Singapore — Hong Kong is excluded here because it used to be a British colony and is now a special administrative region of China — and still later by some ASEAN countries like the Philippines and Thailand. More importantly, all these economies started to open up their political systems after, but not before, their industrial takeoff. Such is the theory of "development first, democratization later". How do we explain this?

To begin with, East Asia's dynamic economic growth can be adequately explained by the standard neoclassical economic theory. East Asian economies have consistently chalked up high rates of economic growth, simply because their high GDP growth has all along been the direct result of their high levels of high investment matched by their high savings. Political democracy or lack of it has little to do with East Asian economic growth.

In fact, development economists have long been arguing that political democracy, whilst desirable on its own, is actually not an essential precondition for successful industrialization, and not even crucial for rapid economic growth. Historically, successful economic development has taken place under almost all sorts of political regimes, be they truly democratic or not. Beyond the basic political and social stability, what is really needed for economic development is an effective and enlightened political leadership which can galvanize consensus and mobilize all resources for the single-minded pursuit of economic growth. Good government and good policy are, in fact, more relevant for economic development, while a pseudo-democracy or a half-baked democracy may not be conducive to economic development. One can find numerous Third World countries as examples of this phenomenon.

Economic growth is measured by increases in GDP. Any political and social system which can generate more GDP and create more wealth by increasing production, consumption, investment and exports is good for growth. Not surprisingly, many democratization experiments in the Third World have turned out to be "anti-growth" or just "growth-unfriendly", especially in the short-run. Too much politics can actually hurt the investment climate. Overcontentious election campaigns can disrupt production and hence reduce GDP. The call for greater workers' rights can frighten away foreign investors. Advocacy for more equal income distribution can reduce or slow capital accumulation. In short, there can be unacceptable economic tradeoffs in terms of poor economic performance for a developing economy rushing into a full-fledged liberal democracy.

It is to be remembered that in the East Asian context, Japan's industrialization occurred before World War II when Japan was under an aggressive military dictatorship. More recently, South Korea's industrial takeoff took place also under a military dictatorship, while Taiwan's was under the martial law. Hong Kong's industrialization occurred under a colonial rule with no political democracy whatsoever. For years, only Singapore had operated a one-man one-vote parliamentary system. But some western scholars would label Singapore's system as a form of illiberal democracy because of its one-party domination.

The Philippine case can even end up as a counter-argument. The Philippines' economic growth had actually plunged and remained at low levels after it toppled Marcos through "People's Power" and achieved the so-called democracy! In the Philippines (as in many other developing countries), corruption was rampant before democracy. After democratization, corruption is still rampant. If anything, such a nominal form of democracy offers a fertile ground for new patterns of corruption such as rent seeking and pork barrel politics or vote buying. The same is true of Indonesia, whose economic growth plunged after the emergence of democracy in the post-Suharto era.

Democracy After Successful Development

While the implications of the foregoing arguments, based on the East Asian development experience, show no direct relations between political democracy and economic development, they nonetheless strongly suggest that the democratization process follows closely at the heels of economic development. In other words, all successful economies will, in time to come, become politically democratic. Once they have achieved their economic takeoff, domestic political forces and social changes will be fast at work to push the country towards a more democratic system. The reasons are very simple. Successful economic growth, in bringing about a general rise in incomes, will also bring about the rise of the middle-class, who will demand a greater say in social policy as well as the political process. And that is the very seed of democracy. Therefore, it is just a matter of time and a matter of sequence. Every country will get there, first economically and then politically.

Once these East Asian economies had taken off into self-sustained growth, political and social conditions surfaced to bring about a smooth transition to political liberalization and democracy: Japan in the 1950s, Korea and Taiwan in the late 1980s, and Hong Kong after 1997. In other words, knowledge will first be used to promote economic growth and create wealth, and later for political and social transformation.

The China Case

The Chinese pattern of economic development and political reform can also fit in quite well with the East Asian model of economic and political development. Deng Xiaoping (who started economic reform and opened up China to the outside in 1978) firmly believed that it would be plainly unrealistic for a big and diverse country like China at its early stages of development to take to such drastic political transformation as instituting a western-style liberal democratization. This could simply bring more disorder (*luan*) to China.

Today, China's economic reform and development has been highly success-ful because it has been carried out gradually, step by step. Such is the "reform and development with Chinese characteristics". China's political reform, on many indications, is now also being carried out gradually and experimentally. Can we be equally optimistic about the successful outcome of such "democ-ratization with Chinese characteristics" any time soon?

Looking from the outside, one can identify at least three favorable precon-ditions for China to move faster towards greater liberal democracy. First, the Chinese economy today without doubt has achieved successful takeoff, and its growth is sustainable. With its per capita GNP now over US$1,700, China has fulfilled its broad development goals of providing basic needs for its people and significantly reducing poverty — i.e., moving towards what the Chinese government called the *Xiao-kang* society. This is by no means a small achieve-ment for the Chinese leadership, which has really earned its well-deserved eco-nomic legitimacy. Hence, we can see in China an increasingly confident and adaptive political leadership. This should provide optimism for greater politi-cal reform in the near future.

Secondly, China at its present stage of development is actually facing many political and social challenges from rising income and regional disparities to rampant corruption and rent-seeking activities. To be sure, many of these problems are the by-products of fast economic growth and successful mar-ket reforms. With further economic growth, many of these problems can be resolved or alleviated. But a more pluralistic political system and a more open society can certainly help the government to cope with these problems. The Chinese leadership will sooner or later come to realize this and move ahead with faster political reform. Hence, another ground for optimism.

Third, on account of globalization and the information revolution, knowl-edge is being transmitted and transferred much faster. Knowledge today has become a much more powerful force, not merely for economic development and social change, but also for political transformation of societies. News and information spread fast in this IT age. People can quickly learn and easily get inspired by what others are doing or how they are behaving. It is well-nigh impossible for any country to operate an open economy within a closed society.

There is therefore strong ground for optimism that China will eventually be democratized, albeit slowly and gradually at first. In response to the demand for greater political and social liberalization, the Chinese Communist Party has started to introduce "intra-party democracy" and local elections. The latest breakthrough in this direction was the open declaration by President Hu Jintao during his visit to Washington (April 2006) that "without democracy, there would be no modernization".

East Asia has experienced remarkable economic revolutions, and is about to accomplish equally successful political revolutions. By then, a great deal of East Asian uniqueness would be no longer unique, but universalized. Increasingly, under the powerful growth of knowledge (information), we find ourselves all living essentially in one world. As knowledge in this IT age is becoming universal, the end products of knowledge application cannot be particularistic or East-Asia specific.

John Wong

22

Promoting Mutual Understanding

CHINA PERSPECTIVE

Introduction

The joint statement of the Helsinki EU-China Summit in September 2006 reaffirmed the intention since 2003 to build a "strategic partnership" and took a step further in declaring that: "In order to reflect the full breadth and depth of today's comprehensive strategic partnership between the EU and China, the two sides agreed to launch negotiations on a new Partnership and Cooperation Agreement which will encompass the full scope of their bilateral relations, including enhanced cooperation in political matters."

We may still have to wait for the new agreement to see what this "comprehensive strategic partnership" will actually encompass, but common sense suggests that a strategic partnership denotes a relationship which is long-term and stable, comprehensive and not casual or convenient, honored and committed by the parties, and, above all, based on mutual interests and shared values. If this generalization is acceptable, then the big question is: do the EU and China between them share common interests and values? And if they do, to what extent?

It does seem that, after 30 years of formal relations and with the recent rapid developments, this question is not altogether solved and there are still doubts and scepticism among politicians, academics, functionaries, businessmen and ordinary people alike, as to the existence of common interests. This paper argues that to build a true EU-China strategic partnership, there is still the preeminent need first to deepen each party's understanding of the other, so as to base the relationship on mutual trust. It will attempt to provide a Chinese perspective on some salient questions concerning EU-China relations where misunderstandings exist and often lead to arguments and disputes. The views presented here are, however, personal, based on the author's own experience and observations from years of studying EU-China relations.

How Mutual are the Benefits from EU-China Economic Relations?

After 30 years of development, the trade and economic ties between the EU and China are now very close and of a very high order. In terms of trade, the volume increased more than 70-fold between 1975 and 2004. The EU is now China's number one trade partner, taking up some 16.3% of its total foreign trade in 2005, while China has become the EU's number two trade partner, taking up 9.4% of the latter's total foreign trade, next only to the US. In parallel to the increase in the EU's exports to China, of which exports of goods increased 100% during the period between 2000 and 2005, and exports of services expanded six times between 2000 and 2004, its investment flows have also increased considerably. In 2004, the EU's total FDI in China reached $35 billion, ranking third after the US and Japan. In technology transfer, the EU is by far China's most important partner, surpassing both Japan and the US in terms of value and growth rate, standing at $5.5 billion and with a growth of 63.3% in 2004. Another factor is the exchange of visitors. According to the statistics of the Chinese National Bureau of Tourism, China received in 2005 more than 20 million visitors from the 10 EU member states monitored.

Over and above these rapid developments are the great potentials for the future. China is now the world's largest developing economy, ranking fourth in terms of GDP volume in 2005. Although its share in the world total — 5% — is not that large, its growth rate is among the fastest, with an average annual rate of 9.5% during the period between 1978 and 2005, much higher than the world average of 3.3% during the same period. The sheer size and rapid growth of its economy, the great potential because of its relative under-development, and the sustained political and social stability have made it the hottest spot for international trade and investment. A recent report in the *Financial Times* points out that China now ranks as the world's seventh largest retail market, with an average growth rate of 13% during the past 10 years, and its total sales will probably reach $596 billion in 2010 from the current $430 billion. It is further estimated that in 2025, around 520 million of the

Chinese population will reach an annual income level of RMB40–100,000, with a total annual disposable income of RMB13,300 billion (about $1,700 billion at the current exchange rate). The EU, as the world's largest trading and economic bloc relying heavily on international inflows and outlets for its growth and development, certainly could not stand to lose the opportunities its economic cooperation with China offer. The enlarged EU is likewise a great attraction to China's expanding economy, especially because of its high dependence on foreign trade and investment.

Of the economic ties between China and the EU, it could well be said that they have reached a state of interdependence, at which neither could probably do without the other. China's great stakes in this relationship are all too evident, as it depends on its economic cooperation with the EU and its member states for a considerable part of its GDP growth, foreign trade, employment, science and technology advancement, development aids, etc., and therefore, social welfare. To Europe, China is not just a source of cheap goods, contributing to keeping the consumer prices and production costs lower, and to maintaining employment. It is also an important outlet for EU exports. These, together with the EU's growing investment in China, contributed greatly to the advancement of general social and economic welfare, including employment in the EU, and to its economic structural adjustment and improvement.

Their mutual economic interests also have an international dimension. Whether we like it or not, economic globalization is an inevitable process. It is the making of science and technology advancement and economic development. When in a twirl of a minuet, huge amounts of capital can be transferred to the other end of the world for transactions just concluded through computers, and when outsourcing, a company does not need to build a workshop or factory anymore to take advantage of local resources and markets. Economic operations are truly running beyond national boundaries, and have to be planned and carried out in a global context.

In macroeconomic terms, the marked acceleration of production and economic factors brought about by globalization entails competition at international level, worldwide reallocation of resources and shortened business cycles — just to mention some of them — which every economy has to reckon with seriously. In this process, "comparative advantage" seems more relevant than before. Either a single firm or an individual industry or a national economy as a whole, has to develop its strengths to the full to take its place in the "industrial chain" and try to move upwards along the chain. Here, overprotection, or what is called "economic nationalism", has the effect of protecting underdevelopment and backwardness, and is therefore to no avail.

This kind of transition is essential to the EU economy at the moment. If we look back at the last decade starting from 1995, its economic performance record does not seem to be that good in comparison with the world economy in general and with the US economy in particular. The two symptoms have been sluggish growth and high unemployment, but behind them is the drop in productivity, and therefore the lag in competitiveness.

Various factors contributed to produce this drop in productivity and competitiveness. There were macroeconomic policy factors, institutional factors and even social-economic model factors, but there were also very important ones coming from the EU's current economic structure.

It does seem that the current EU economic structure based on manufacturing industries developed during the post-war boom years during the 1950s and 1960s is now somewhat obsolete, and more importantly, the EU economy is lagging behind in the transition towards a knowledge economy and information society: in other words, the EU has failed to upgrade its economy along the "industrial chain". This accounts for its relatively bad economic performance against the US economy. Within the EU, we have examples, too. All those better performers, like Sweden, Finland, Ireland and the UK, are ones that have succeeded in climbing up on the ladder. This is just what the EU's "Lisbon Agenda" is driving at.

In climbing up this industrial chain, the EU and China have common stakes and could and should work together. So far, China has been quite a success story in the economic globalization process. By taking an active part in international competition, it has achieved tremendous economic progress in the past 20 or so years, especially after its access into the WTO in 2001, but the question remains: can China rely forever on its labor cost advantage? The intelligent reply is no; it might still enjoy this advantage for another five to ten years, but only if it adopts sensible adjustment policies to upgrade its economic structure as well. China is faced with a series of serious bottlenecks in its development, and can only hope to overcome them through taking part in the globalization process and through developing its relations with the outside world, the EU included.

The EU and China are still on different steps of the ladder, which makes their economies more complementary than competitive. In the face of the challenges of economic globalization, there is a strong case to realize a win-win game in the upgrade of their respective economies through economic cooperation and transfer.

And more than that, they also have the common responsibility to address the negative effects of globalization, which have been part of the root causes for much of the present international disturbance and insecurity. Issues like trade, finance, energy, poverty, epidemic diseases, pollution and climate, are better, or have to be, tackled at multilateral and international levels. As two important international entities, China and the EU share stakes and responsibilities and it would be better for them to work closely together.

Notwithstanding all these common interests, there have come to the fore some issues of concern in recent years. Chief among them is the increasing trade imbalance. In parallel to the increase of trade volume, the EU's trade deficit is rising as well, going up to € 106 billion in 2005 according to EURO-STAT. From an economic point of view, the trade deficit between two countries or regions is the result of market forces, and it is not alarming if a country or region maintains a general balance between exports and imports, just as the EU usually does. And just as a recent Commission document ("Policy Paper on EU-China Trade and Investment: Competition and Partnership") points out, the rise in China's exports to the EU is the function of their replacement of EU's imports from other Asian countries. In other words, if the EU did not import these goods from China, it would import them from other Asian countries anyway. There is still another side to the story. It is estimated that more than half of the recent increase of China's exports was created by foreign firms established in China. In this way, a large share of China's trade surplus might not actually be in China's pocket. Or to put it another way, the EU's trade deficit is partly compensated by the returns on EU firms' investment in China. The fourth point is that the current deficit could be reduced considerably, if the EU were more liberal in exporting high technology products to China, as these are of much higher value than China's manufactured goods.

A further concern is that cheap Chinese exports in the EU market are driving EU firms into bankruptcy and EU workers out of their jobs. An accusation like this is okay for creating a headline in the press, but is misleading for policy consideration. First, at this stage of economic globalization, there is simply no way of ruling out competition.

Neither a national economy nor an industry nor a single firm can avoid global competition; either it survives by braving the competition, or it loses — that is the hard law of economics. Second, in such traditional industries as textile, shoemaking, machinery, etc., the EU will never be competitive again against China, Vietnam, India and other developing economies. It is understandable for the EU to protect these industries for social reasons, but from an economic point of view, such protection is, in the final analysis, protecting inefficiency and backwardness. A more positive policy would be to use the money to create new industries and hence, new jobs. This structural transformation or economic upgrading may be just what the EU economy needs most at the moment, and what is behind the success story of a number of EU member states, such as Finland, Ireland and Sweden. The EU and China are still at very different stages of economic development; their economies are more complementary than competitive; and the theories of intra-industrial trade teach us that even among the competing economies, great scope still exists for trade and investment cooperation.

What are the Common Political Interests between EU and China?

If the common economic interests between the EU and China are apparent and generally acknowledged, common political interests between them are far less perceived and accepted. There is a serious doubt that the EU and China can be political allies, even though they might not necessarily become political foes or rivals. This doubt is mainly based on the perception of the political differences between the two.

It is true that EU and China have different political beliefs and adopt different political systems, but does that prevent the two from sharing common political interests, or from working together towards some common political goals?

First of all, both China and the EU need a peaceful international and regional environment. China had been the most developed economy until the 13th century, but was reduced to one of the poorest in the world afterwards. It is only after the late 1970s that China was able to concentrate on economic development. Too much of its time has been lost and despite its recent rapid growths, it is still very much underdeveloped with a GDP per capita of only 5% of the EU's average in 2004, and with dozens of millions of its people still struggling to make a bare living. To recover its world status, China needs to double and double again its GDP to be "comparatively well-off" by the middle of the century. To fulfill this modest goal, it has yet to break through a long list of bottlenecks. But the prerequisite is a peaceful international and regional environment, and domestic political, social and economic stability, so that all attention and resources can be focused on modernization.

The EU is likewise in need of such an environment. It has achieved tremendously along the integration process in the past 20 or so years, first with the single market, then the economic and monetary union, and now the new enlargements. It needs time to consolidate the past achievements and to plan for the future, especially to build up an international political identity, and to modernize its economic structure and, perhaps, also its social model, in order to live up to its people's expectations and faith in the integration process.

The need for international and regional peace and security is not just rhetoric. With the end of the Cold War came the end of the massive nuclear confrontation, but it is now evident that the world has not become safer or more peaceful because of that. In the past one and half decades, there have been more local wars and military conflicts than before, and new forms of threats to security like international terrorism and nuclear proliferation have arisen. There are other issues with serious security implications such as drug trafficking, arms smuggling, illegal immigration and economic fraud, as well as questions of energy, food, economy, finance, transportation, communication, medical and ecological safety, which are now all of international dimensions, and cannot possibly be addressed and solved through conventional means and at the national level.

The EU and China both believe that current threats to international peace and security, whether in the form of economic, cultural, religious or ethnic conflicts, or of terrorist activities and local wars, are the results of glaringly uneven development, which has to be addressed through international institutions and mechanisms and by international law. So, they really need to work together for their common concerns and stakes.

Technology developments have made today's world virtually a "small village". When nuclear technology is no longer an exclusive secret of a few countries, when terrorist activities have increasingly assumed an international dimension, and when incidents like the bankruptcy of a single bank can induce an international financial crisis, the countries of the world are now actually sharing a common destiny. The EU and China, as two important international entities and actors, cannot escape the political realities and their international responsibilities, and differences in political beliefs and systems should not be a barrier between them in their shared aspirations and responsibility for peace and development.

Much of the European misunderstanding of China concerns China's peaceful intentions. As was mentioned above, the old ideological shadows still hang over the China-EU bilateral relationship and these seem very hard to disperse. An interesting example is the arms embargo, a political sanction the EU imposed on China after the Tiananmen incident in 1989. It is a past story and of little actual effect. When the lifting of this embargo was first brought up in 2004, China welcomed it as an act to normalize their bilateral relations, because it is really an irony for the two parties to talk about building a strategic partnership between them, while one is still imposing a political sanction on the other. Then came the fuss over China's military build-up, the threat to peace across the Taiwan strait, the human rights situation in China, and so on, as if the lifting of the embargo would release a monster in China that would bring to an end peace in the world.

People tend to forget a simple logic: armament trade is a two-party business; even if China would want to buy arms from Europe, the latter could still refuse to sell. If there is a fear that after the lifting of the ban there will be no control of arms trade between the EU and China, then one should not condemn China for the incapability of the EU institutions or the European national governments, nor should it be an excuse for not normalizing bilateral relations. On the other hand, China is such a big country, could anyone with common sense believe that it would depend on imported armaments from Europe to build up its defense capabilities?

As for the Taiwan issue, were China determined to realize its unification through military means, considering the comparative military strengths across the strait, it could well do it without the armaments from Europe; and it does not seem that the US and its allies could afford to enter a full-scale war with China over Taiwan, or that China would be daunted by such intervention. But China has refrained from doing so and has declared repeatedly that it would avoid doing so by all means, because it realizes fully the disastrous consequences it would bring about: the devastation of millions of lives of the people across the strait, who are kin; the destruction of China's achievements in the past decades through reform and opening-up; and it would mean the loss of peace and stability in the region and in the world. China's policy over Taiwan shows that it is rational and responsible as an international actor. The baseline is no secession of Taiwan. The EU and the international community can contribute to a peaceful solution by not encouraging the secessionist tendency of the current Taiwanese government. Keeping the status quo and left to themselves, the people across the strait should be able, if not in this generation then in the next generations, to find a settlement satisfactory to both sides and to the international community. The increased across-strait economic and cultural exchanges (in the Shanghai region alone there are now more than 400,000 Taiwanese businessmen with their families) and communications will certainly contribute greatly towards this end. So, talk that lifting the arms embargo will disturb the military balance and therefore increase the threat of war across the strait is ill-founded.

It might be a bit naïve on China's side to have thought that the arms embargo issue could be easily solved when it was first raised in 2004. All the subsequent happenings have taught China a lesson that the so-called European common foreign and security policy is still very far away, nor is the EU ready or able to resist political pressures from the US and others. Now that it understands the difficulties and the twists, China will have the patience to wait. After all, except as a political irony, the arms embargo is of little effect.

The arguments raised around the arms embargo issue show that there is still a kind of distrust in the EU of China's peaceful intentions. By nature, China has never been a bellicose nation, neither posing a threat to any country, nor having the intention or the capability of gaining international or regional hegemony. People will find, if they look at the historical maps, that its territorial space shrunk greatly between the 16th and 19th centuries. In the past two centuries, China has repeatedly suffered from foreign military invasions and interventions; and during World War II, China fought eight hard years against military occupation by a neighboring country, at the cost of 30 million lives. It is because of this painful past that China cherishes its hard-won national independence and sovereignty more than anything else.

China has a territorial area of 9.6 million km^2, which is larger than both the whole of Europe and the US, and with a land border stretching over

20,000 km and a coastline nearly as long. It is justified to maintain a reasonable level of defense capability. China is often accused of increasing its military spending (15.36% on average between 1990 and 2005), but few seem to notice that its percentage in the total national budget is only 7.29% in 2005 as compared to 9.51% in 1994. In 2005, its defense budget ($30.6 billion) was only one-sixteenth of that of the US ($495 billion) and even less than non-military Japan ($45.4 billion) and Germany ($31.1 billion). And of this amount, one-third was spent on improving the living of its officers and men, the number of which stands at about 2.3 million, after several reductions in recent years. China's yearly military spending in 2005 was only $1,332 per military man compared with $35,661 for the US.

Another accusation often heard against China is that its military spending is not transparent enough, much of the spending is not included, and the actual defense budget could be twice or thrice the announced figure. There is no telling on what this guess is based, but the question is: is China that different from other countries in this respect? And even if China's defense budget were thrice of the current figure, it could still be a very small fraction of the US'. So, why should the modest increase in China's military spending cause such concerns and even alarms, whereas no one has ever challenged the soaring military spending of the US? If the US military build-up is not for war, why should China's necessarily be so? It does seem that the problem is apparently with sentiment, not with reason. Times have changed, and the European integration experience has taught us that what could not be achieved by means of war, could be better achieved through national reconciliation and cooperation, but unfortunately some people's minds still refuse to change.

China is now among the major nuclear powers. But ever since it exploded its first atomic bomb in 1964, it has been repeatedly declaring that: (1) it will not use its nuclear weapons in the first instance; (2) it will not use them against any non-nuclear countries; and (3) it is for total nuclear disarmament amongst all nuclear powers. This is peaceful intention, and no other nuclear power has made a similar declaration.

The arms embargo issue does show that there is still a political and ideological barrier between EU and China. If misunderstanding in this respect could be overcome, EU-China political cooperation will have a much broader basis.

Do EU and China Share Common Values?

In relation to a China-EU partnership, many people think there is one weak or missing link, that is, common values. To them, with its Communist background and its insistence on socialism, China is synonymous with totalitarianism and therefore belongs to, in their hearts if not in their words, the camp of "evil forces", and has no respect for human values. Nothing could be more wrong. The socialism China is now seeking — a better balance between economic efficiency and social equity — originates from Europe and is better achieved in Europe than anywhere else. Just as we know that the present capitalism in Europe is no longer the capitalism of when Karl Marx wrote "The Capital", and as described in the novels of Charles Dickens, Victor Hugo and Thomas Hardy, the socialism in China today is neither the socialism of Stalin's time or that of Mao Zedong's time.

In talking about common values between the EU and China, the most apparent one is market economy. It took a few decades and several national political debates for China to adapt to this value and economic system. Ever since China began its reform and opening-up in the late 1970s, market economy has always been the central theme, and no one would doubt that after 25 years this value is now deep-rooted in the Chinese economy, even though it is still very much in transformation. To China, which practised a planned economy after the Soviet Union's model for 30 years, the return to market economy is not just the institution of an economic system, but entails also profound political and legal reforms and a change in the pattern of life. A recent example is the passing of the Property Law by the National People's Congress after several years' heated debates. This law marks a very significant step forward towards the transformation to market economy in proclaiming, for the first time, that private property is protected by Chinese law as much as public property. China paid a much higher price in comparison to other developing countries for joining the WTO, and one of its strong political motivations is to ensure that there is no going back from the market economy.

What about democracy? Democracy is not in the traditional Chinese culture, and China had been under feudalistic rule for thousands of years until the beginning of the 20th century. The present Chinese political system is quite different from the social democracy practised in Europe, and is admittedly not as democratic as it should be. But that does not mean that China is against democracy or that there is no democracy in China. China's political life is much more democratic now than it has ever been in its history. There is much more free speech, and nearly every government policy move stimulates people's discussion and comments in the press and on the internet. Decision-making is, likewise, more transparent and usually coupled with public debates and hearings. In this way, a legislative proposal often involves several rounds of revision before it is voted. The current problem of democracy in decision-making is not so much with the public participation, but rather with the public monitoring of policy execution. The present Chinese political system may be far from perfect yet, but it should be looked at from another perspective: it might be just what China needs, or can have, at this juncture of economic, political and social transition.

European social democracy has its well-proven merits, but it is also the result from several centuries of social and political development and reform with blood and deaths. It is so well-established in Europe that the people take it for granted and accept it as part of their lives. But to a country like China, democracy needs a process of learning and practising. And it does not mean that the European social democracy or any other democracy is the best and suits everywhere. The essence of democracy is faith in the people. Democracy cannot be imposed or imported, and has to grow by itself and through people's own choice. If we believe democracy will be the final human destination, the world and Europe should have faith in the Chinese people and patience: they will be able to find and choose what kind of political system and institution suits them the best.

The concept of human rights and respect for fundamental freedoms is also comparatively new in China. In the past few decades after the founding of the new People's Republic in 1949, China emphasized "collectivism" rather than individualism. For instance, 10 or 15 years ago, Chinese traffic rules still gave priority to cars and trucks rather than to pedestrians on the basis that the former were doing public good. Admittedly, the human rights situation in China is not that good yet and a lot of bad practices and instances in violation of basic human rights can still be found in daily life. But it should be pointed out that the human rights situation in China is not particularly bad compared with other developing countries. While this should not be used as an excuse, it does imply that the practice of human rights, just as of democracy, has to be based on economic development and education. The important thing is that the human rights situation in China has been improving rapidly in recent years, as is witnessed by the passing of many related legal acts. China has been emphasizing the right to exist, not without reason. When there are still millions and millions of people who could still not make a basic living, how much room is there to talk about human dignity or equality? And what right is more humane and important than their very existence? China's "one-child" policy is often criticized as inhumane, too. But from a Chinese perspective, when and where poverty still exists, it might be much more humane to give a better existence to the living than to the unborn. Another criticism is that China has not yet ratified the international convention on political rights. China is cautious in this respect, as it involves the amending of the Constitution on the one hand, and there is the concern for domestic stability on the other. The concepts of human rights and fundamental freedoms have been in the American Constitution ever since its founding, but a national civil war had not been enough to solve the problem, and after nearly 200 years, black people were still not allowed to sit in the same carriage as white people in the southern states in the early 1960s. So, allow some more time for China to catch up in this respect, too, and it will definitely not need 200 years to solve its human rights problems if the current progress could be kept.

Another important value in question is the rule of law. This is also not in the Chinese historical and cultural tradition, and it is an area where China has had to start from the very beginning and with great effort. Looking at the law-making records at the national and provisional levels, you will be amazed to find so many laws have been erected or revised in China in recent years. The process of legal modernization is far less conspicuous than economic modernization, but it constitutes a very important part of the total reform in China. The problem with the rule of law in China is also not that China is against it, or even that it is in lack of laws and regulations of the sort, but rather with their enforcement, which at the moment has to depend very much on the people's education on and acceptance of rule of law. Maybe because China had been under the feudalistic rule for so long, in social life there is still the habit of needing someone to give the final word. That habit does in a way impede the rule of law.

The Cold War has ended, but unfortunately China is still very often judged by the Cold War mentality. The world has changed tremendously in the past century. When China reopened its doors to the world, we came to realize that the outside world was very different from what we had believed to be. The same should be true that with its reform and opening-up, China is also no longer the country that it was.

How to Improve EU-China Mutual Understanding

There is still a need to improve EU-China mutual understanding so that their partnership is based on better mutual trust. Misunderstanding comes more from the EU side than from the Chinese side. Most Chinese people may be still quite ignorant of what is taking place in Europe, but they generally have no bad feelings or prejudices towards Europe. The case in Europe, however, is different, and distorted allegories and assertions are often heard, for instance: "The Chinese government is turning Tibet into an area for prostitution"; "It adopts a forced migration policy in Xinjiang to drive the local minorities abroad"; "It is increasing military spending irrespective of the people's poor living conditions"; "It tries to develop its economy at the costs of biological equilibrium and by transferring pollution abroad"; "It violates the WTO rules to rob the world markets"; "It indulges in the violation of the intellectual property rights"; "It abuses the exchange rate advantage of its currency to dump on US and European markets and to drive the local workers out of their jobs"; "It indulges intentionally on pirate production in violation of the intellectual property rights"; "Its efforts for economic development is to replace the US and Japan and to get Asian and world hegemony".

Whereas misunderstanding is more on the European side, the cause may be more on the Chinese side: it is a failure of China's foreign policy not to create a better image. With one-sixteenth of the world's arable land, China has managed to feed one-fifth of the world population and contributed three-fourths of the world's recent reduction in poverty population. An economically prosperous and politically stable China is indeed a great asset to world peace and development, but unfortunately the world's increased attention to China is still often accompanied by a distorted image. China has done more than a developing country's share in its recent move to increase cooperation with African countries, where it is very positively welcomed. But there are many accusations that it is selfishly motivated and even neocolonialist. This example shows the awkward dilemma China now encounters. On the one hand, there are voices asking China to shoulder its international responsibilities, but on the other hand, all its moves in that direction tend to attract some sort of suspicion.

China should learn from the EU and set about improving China's image in Europe as one of the objectives of its EU policy, and to take serious measures to make China better understood in Europe. It could begin with diffusing information on China. Because of the language barrier, China will have to translate into European languages serious works that give true pictures of the changing China. Nearly all of the books on China published in English have not been written by home authors. We should also promote academic and cultural exchanges. China's Education Ministry has made a good start by supporting cooperation between foreign and Chinese universities to set up "Kongzhi Colleges" (Confucius Institutes) abroad. While it is good to encourage the learning of the Chinese language, emphasis should be put on modern China studies. Shanghai hosted the "World Forum on China Studies" in 2004 and 2006, when 200 or 300 foreign scholars gathered together to discuss in different panels questions concerning China. The exchanges are valuable but the links thus created are even more valuable.

Conclusion

Although both the EU and China have repeatedly confirmed their intention to build between them a strategic partnership, doubts and scepticism still persist. Such a partnership is necessary and new circumstances have made it more relevant and extended its scope. On the other hand, much still has to be done for the building of a true strategic partnership.

To conclude, we should be content with the improvement in EU-China mutual understanding. There are still misunderstandings, but that is natural, and after 30 years of "grinding-in", both the EU and China understand each other sufficiently to compromise in times of difficulty, and so we can be optimistic about further improvement.

Dai Bingran

EU PERSPECTIVE

Introduction

This commentary is confined to a number of issues which Dai Bingran raises in his thorough Chinese perspective on understanding EU-China relations, and concludes with some specific thoughts on how to improve mutual understanding.

Strategic Partnership

The word "strategic" is overused and, while PRC and EU leaders have agreed to enter into a strategic partnership, the term has not been defined. Any such partnership must be based on equality, mutual trust, respect and understanding. It must also be comprehensive, holistic and long-term, and there must be an intensive, on-going and stable commitment to it. The relationship must be based on mutual interests, but not necessarily shared values.

Economic Relations

Economic relations have indeed reached a state of interdependence with their mutual economic interests also having an international dimension. The EU and China have common stakes and need to work together. Their economies are more complementary than competitive. They also have the common responsibility to address the negative effects of globalization, one of the causes of international disturbance and insecurity.

Dai Bingran is right to express concern about the rising trade imbalance, but is correct to remind us that Europe can never be competitive against several developing economies. It follows that many Chinese exports to Europe merely displace exports from other Asian countries. It must also be remembered that the majority of Chinese exports to Europe come from production wholly or partially foreign-owned.

Common Political Interests

Unlike in the United States, Europeans are worried about China as an economic rival but do not worry about the country as a growing military power.

The EU has no treaty obligation towards Taiwan. Both China and Europe are concerned about current threats to international peace and wish them to be addressed through international institutions and mechanisms.

This having been said, greater transparency over China's military expenditure would be welcome and reassuring. China's destruction of one of its weather satellites with a ballistic missile in January 2007 gave rise to concern in Europe as well as the US as to China's reliability as a global partner. No notice was given nor concern shown over the danger resulting from the space debris which puts at risk satellites for years ahead. The Chinese Ministry of Foreign Affairs appeared to know nothing about the project, which led to speculation that it was the responsibility of the PLA.

Common Values

The extent to which China and Europe share common values, as well as common interests, depends upon how values are defined. Often, one can have common objectives but differ as to means (as, for example, the US and the EU). Despite their differences in political history and current systems, both seek a society based upon market economy but socially equitable. However, attitudes towards democracy and human rights fundamentally differ. It is not for Europe to seek to impose its rules on China, which must choose its own societal model. It is to be hoped that there will be democratization within the CCP as well as increased local elections and grassroots participation in decision-making.

Dai Bingran's claim that there is more free speech than there has ever been in Chinese history may be true, but the standards fall seriously short of those prevailing in Europe. It is in China's own interests that there is greater freedom of expression as this is essential in creating an environment conducive to innovation.

Europeans still see in China the rule by law, rather than of law, the latter being understood not to accord with Chinese historical and cultural traditions.

Improving EU-China Mutual Understanding

Mutual understanding is a prerequisite to mutual trust. We must try to understand each other's historical, cultural and social differences which help determine our attitudes and create misunderstandings. Above all, we must explain to each other our policies and decisions — not just to the cognoscenti, but through the media — to the public at large. The EU is not very good at this but China is a very poor public communicator — one reason why China's image is poor in Europe.

Working together helps to increase mutual understanding and trust. A priority should be the promotion of exchanges in all sectors and at all levels of society. Learning each other's languages is another priority.

Conclusion

Although both the EU and China have repeatedly confirmed their intention to build between them a strategic partnership, doubts and scepticism still persist. Such a partnership is necessary and new circumstances have made it more relevant and extended its scope. On the other hand, much still has to be done for the building of a true strategic partnership.

Dai Bingran is right to conclude that we should be content with the improvement in EU-China mutual understanding and that both the EU and China understand each other sufficiently to compromise in times of difficulty. His optimism as to the future relationship is shared and should spur us to ensure that this optimism is not misplaced.

Stanley Crossick

Epilogue

The opinions and thoughts expressed in this book strike by their diversity and also by their entrenched assertiveness. Coming from different backgrounds and reflecting different interests, the authors highlight some of the problems and prejudices that affect China's relations with the EU and other countries. China's reemergence as a first-rank economic and political power, her nationalism, her production and exporting capacity are one side of a coin mirrored by anxieties, concerns and sometimes clamors for protectionism in the EU and US on the other.

There is also the clear perception of a new reality. No big issue on the world's agenda — energy, the environment and climate change, poverty alleviation, peace and stability — can be solved without China's active participation. The EU and China have an inescapable common future, sharing stakes and responsibilities. After 30 years of interaction and cooperation, China and the EU are at a crucial crossroads. They need to generate the political will to upgrade their relationship, to transform it into a strategic partnership transcending trade and investment issues, that will lead internationally to diplomatic complicity and internally to civil society dialogue.

These are historic times. The EU now has 27 member states and is confronted by the necessity to adapt its decision-making, to ensure a balanced economic growth and to restore its political and societal cohesion. The arrival on the scene of new political leaders gives a special relevance to this moment of opportunity. China too is in a phase of redefining its policies, declaring its intention to care for the poorest in its society, but also promoting space exploration and industrial innovation. She is preparing to welcome the world for the Olympic Games and, two years later, the World Expo. But for her leaders and the next generation of leaders, internal cohesion as well as regional stability will remain on top of the agenda.

What can the harvest of ideas and suggestions advanced by the authors contributing to this book bring for those in the EU and China, who are now involved in developing the new partnership and cooperation agreement that the political leaders on both sides have called for?

The fact is that cooperation between China and the EU — covering over 25 policy areas — is good. The need for a strong political signal for an upgrade of the partnership should not lead to complex and arcane negotiations which will consume time and resources without guaranteeing added value.

Without waiting for progress in the formal negotiations, lessons can be drawn from this book. They include recommendations that China fully comply with its WTO obligations, in particular market access in services, and that China ratify the UN International Covenant on Civil and Political Rights. The new strategic partnership should give priority to cooperation in the energy field (security, alternative sources, renewable energy and energy conservation, technology, etc.). Working together on development cooperation (Africa, but not only Africa) should also be a shared goal. Finally, a recurrent theme in the comments in this book is the importance of promoting mutual understanding and people-to-people exchanges at all levels between China and Europe. Mutual understanding helps working together, and working together builds trust.

This book conveys one clear message: Europe and China have a common future, and for the sake of the well-being and prosperity of their people and their countries, and for the sake of peace and stability in their regions and worldwide, they must forge closer cooperation on the whole range of challenges that our planet faces in the 21st century.

Stanley Crossick
Etienne Reuter
Autumn 2007

Jan Willem BLANKERT has worked in the European Commission on issues relating to European integration and EU enlargement and, more recently, on EU relations with China, in particular trade and economic issues, and Taiwan and the cross-strait question. He is currently visiting professor at the Lee Kuan Yew School for Public Policy, National University of Singapore.

Fraser CAMERON is Director of the EU-Russia Centre, a Senior Advisor to the European Policy Centre and Adjunct Professor at the Hertie School of Governance in Berlin. A former diplomat and EU official, he is the author of numerous books and articles on the external relations of the EU.

David CAMROUX is Senior Research Associate within the Centre d'Études et de Recherches Internationales (CERI), and also a Senior Lecturer seconded to the Institut d'Études Politiques (IEP) at Sciences Po in Paris. He has authored numerous articles on Southeast Asian and Australasian politics and history, and is currently preparing a book on foreign relations, nationalism and regionalism in Southeast Asia.

CHEN Zhimin is currently head of the Department of International Politics, School of International Relations and Public Affairs, and also Associate Dean of the Institute of International Studies, Fudan University, Shanghai. His research interests include international relations theory, diplomacy studies, Chinese foreign policy and EU studies.

Stanley CROSSICK, an English solicitor and founding chairman of the European Policy Centre, is also Senior Advisor to the EIAS (European Institute for Asian Studies) and member of the Council of La Fondation de l'Innovation Politique. He is a regular visitor to China and speaker, writer and media commentator on EU-China relations. He is an Officier de l'Ordre National (français) du Mérite and an Officer of the Order of the British Empire.

DAI Bingran is the Jean Monnet Chair and former Director of the Centre of European Studies, Fudan University. Active in the area of European studies, he is Vice Chairman and Secretary-General of the Chinese Society for EU Studies, and Vice President of the Shanghai Institute of European Studies.

Pierre DEFRAIGNE presently heads eur-IFRI, the Brussels-based think-tank of the French Institute for International Relations (IFRI). Recently retired as Deputy Director-General of DG Trade, he was formerly Head of Cabinet for Pascal LAMY, European Commissioner for Trade (1999–2002), and previously Head of Cabinet for Etienne DAVIGNON, Vice President of the European Commission (1977–1983).

DING Yifan is Senior Fellow, Deputy Director of the Institute of World Development, under the State Council's Development Research Center in China. He has published numerous papers on international economics, international relations, and European and US politics in leading Chinese academic magazines and newspapers. He has also published several books on globalization, the Euro and US global hegemony's paradoxes.

Glyn FORD has been a Member of the European Parliament since 1984, and is a member of the Foreign Affairs Committee and the Korean Peninsula Delegation. He is a specialist on East Asia, particularly North Korea.

David FOUQUET is a European-based journalist who is the Director-Editor of the Asia-Europe Project Information Service. He has travelled, lectured and been a consultant in Europe and Asia, and served as Secretary-General with the European Institute for Asian Studies in Brussels. Specific fields of interest include international and economic relations, arms control, conflict management and environmental protection.

Gustaaf GEERAERTS is Professor of International Relations and Dean of the Faculty of Economic, Social and Political Sciences at Solvay Business School, and the Director of the Brussels Institute of Contemporary China Studies, both at the Vrije Universiteit Brussel. His research interests center on international relations theory, global governance and EU-China Relations.

GUO Xiaobin is a researcher at the China Institute of Contemporary International Relations and recently was a visiting scholar at the University of Georgia's Center for International Trade and Security. His research focuses on export control, non-proliferation and space cooperation.

Gary HALLSWORTH has been Director of Governance and Development for the British Council, China since 2002. He has developed governance programs in Vietnam and China, working with both government ministries and the non-government sector.

Thomas HEBERER is Professor of Political Science and East Asian Studies at the University of Duisburg-Essen, Germany. Having worked and lived in China for many years, he regularly conducts fieldwork in various regions of China and has published extensively on various issues of social and political change in China.

James KYNGE spent 19 years as a journalist in Asia and was the China Bureau Chief for the *Financial Times* for seven years until 2005. The recipient of several journalism awards, in October 2006 he won the *Financial Times* & Goldman Sachs Business Book of the Year Award for his bestseller, *China Shakes the World*. He currently heads up the business operations of a publishing multinational in Beijing.

LI Jinshan is the Director of the Centre for European Studies and head of the Department of Public Policy & Public Economy at Zhejiang University. Prior to that, she was based at the East Asian Institute of Singapore National University (1996–1998) and at the Research Institute for Public Finance of the Ministry of Finance, PRC (1998–2005).

Gjovalin MACAJ is a researcher at the Vrije Universiteit Brussel. His current research project is on the European Union as a multilateral actor and the reform of the UN Security Council.

MEN Jing is an assistant professor at Vesalius College in Brussels, specializing in Chinese foreign policy and external relations. She has published in peer reviewed journals such as *European Law Journal, Global Society* and *Studia Diplomatica*.

Dermot O'GORMAN joined the World Wildlife Fund (WWF) in May 1998. During this time, he has worked as Head of Government and Aid Agency at WWF UK, as Regional Representative of WWF South Pacific Program based in Fiji, and as Deputy Director, Asia Pacific Program for WWF International. He is currently the Country Representative for WWF China.

Chris PATTEN is Chancellor of the University of Oxford and of Newcastle University. After studying at Oxford, he became a conservative politician, was a member of Parliament from 1979 to 1992, and held a number of ministerial and cabinet posts. He was the last Governor of Hong Kong from 1992 to 1997 and EU Commissioner for External Relations from 1999 to 2005. Currently, he is co-chair of the International Crisis Group.

Etienne REUTER is a senior official of the European Commission in Brussels, having first joined as an advisor to President Roy Jenkins in 1977. An Asian affairs specialist, he worked and lived in Hong Kong and Tokyo from 1993 to 2005. He was the 2006/2007 EU Fellow at the Lee Kuan Yew School for Public Policy at the National University of Singapore.

Andrew SMALL is a program associate at the German Marshall Fund of the United States, where he coordinates GMF's work on China. He was previously Director of the Foreign Policy Center's Beijing Office and a visiting fellow at the Institute of European Studies at the Chinese Academy of Social Sciences.

Willem VAN DER GEEST specializes in the study of global economic and financial institutions and their impact on local, national and regional development. In his present position, directing a think-tank for the EU, he has developed unique insights into the processes of regional integration and accession, especially in the contexts of EU-China and EU-ASEAN.

Willem VAN KEMENADE is Senior Fellow at the Clingendael Institute in The Hague. He has been a long-time China analyst for Dutch and international media. In recent years, he has been a consultant and lecturer at business schools and the Clingendael Institute. He is currently writing a new book on global responses to the rise of China.

Gudrun WACKER is currently Head of Research Unit Asia at the German Institute for International and Security Affairs (Stiftung Wissenschaft und Politik, SWP) in Berlin. Her research focuses on Chinese foreign and security policy, especially on EU-China, Sino-Russian and Sino-Central Asian relations; China and the Asia-Pacific region; and Chinese domestic development and minority policy.

John WONG is Research Director of the East Asian Institute (EAI) of the National University of Singapore. He has done consultancy work for the Singapore government and many international organizations, and has written and edited over 20 books and numerous articles and papers in learned journals on the development of China and other East Asian economies.

WU Baiyi is Research Fellow and Deputy Director at the Institute of European Studies, the Chinese Academy of Social Sciences. His research interests broadly range from power relationships, regional security regime and crisis management, to Chinese foreign policy-making.

XING Hua is senior research fellow and director of the China Institute of International Studies (CIIS). His main research fields include the EU, NATO, transatlantic relations and Europe-China relations. He has previously worked at the Chinese embassies in Guinea, Mauritania, Switzerland and Mali.

YU Keping is currently Professor and Director of the China Center for Comparative Politics & Economics (CCCPE), and also Professor and Director of the Center for Chinese Government Innovations, Peking University. His major fields of research include political philosophy, comparative politics, globalization, and governance and politics in China.

Marcin ZABOROWSKI is Senior Research Fellow at the European Union Institute for Security Studies. From 2002 to 2004, he directed the Transatlantic Program at the Center for International Relations in Warsaw, Poland. He was formerly a NATO Research Fellow (1999–2000) and a EUISS Visiting Fellow (2004).

ZHANG Jun is an Associate Professor at the Institute of European Studies, Chinese Academy of Social Sciences. She specializes in both the EU's external relations and foreign aid. Her main works include "EU within the ASEM process: The institutional power of the EU vis-à-vis the Asian members" and *Donors in China* (co-authored with ZHOU Hong).

ZHANG Tiejun is Acting Director of European Studies at the Shanghai Institute for International Studies. His research interests lie in the areas of China's foreign policy, East Asian regionalism, Sino-European relations and Asia-Europe cooperation. He has published in both China and the West, including two books and numerous papers.

ZHENG Yongnian is Professor and Head of Research at China Policy Institute, the School of Contemporary Chinese Studies, University of Nottingham, UK. He has published extensively on China's transformation and its external relations, and is Editor of the Series on Contemporary China (World Scientific Publishing). He is also an academic activist, having served as a consultant to United Nations Development Program on China's rural development and democracy.

ZHOU Hong is Professor of European Politics and Modern History, Director of the Institute of European Studies at the Chinese Academy of Social Sciences (CASS). She is an elected Member of the Academic Divisions of CASS and is serving as Deputy Director of the Division of International Studies. She also chairs the Chinese Association for European Studies.

ZHU Chunquan has been the Head of Conservation Operations Program since September 2005, and before that, was the Director of Forest Program, at WWF China. He has worked with various partners, including government agencies and international organizations at different levels.

ZHU Feng is currently Professor at Peking University's School of International Studies and is the Director of its International Security Program. A leading Chinese security expert, he writes extensively on regional security in East Asia, the nuclear North Korea issue, American national security strategy, China-US relations and missile defense.